How March Became Madness

How the NCAA Tournament Became the
Greatest Sporting Event in America

Eddie Einhorn with Ron Rapoport

TRIUMPH
B O O K S
CHICAGO

For Ann, Jennifer, and Jeff, who helped me live my fantasy life.

And for Julian Lopez, who allowed me to live it again.

Library of Congress Cataloging-in-Publication Data

Einhorn, Eddie, 1936–
    How march became madness : how the NCAA tournament became the greatest sporting event in
America / Eddie Einhorn with Ron Rapoport
        p. cm.
    ISBN-13: 978-1-57243-809-5
    ISBN-10: 1-57243-809-6
        1. NCAA Basketball Tournament—History. I. Rapoport, Ron. II. Title

    GV885.49.N37E56 2005
    796.323'630973—dc22

                                                                    2005054903

This book is available in quantity at special discounts for your group or organization. For further information, contact:

        Triumph Books
        542 South Dearborn Street
        Suite 750
        Chicago, Illinois 60605
        (312) 939-3330
        Fax (312) 663-3557

Printed in U.S.A.
ISBN-13: 978-1-57243-809-5
ISBN-10: 1-57243-809-6
Design by Wagner|Donovan Design, Chicago, IL
All photographs courtesy of AP/World Wide Photos unless otherwise indicated.

CONTENTS

ACKNOWLEDGMENTS

I would like to thank a number of people whose thoughts and insights were a great help in writing this book. They include Roger Valdiserri, Les Keiter, Larry Conley, Joe Dean, Jack Ramsay, George Gallup, Bob Pettit, Bob Vetrone, Dan Caesar, Bill Raftery, Dr. Cedric Dempsey, Tony La Russa, Beano Cook, Dan Rather, Norm Stewart, Rich Hussey, Jay Randolph, Gary Thompson, Dr. Charles Young, Ed Steiner, and John Sias.

The only person I asked to speak with me who declined was Walter Byers, the first executive director of the NCAA. Now retired to his farm in Kansas, Walter sent me a very kind letter in which he said he had nothing to add beyond what had been published in his own autobiography. I hope the reminiscences of those who knew and worked with Walter will give some indication of how important he was to the growth of college basketball. Walter, Wayne Duke, and Tom Jernstedt, at the NCAA office, opened the door to a young dreamer, and I hope I lived up to their trust.

Thanks to Ron Rapoport, who has been telling me for years I should write a book and who particularly encouraged me to write this one. When I wondered if my inexperience as an interviewer might be a problem, Ron said that, on the contrary, my long association with many of the people in this book would encourage them to talk to me more freely than to someone they didn't know well. "Look," he said. "Bob Knight isn't going to pick *me* up at the Lubbock airport."

Thanks also to Nancy Mack, who typed the transcripts of these conversations. As Ron and I read them over, we were constantly amazed at her ability to decipher what was being said in the midst of ringing phones, waitresses taking lunch orders, people stopping by to say hello, and other interruptions. Every time I saw Nancy's notations "overlapping voices" and "laughter," I was afraid the fun I was having might have obscured some valuable information, but somehow she always managed to figure out what we were saying. And a special thank you to my partner and loyal friend, Jerry Reinsdorf, who got me started on a new 25-year career in baseball.

Thanks to Mitch Rogatz, Tom Bast, Kelley White, and all the folks at Triumph Books for their enthusiasm for this project and their efforts on its behalf. And our personal thanks to Ann Einhorn for her important contributions, and to Joan Rapoport for giving the manuscript one last careful read.

Thanks to my law school roommate Bob Hatch, a true friend and adviser over the past 46 years, and to the hundreds of announcers, producers, and office personnel at TVS for their dedication and loyalty. Thanks in memoriam to the many friends of TVS and college basketball: Harry Fouke, Jim Corbett, Bernie Moore, Bernie Shively, Harry Lancaster, Adolph Rupp, Henry Iba, Bob James, Harry Litwak, Bill Sheehan, Carl Lindeman, Dick Bailey, Art Watson, Al Rush, Castleman D. T. Chesley, Jim Grainer, Ed Thilenius, Don Canham, Jim Valvano, and Al McGuire.

Finally, I would like to say that the more I worked on this book, the more I missed former UCLA athletic director J. D. Morgan. He had the vision to see that the television exposure of UCLA's basketball team during its dynasty years could only help the growth of the game. I know J.D. would have enjoyed reliving those days as much as I did, and I believe college basketball owes him as great a debt as I do.

INTRODUCTION

I was 22 years old when I produced the first nationally syndicated radio broadcast of the NCAA basketball tournament in 1958. My office was my dorm room at the Northwestern University School of Law in Chicago, my mailbox was a box at the main post office, and the office phone was at the end of the hall.

"Hey, Einhorn, it's for you," somebody would yell, and I would run down to answer, always a little afraid the universities and the radio stations I was dealing with would get wise to me. Somehow, they never did. To pick up a few extra bucks, I worked as a vendor at Comiskey Park that year—it was 1959 and the White Sox lost the World Series to the Dodgers—never dreaming that one day I would return as an owner of the team and, in 2005, after a wait of 25 years, be hoisting the World Series trophy in the White Sox locker room.

To this day, I wonder how a guy like me, a young law student with no money and no background in broadcasting except the basketball games I had announced on the campus radio station when I was an undergraduate at Penn, could acquire the rights to a national radio hookup for the NCAA basketball tournament. It was easy. Hardly anybody cared about college basketball then except for the fans of the individual teams who listened on their local stations. Nobody could foresee the day when it would become March Madness, the Final Four would be one of the top sporting events in the country, and the television networks would be paying billions of dollars to put it on the air. So the NCAA was happy to sell me the rights for a small fee. They were just happy someone was interested.

I couldn't figure it out. The game was so exciting and the players were so great. How could people not care? But there I was at the 1959 Final Four in Louisville—California beat West Virginia by one point that year—sending back play-by-play to the radio network I'd put together. The network didn't amount to much—I only had a few stations—but one was WOR in New York, and as far as I was concerned that made me a big-time radio broadcaster. My fantasy life was beginning.

The first Final Four I ever saw was three years earlier in Evanston, Illinois, when Temple made the semifinals, and I talked my way into sending some interviews back to my campus radio station. I wasn't doing play-by-play, so I could do reports from the press room after the games without paying any rights fees at all. The tournament featured Bill Russell and the University of San Francisco, which I still think is the most dominating team I've ever seen in the NCAA Finals.

My station had just enough money for the train fare—the only ad we sold was to the university bookstore—so I had no place to stay. After I slept in the press room the first night, Herb Good and Bob Vetrone, two Philadelphia sportswriters, pulled a mattress off a bed in their hotel room and let me sleep on their floor. I was in heaven. Though I loved announcing the games back at school, I knew I was never going to be the next Marty Glickman, but there I was, dealing with NCAA executives, meeting all the greats of college basketball, announcing the biggest games, and sitting in the best seats in the house.

The next year, 1957, was even better. I went to Kansas City—I had a budget then and my own hotel room—and saw maybe the greatest Final Four ever: an undefeated North Carolina team beating Michigan State in overtime in the semifinals, then getting past Kansas and Wilt Chamberlain in the championship game. This time, I broadcast the games via tape delay, and somehow I convinced NBA Hall of Famer George Mikan to be the commentator. I learned a valuable lesson at that tournament, one I often applied to my broadcasts in the years to come: if you called an announcer a guest analyst instead of a color man, you didn't have to pay him. Usually he was just happy to get a better seat.

After I graduated from law school, my next step was to try television, and I learned one thing very quickly: if radio didn't think college basketball was national programming material, television *really*

didn't care. When I broadcast the 1962 NCAA championship game, for instance, it featured the two best teams in the country, Cincinnati and Ohio State, but the only viewers who saw the game live were in the state of Ohio. I know it sounds crazy, but the rest of the country had to wait for ABC to show the tape the following afternoon on *Wide World of Sports*. It was this indifference that gave me my opening.

In 1960 my dad died, and I was sitting at home running his insurance business but longing to stay in broadcasting when I read about St. Bonaventure playing Bradley at Madison Square Garden. They were the top two teams in the country, and I wondered if I could do on television something similar to what I had done on radio—broadcast the game back to the teams' home cities. I called a station in Peoria and another in Buffalo, and they couldn't say yes fast enough. So all of a sudden, I was hiring the equipment, arranging the transmission lines, and booking the team's radio announcers—Tom Kelly from Bradley and Bill Mazer from Buffalo—to do the play-by-play. At halftime I interviewed Red Auerbach myself.

Not long before the game, the phone rang. It was an executive from Madison Square Garden wanting to know what I thought I was doing. "We own the television rights to this game," he said.

"Well, nobody told *me*," I said, and pretty soon we were yelling at each other. Eventually, I paid the Garden a rights fee and everybody was happy. And when I found out I could charge the stations $2,000 instead of the $200 I had made in radio, I was hooked. I was now a television producer.

I called my network TVS—for television sports—and bit by bit, station by station, conference by conference, independent team by independent team, I started reaching out across the country. I got my foot in the door by offering to do what I had done in the Garden: broadcast road games of the major college teams back to stations in their home cities. It seems obvious now, but back then it was a radical idea.

My office wasn't a dorm room anymore; it was the $117-a-month garden apartment in Paterson, New Jersey, where Ann and I lived. We had met when I was a cashier at the law school cafeteria and had gotten married when I graduated. During the day, I would make my calls, and in the evenings Ann and I would sit on the living-room floor cutting, pasting, and stapling the program formats to mail out to stations around the country.

Our first network logo was a picture of our one-year-old daughter, Jennifer, in a basketball uniform that said TVS on the front and ½ on the back. When our son, Jeff, was born two years later, he wore the uniform, and Jennifer, dressed in a cheerleader's outfit, sat on a basketball and waved pom-poms. Pretty soon they were getting fan mail.

Later, when I needed a New York address for appearance's sake, that's what I got: an address. There was a building on Fifth Avenue that had some one-room offices with phones on the wall in the lobby that used a common answering service. It was six months before I could afford an office, but in the meantime, I had one of the phones. I'd come in, get my messages, and make my calls from the lobby. Finally, I moved into an office that had two desks, one for me and one for my new salesman.

I had to hire a salesman not only because I had been doing everything myself—booking the stations, producing the games, selling the advertising—but also because I needed some legitimacy. Once, a guy offered to buy some commercials, and, trying to stall him a little to see if I could get a better price, I said I'd have to check and get back to him.

"You have to *check*?" he said. "Who are you going to check with, your wife?"

In 1965 I started regional networks with the college conferences that didn't already have their own packages. I began with Southeastern Conference games, and during the next few years I added the Mid-American Conference, the Big 8, the Southwest, the Western, the West Coast, and the Missouri

Valley. By the time TVS added the Big Ten and the Pac-10 in 1974, in fact, the only conference we *didn't* have a deal with was the Atlantic Coast Conference. The ACC was probably the best basketball conference of them all back then, but thank goodness it covered only 7 percent of the country. I also signed up some of the leading independents: Notre Dame, DePaul, Marquette, Houston, Air Force, Detroit, and a few others. I was on my way.

I had competition, of course. I was afraid other networks would combine to swallow me up, but they seemed content to stay regional, whereas my plan was to operate on a national basis. And after a while, TVS had deals with almost 200 stations that reached more than 95 percent of the country.

The one thing we had going for us was the lack of interest on the part of the three major networks. None of them saw the national potential of college basketball, so it was left to those of us with local and regional contracts to fill the void. Even when I started booking games on the local stations the networks owned in some of the largest cities in the country—preempting their own shows, in other words—they were slow to react. I guess I always knew in the back of my mind they'd get smart one day, but for now I was building TVS into a national brand and broadcasting some great games that were spreading the appeal of college basketball.

The fact that I wasn't making much money didn't really bother me. We always seemed to be scrambling to pay our bills, floating loans, and depending on the revenue from the coming year, but we told ourselves things were sure to get better. It was seven or eight years before we made more than our expenses, and I never really did get rich. But Ann and I were able to move out of the garden apartment, our kids were healthy and happy, and I was doing exactly what I wanted.

My biggest break came when I telecast some UCLA games back to Los Angeles from the Chicago Stadium in the midsixties. That's when I met UCLA's athletic director, J. D. Morgan, who was one of the few real visionaries in the college game back then. He wanted to build on UCLA's great success beyond the West Coast, and, unlike so many of the athletic directors of other teams in major conferences, he wasn't afraid to book intersectional games with top independents during the season. And he always had great faith in me.

Our relationship led to the telecasts of UCLA's great series with Notre Dame and to what was by far my greatest TV success: the 1968 game in the Astrodome between UCLA and Houston, which were both unbeaten at the time, that starred Lew Alcindor and Elvin Hayes. More than any other game, it showed college basketball's potential as a national, prime-time attraction. And in a way, it sowed the seeds of my own destruction.

The networks were finally beginning to understand the game's potential, and they were tired of seeing me preempt their shows, so they started bidding up the rights fees. In 1972 I sold TVS to Corinthian Broadcasting, a division of Dun & Bradstreet, which had more resources to compete with the networks. For tax purposes, we couldn't close the deal in New York, so we all took the ferry to Hoboken, New Jersey, where we signed the papers in a little room with Jennifer crawling around on the desk. It was not exactly what I pictured for the biggest deal of my life.

No tears, no recriminations, no regrets. I'd had my fun, and besides, I wasn't going anywhere. I worked for Corinthian for five years doing exactly what I had done when I was on my own, booking college basketball games around the country. And when Corinthian and TVS went out of business, I moved over to *CBS Sports Spectacular,* where we broadcast everything imaginable.

What did we put on television back then? Heck, what didn't we? We did figure skating, gymnastics, boxing, auto racing, swimming, you name it. We pioneered "trash sports" too, like Acapulco cliff diving, the "battle of the NFL cheerleaders," and a fight featuring Ed "Too Tall" Jones of the Dallas Cowboys. A lot of people criticized us, but audiences ate it up.

When we finally beat ABC's *Wide World of Sports* one Saturday, I explained it to my sportswriter pal Vic Ziegel by saying, "Our crap was better than their crap." When CBS boss Bill Paley read that in *New York* magazine, I nearly lost my job.

The thing I loved most about those early days was the way we lived by the seat of our pants. For instance, after we sold a series of IndyCar races to Andy Granatelli, the owner of STP Oil Treatment, I realized there was one little detail I hadn't taken care of. So I went out and bought the rights. I had other adventures too, such as the time I was having some success televising professional wrestling as a side venture until Vince McMahon and the other promoters called one of Corinthian's lawyers and convinced him it was bad for Corinthian's image. After three straight sellouts in New York, I had to get out.

In 1981 I started a new career when Jerry Reinsdorf, whom I'd met in law school, and I bought the White Sox. It was crazy right from the start. We had feuds with Bill Veeck, George Steinbrenner, Harry Caray, and Jimmy Piersall, and we had to deal with the labor-management problems baseball was going through at the time. Along the way, Bill Giles, of the Phillies, and I negotiated the game's first billion-dollar television contract, although sometimes I found the team owners' lack of vision concerning television similar to that of the networks when it came to college basketball. Can you believe there was a time when ESPN, which was just starting out, was looking for a partner, and baseball could have bought a major interest for very little money and passed? I could cry just thinking about it.

Then in 1993 I began a bad run with my health. A very bad run. You name it, I had it. Pancreatitis that put me in a coma for three weeks. Anemia. Tremors throughout my body that made me look and feel shaky much of the time. And then, to top it all off, prostate cancer. But even when radiation treatment cured that, I knew I wasn't out of the woods because for years it had been clear that one day I was going to need a new kidney. That day arrived in 2002.

I don't mind telling you how scared I was. I was told I was a good candidate for a transplant, but when no one in my family was a suitable match, I had to get in line like everybody else. I had no quarrel with that—I'm not a special guy—but I won't lie to you: I went into a real depression. For the first time in my life I felt I wasn't in control, and I couldn't handle it. If a donor wasn't found immediately, I would have to go on dialysis for four-hour sessions three times a week. I learned that people can live 25 years on dialysis, but not to be able to travel, to pick up and go the way I always had, seemed unbearable to me.

Then one day, I got a call from my friend Julian Lopez, a gastroenterologist in Las Vegas I had met when he treated me while the White Sox were training there in 1993.

"I've got a volunteer for you," he said.

"You *do?*" I said. "That's *great*. Who?"

"Me."

"*You?* Are you sure you'd want to do that? I'm not strong enough to say no."

"What are friends for?" he said. "And besides, I only need one. I don't know if we're a match yet. We're going to have to find out if tacos and bagels mix." Luckily, they did.

Later Julian told me that of course there had been some risk. "But you take risks in life all the time," he said. "The risk here was less than I run leaving the house each day. When you try to do something good, it's hard to envision something bad coming out of it."

The operation was performed October 4, and I was home less than two weeks later. Julian was back seeing a full schedule of patients in less than a week. "I could have gone back sooner," he said, "but I wanted to keep an eye on you. I went from being a donor to a doctor. I don't have a big scar—maybe three inches long—my life expectancy won't change, and it doesn't affect my eligibility for life insurance or health insurance. People need to know these things."

How do you thank someone for saving your life? You don't. You just try to be as good a friend to him as he was to you. Julian is a big Raiders fan, so a few months after the operation, I took him to the Super Bowl in San Diego.

"Well, here you are," I said, as we sat watching the Raiders get obliterated by the Buccaneers. "America's number-one sporting event. What do you think?"

"It's great, Eddie," Julian said, "but with all due respect, I don't think so. The way March Madness grips the whole country for an entire month makes me think *it's* number one."

"You know," I said, thinking out loud, "I once had something to do with that. . . ."

The more I thought about it, the more I realized Julian was right. March Madness *is* a national phenomenon, isn't it? It stirs up passions in every part of the country. It dominates sports television programming for weeks at a time. The TV contracts alone are worth billions. But it hadn't always been that way—far from it—and who knew that better than I did? I had hundreds of stories about what it was like to try to promote college basketball, build it, and televise it when so few people seemed to care. And it really wasn't that long ago, was it? No more than 30 or 40 years. Most of the people who were a part of the game back then were still around. The coaches, the players, the announcers, the executives, the producers, the cameramen, the salesmen, the sportswriters . . .

And then it hit me. I knew almost all of them. Hell, I'd worked with them, hired them, conspired with them, and sometimes fought with them. Why not go see them? Why not sit down and talk to them? Why not re-create that era of college basketball with them? I got excited just thinking about it. I was feeling good. I was ready to tackle a new project. I was ready to hit the road again.

So I did. I bought a little handheld tape recorder, and I started traveling. In the next two and a half years, I went all around the country. I went to Los Angeles to see John Wooden, Kareem Abdul-Jabbar, and some of the great coaches and players from the glory days of UCLA. I went to Houston to see Guy Lewis, Elvin Hayes, and others who had been involved in maybe the most important game in the history of college basketball—Houston vs. UCLA in the Astrodome. I went to the 2004 NCAA Finals in San Antonio, the 2005 Finals in St. Louis, and some regional tournaments, and talked to a who's who of college coaches: Dean Smith and Bob Knight, Digger Phelps and Ray Meyer, John Thompson and Jerry Tarkanian, Roy Williams and Denny Crum, Joe B. Hall and Rick Pitino, and more.

I talked to announcers like Bill Walton, Dick Enberg, Billy Packer, Dick Vitale, Jim Nantz, and Rod Hundley, many of whom had worked for me when we were all a lot younger. I talked to network executives like Chet Simmons, Neal Pilson, and Sean McManus, and to the men who ran the stations that broadcast our games. I talked to NCAA and conference executives. I talked to some of my old producers, cameramen, and ad salesmen. You may not know their names, but wait until you hear some of their stories.

I talked to more than 50 people before I was done, and I had a ball. It was wonderful to see all these old friends and to listen to their stories—some I had forgotten and others I never knew. I was delighted to see how eager they were to tell me how they got started and to remember the times we lived through together, and I thank all of them for opening their doors to me.

As my collaborator, Ron Rapoport, and I were trying to decide the best way to present their reminiscences, it occurred to us that we should just let them talk. Let the television executives talk about how little respect college basketball received from the medium back then. Let the coaches talk about their small gyms and small salaries in the days before they became television personalities and millionaires. Let the announcers talk about their crazy schedules and primitive working conditions, and about the man they all revered and lost too soon—Al McGuire. Let the producers talk about the subterfuges they pulled just to get some commercials on the air. Let everyone who had played a role in the game in the Astrodome tell *that* story, which somebody will make a movie about someday, I promise you.

Working on this book was a labor of love for me, but in a way it was much more than that. It gave me a goal again, a sense of purpose. Reliving that wonderful time of my life made up for those days when I was sitting at home, feeling depressed, and waiting for the phone to ring with good news.

One of the first calls I made was to John Wooden, and I was a little nervous, wondering if he'd remember me and feeling a little sheepish for not having been in touch for so many years. But the first thing he said when he picked up the phone was, "*Eddie! Where have you been?*"

The next thing I knew I was sitting with one of the great figures in the history of college basketball, who had been one of my closest friends in the old days, talking about how much the game has changed since March went mad.

How March Became Madness

James Naismith invented the game of basketball in Springfield, Massachusetts, in 1891. Later, at the University of Kansas, he coached Phog Allen, who coached Dean Smith, who coached Michael Jordan. Can any other sport trace its lineage this directly?

PART I

In the Beginning

From the turn of the century, football was firmly entrenched as the king of college sports. Basketball was such an afterthought that the NCAA championship tournament didn't even exist until 1939, and for years the NIT was actually more important.

Ray Meyer's coaching career began at Notre Dame in 1940 and spans the generations. His first appearance in the Final Four with DePaul was in 1943; his second was in 1979. In 42 seasons his teams won 724 games, lost 354, and made 21 postseason appearances. Meyer was 91 years old when we talked near Chicago, where he has long been regarded as a civic treasure.

CHAPTER 1

Ray Meyer Remembers the Early Days

Arlington Heights, Illinois, January 2005

If you think you're glad to see me, Eddie, just think how glad I am to see you. I get up in the morning, look in the mirror, and think, "I'm still alive." (laughs)

How did I get into coaching? It's a long story. I was playing high school basketball in Chicago, and I was walking by St. Agatha's Church when the monsignor came out and said, "I want you to tell me what that priest coaching the girls knows about basketball." Well, I took one look and said, "That guy doesn't know whether the ball's got air in it or rags."

The next week, the priest called and said, "The coach is sick. Will you take his place?" I thought it was for one night, but it was for every night. It was a good thing, though, because that's how I met my wife, Marge, who was on the team, and that's how I started coaching basketball.

I played basketball at Notre Dame, and in 1940, which was still the Depression really, I got laid off from my job. George Keogan, my coach at Notre Dame, wanted to help me out, so he hired me to go around the area looking at teams for him. I'd go to Northwestern, Illinois, Wisconsin, the University of Chicago, and he'd pay me $25 per game. In the middle of the season, George called and said, "You have a good mind for basketball. You ought to be a coach."

> The priest came out and said, "I want you to tell me what that priest coaching the girls knows about basketball." Well, I took one look and said, "That guy doesn't know whether the ball's got air in it or rags."

I told him I wasn't really interested, that I was thinking about a business career, but he said, "Well, too bad, I made an appointment for you at Joliet Catholic High School. I want you to go out there today. Talk to them and you've got the job."

3

So I drove out to Joliet, and they offered me the job. But when they said I'd get $1,800 a year, I said, "I can't live on that. I need $1,900." They wouldn't give me that, so I went home. That night, I got a call from the president of Notre Dame, and he said, "Ray, George Keogan had a heart attack this afternoon. We asked the players who they wanted to coach them, and they said you. Would you come do it?"

So I went down to South Bend and moved in with George and his wife—they were so nice to me, very welcoming—while he recovered. Marge didn't move down with me because we knew it was temporary until George got back. So I finished out the season, and the next year George coached the home games and I did the road games.

We played DePaul at home that year, and after the game, a couple of their people got me in the corner of the locker room and said, "How would you like to coach at DePaul?" I said, "I don't even know if I want to coach. I'm just doing this until George is ready to take over again." I still thought I could do better in the business world.

> I'm a little ashamed of some of the things I did: I got a boxing coach to teach [George Mikan] how to hit the bag to develop his reflexes, I had him jumping rope every spare minute, and I even got a girl to teach him how to dance because I thought it would make him more graceful.

"Look," one of them said, "take it for a year. You can always go back to Notre Dame." And when they said the job paid $2,200, I took it.

Probably the best thing that happened to me when I took the job was that I took George Mikan with me.

He was a big gangly kid, very raw, and he came down to Notre Dame for a tryout, which was legal then. They told him he should go to a small school where they'd work with him and he could play more. So I brought him with me to DePaul.

I knew George would be my bread and butter, so for the first six weeks I didn't bother with the other players. I spent all my time with George and made him do everything I could to develop agility and learn the game. I'm a little ashamed of some of the things I did: I got a boxing coach to teach him how to hit the bag to develop his reflexes, I had him jumping rope every spare minute, and I even got a girl to teach him how to dance because I thought it would make him more graceful.

I set up a bench for George to jump over before he could retrieve the ball. I'd make him throw the ball over the bench and then go get it maybe 300 times a day. I'd stand and shoot the ball over and over again and make him bat it away, bat it away—never dreaming we'd find a way to use that. George became one of the first centers to make blocking shots part of his game. He'd just stand under the basket and bat the ball away just like we had done in practice.

I learned something from George, too, that helped me my entire career. I learned it's easier to coach an intelligent man than a dumb one. A dumb one learns like an animal, by repetition. With George, you just told him something and it was done. I also learned it's easier to teach a boy from nothing, rather than one who has a habit of doing things wrong. It's hard to break a habit.

George's height made him great, but he could run the floor too. He'd have been a good player if he was 6'1" or 6'2". And he did whatever he needed to do to win. If we won by 30, he'd have 6 or 8 points. If we won by 2, he'd get 30. He was smart that way. He kept the other players happy. But everybody on the team knew that when he raised his right hand it meant, "The ball goes here."

George really put DePaul on the map. When we played at Madison Square Garden, it was like a home game for us because he was the best player in the country then, and very popular. I'll always remember walking down Broadway to practice once, and a vendor shouted, "Hey! George Mikan! Come here!" So George went over and the vendor said, "Something

I hear John Wooden says the most he was ever paid was $32,500. He's a piker.

is going to happen now that never happens in New York: it's a free hot dog—on the house."

Another time we were in town for a few days and I wanted to take the team to see a show. So I sent the student manager over to get tickets, and they told him it was sold out. He said it was for DePaul, and they put us right on the stage. When you win, people want to do things for you.

One thing I learned early is that you learn more from losing than you do from winning. When you win, you savor the game, you have a beer and a sandwich, and you go home and you go to sleep. You're happy. But when you lose, you have to know why. I used to walk the streets after we lost, trying to figure out what had gone wrong. Did we have the proper approach to the game? Did I do a good job of substituting? After a few years, I figured if I kept walking the streets people might begin to wonder about me, so I got over that habit.

Once, after we lost to Kentucky on the last play of the game, I drove home and the phone rang. It was Marge, and she said, "I'm waiting for you."

I said, "What for? I came home right after the game."

"Yeah," she said, "but don't you remember? You took me to the game."

She was standing outside the stadium waiting for me. I had to drive back and get her. I heard about that for a long time. (laughs)

I spent 42 years at DePaul. That's pretty amazing, isn't it? When I got there, we played in a little gym

across the street from where they later built Alumni Hall—we called it the Barn—and we didn't lose very many games there. I was sorry when they tore it down because it was to our advantage to play there. We played our major games at Chicago Stadium, maybe 15 a year, often as part of a doubleheader with Loyola and Northwestern.

Arthur Wirtz, who owned Chicago Stadium, always had me signing up other schools to play in the doubleheaders. He'd give me my orders: get this school, get that school. And every time a team won the NCAA Tournament, it was my job to get them to come play in the stadium the following year. So for years we played the NCAA champion from the preceding year. We played Hank Iba's Oklahoma A&M team. We played the University of Kentucky and Adolph Rupp. We only played him once when George Mikan was on the team, though. Adolph wouldn't play us again until George graduated. (laughs)

I shouldn't tell you the stories of what traveling was like in the early days. If any of the parents are still around, they'll kill me. We flew into Kansas City once in the middle of a snowstorm and had to take a bus to Kansas State. It was a huge blizzard, and I was telling the driver, "Slow down, just get us there in one piece."

"I've been driving for Greyhound for 20 years," he said. Well the next thing I knew we were off the highway and metal was coming up from under the bus through the floorboards. I was sitting in the front seat on the right, and I did a somersault and hit the windshield. Everybody was flying all over the bus. We couldn't even open the doors until the rescue workers got there, and we had to wait four or five hours in a police station before another bus came to pick us up.

Once, after a game in Louisville, the plane's heating system went out and the whole cabin filled up with smoke just as we were taking off. The pilot made a U-turn and landed on a highway. The fire engines were right behind us, and we got out of the plane right on the highway and waited about two hours until they fixed it. Then the pilot took the plane up by himself

Ray Meyer's coaching career began in 1940 and ended after he spent 42 years at DePaul. His first appearance in the Final Four was in 1942, when George Mikan was college basketball's biggest star. His second came in 1979 with All-American Mark Aguirre leading the way.

to test it before he came back for us, still standing near the highway.

Another time, we were supposed to play in Bowling Green, Kentucky, but we were grounded in Chicago. So I called and said, "Look, we're renting a bus, but

One thing I learned early is that you learn more from losing than you do from winning. When you win, you savor the game, you have a beer and a sandwich, and you go home and you go to sleep. You're happy. But when you lose, you have to know why.

we're not going to get there in time. We'll play you tomorrow."

But they said, "No, we've got a full house here waiting for you. We'll have a police escort when you get to town."

Everybody cheered when we got there, and when we went down to the locker room, I said, "We've been on the bus all this time. You have to give us five minutes to warm up." But when we walked out on the floor, the whistle blew, and the game started. Oh, I was mad about that.

Signing up with TVS was one of the best things that happened to us back then, Eddie. People used to say, "Don't put your games on TV. You're not drawing well, and if you're on TV you won't draw at all." But I thought it was good for us. I thought we'd make fans and it would help us at the gate, which is what happened. I never thought that because people could see us on TV they wouldn't come out in person. I thought they'd say, "That looks like a good place to go for some entertainment," and we'd make more fans.

Where it really helped was with women fans. A lot of them had no conception of basketball and no interest in going to the games, but they started watching it on television with their husbands and all of a sudden they got interested. You'd be surprised at how many women have told me they got interested in basketball through television.

The fact that we were an independent meant that we could play against any teams we wanted. So pretty soon we became known as a national team, and that was a great recruiting tool for us. We once recruited a player in Los Angeles UCLA was interested in by telling the parents that they would see him more if he played for us. All our games were on television, so they would see him more than if he stayed home and they went to the games there. We could also tell parents that if their son was good, he'd have a better chance to go to the pros because they would see him on television. Of course, I didn't say that if he *didn't* have much talent, the pros would see that too. (laughs)

We needed all the help we could get recruiting the top players, because if they were recruited by Duke or another school with a beautiful campus and a football team, that was a big advantage over us. The other schools could bring them down for homecoming and get them all caught up in the glamour of it. We didn't have any of that in Chicago.

A lot of people think the 1979 NCAA championship game between Indiana State with Larry Bird and Michigan State with Magic Johnson had a lot to do with making the tournament so popular, but what they forget is that that game almost didn't come off. We beat Marquette and UCLA in the regional, and I thought we were good enough to beat Indiana State in the Final Four. But Curtis Watkins, who was our star forward, got hurt, and we weren't going to play him.

Bird had a great night—he scored 35 points—but we were ahead by one point with 16 seconds to go. When we ran out of substitutes, we had to put Curtis in. Clyde Bradshaw passed him the ball and Curtis couldn't bend over, so the ball went out of bounds. Indiana State got it, and they scored to go ahead. Mark Aguirre, who was our top player, got the last shot, and it hit the rim and rolled out. That one killed me. Those are the ones you remember—not the ones you lost by 30, but the close ones.

Here's a funny story from the tournament that year. We were playing UCLA in the regional in Provo, Utah, and we were leading by 17 points at halftime. When we came out for the second half, everybody in the stands was cheering for us. I went to the scorers' table and asked what was going on, and they said Brigham Young had some dancers out on the floor at halftime. When the UCLA players came out, they started practicing, the band started playing their fight song, and the girls had to stop their dance. For that everybody hated UCLA, and I think it affected the refs. We could have committed murder out there and they wouldn't have called a foul on us in the second half. We won by four points.

I hear John Wooden says the most he was ever paid was $32,500. He's a piker. I made $50,000. Of course, I coached longer than he did. The year we went to the Final Four, 1979, I was making $30,000 a year, and I had been coaching 37 years by then. That wasn't going to raise my family, so I ran a boys camp in Wisconsin for many years.

I first met John when I was at Notre Dame and he was coaching at South Bend Central High School. That's how far back we go. He used to come out and watch us practice, and I got to know him a little, but we spent more time together at NCAA Tournaments through the years. The thing that always impressed me about John is that he had time for people. He would sit in the hotel lobby at the tournament and talk to anybody who came by. Here he was, the most famous college coach in America, and he always had time for the little guy. Most coaches wouldn't go down to the lobby like that to mix with the crowds.

We kept up our friendship through the years. When he played in the Chicago Stadium or at Notre Dame, he would practice at DePaul, and we always had a nice visit. Bill Walton came up to me one day and said, "We love it when we practice at DePaul." I said, "That's nice, Bill, but why?" And he said, "Because Coach sits down and talks to you, and we have a nice lazy practice."

The biggest change in the game since I came in would have to be the development of the big man. It seemed they were always legislating against him. First they got rid of the center jump where he had a big advantage. Then they put in the three-second rule so he couldn't stand under the basket. They put in a rule that you couldn't bat the ball away the way George

People used to say, "Don't put your games on TV. You're not drawing well, and if you're on TV you won't draw at all." But I thought it was good for us. I thought we'd make fans and it would help us at the gate, which is what happened.

Mikan liked to do, and that you couldn't throw the ball in over the backboard from behind the court.

Then they put in a 6' lane, and when Wilt Chamberlain came along, they widened it to 12'. I remember being at the coaches convention that year and Hank Iba standing up and saying, "We're spending all this time legislating against the big man. Why don't we worry more about *coaching* against him?"

I coached against Al McGuire a lot of times, and, oh, he was tricky. I remember once when Tom Collins, Marquette's announcer, said, "Can you explain your defense to me?" Because we were on TV, I wanted to sound intelligent, so I explained exactly what we were doing. Then later I walked by the Marquette locker room and there was Tom playing the tape for Al. So I went into the men's room, which was right next to their locker room, and started flushing all the toilets so they couldn't hear what was on the tape. (laughs)

When I turned 70, I said, "That's enough," and I retired. I wanted to give my son, Joey, a chance to coach. He'd been my assistant, and I'd given him more and more to do over the years. He'd played for me and been my first full-time assistant.

I'll tell you a story that sums things up, I guess. We had just lost a game to UCLA, and I was sitting in the office the next morning feeling lousy when the phone rang. It was George Ireland, a friend for years who won the NCAA Tournament at Loyola in 1963.

"How do you feel?" he asked.

"Lousy," I said. "We lost the game."

"Well, I'll trade places with you," he said.

"What do you mean?"

"I just had a heart bypass."

"No, thanks, George. I don't want to trade."

I remember being at the coaches convention that year and Hank Iba standing up and saying, "We're spending all this time legislating against the big man. Why don't we worry more about *coaching* against him?"

OK, here's one more. I was driving home last year and listening to the *Score*—the big sports-talk station in town—and they've got a contest: which Chicago sports figure is going to die next? One guy says, "Ray Meyer because he's getting old." Then another guy calls in and says, "I'm never going to listen to this station again because I think Ray Meyer is going to live forever." (laughs)

Photograph courtesy of ASUCLA Photography.

PART II

UCLA, Inc.

Nothing drives interest in sports like a contest between David and Goliath. Whether it's the Yankees, the Celtics, Notre Dame, or the Green Bay Packers, we are all fascinated at the sight of the little guy playing against— and possibly upsetting—the giant, which is why dynasties always have had such a great impact. And college basketball had one of the greatest dynasties of them all: UCLA.

TVS televised many of the Bruins' most exciting games over the years, which went a long way toward establishing college basketball on television. Here is their leader and two of their biggest stars

In 27 seasons at UCLA, John Wooden established a record that will never be equaled in any sport: 10 national championships, including 7 in a row; 4 unbeaten seasons; an 88-game win streak; and an overall record of 620 wins and 147 losses. He was 92 years old when we talked at his home in Los Angeles.

Kareem Abdul-Jabbar, who was known as Lew Alcindor in college, led UCLA to three consecutive NCAA championships from 1967 to 1969: the Bruins were 88–2 in his three seasons. He later won six NBA championships with the Milwaukee Bucks and the Los Angeles Lakers. No ranking of the greatest basketball players of all time fails to include his name. Today he is a distinguished author of historical books.

Bill Walton won two titles at UCLA and was named college Player of the Year three consecutive times. During his three years in Westwood, the Bruins won 86 games and lost 4. His professional career was cut short by injury, but not before he led Portland to the NBA championship in 1977. Today he broadcasts NBA games for ESPN and ABC.

CHAPTER 2

John Wooden on Building a Dynasty

Los Angeles, California, January 2004

It has been said that I never had a losing season as a coach, but that's not true. My first two years of teaching after I graduated from Purdue were at a high school in Dayton, Kentucky, and my first year there we had a losing season. They weren't hiring coaches back then: you were hired to teach, and you coached because you loved it.

For a long time, I would teach several English classes a day, and for each sport I coached, maybe I'd have one less class. Since then, I have always referred to myself as a teacher/coach. I think that's what a coach should be: a teacher first and a coach second. We were better my second year at Dayton, and then I left and went to South Bend, Indiana, where I taught high school for nine years. I loved every bit of it. Had I not enlisted in the service during World War II, I don't believe I would ever have left that high school job in South Bend.

But when I came back from the service, things weren't the same. I didn't like the way that school was treating some of the returning servicemen, and though I had no complaint about my own situation, I decided I didn't want to work for them anymore. So when Indiana State called and said their coach was just leaving—he had been my high school coach and had recommended me—I talked it over with Nellie, my wife.

I have always referred to myself as a teacher/ coach. I think that's what a coach should be: a teacher first and a coach second.

We said, "Well, let's try it. If we do all right, maybe I'll have a chance to get a job in the Big Ten, and if I don't, I've got a lifetime teacher's license." I've never worried about a job because I knew I could always get one. Maybe not the job I wanted, but a job.

After two years at Indiana State, I had opportunities at Purdue, Minnesota, and UCLA. I said no to Purdue because I didn't like the way they were treating the man I would be replacing, and I decided to take the Minnesota job. But they were supposed to call me at a certain time and they didn't. While I was waiting, UCLA called wanting a final answer and I said yes. Minnesota called and said everything was OK. I said, "Well, I'm sorry, I've just given my word and I can't renege on that."

I really believe that one's greatest joy comes from knowing that something you've said or done has been meaningful to someone else, especially when it was done with no thought of something in return.

And that's how I happened to come to UCLA. After a few years here, I never wanted to leave. I had a lot of opportunities to go back to the Big Ten, but I had settled here, my children were happy, and California is a pretty nice place to live. So I chose to remain here the rest of my career.

The phone rang. "This is a message for the great John Wooden," a voice said into the answering machine. "I just wanted to tell you what a great book you wrote—A Lifetime of Observations. I coach fourth-grade basketball, and I'm going to give it to all the kids on the team so that hopefully they can follow in the path you did. Thank you, Mr. Wooden."

I get a lot of calls like that, and they give me a lot of pleasure. I really believe that one's greatest joy comes from knowing that something you've said or done has been meaningful to someone else, especially when it was done with no thought of something in return. The fact that I've helped someone makes me feel good.

A lot of my players write me poems. Here's an example:

For My Teacher with Love and Appreciation

You teach me to believe in work.

There is no other way.

There is no substitute for it and I've always heard you say.

You teach me to believe in love,

A word forever true.

But warn that it remains a word until it's what I do.

You teach me to believe in books,

Especially the one.

And I have caught the fever now and joined you in the fun.

You teach me to believe in faith

and shun the fear to fail.

I know mistakes are weaknesses and fixed can cure the fall.

Of all the things you teach me, Coach,

And God knows there's a host.

You teach me to believe in me and that's what I love the most.

When your players are writing you things like that it makes you realize you've accomplished something.

The most money I ever made at UCLA was $32,500. That was in my final year. I was offered a shoe contract for more money than that, and I turned it down because I don't believe a coach should be paid to make his players wear certain shoes. In retrospect, though, I think I should have taken the money and put it in a scholarship. But for me to take it personally—I don't think it's correct now and I didn't think it was correct then.

The current coach at UCLA is probably making more in a season than I did in my entire 40 years of coaching. That's not uncommon now, and there are coaches making more money than he is. Am I envious of him? Not at all. I like the guy. I'm not against him getting it. Do I think coaches are overpaid? Of course I think they're overpaid.

Coaches don't like to hear me say this, but I don't believe a coach should be making more money than the president or chancellor of the college. And I'm not so sure that any coach should be making more

Between 1967 and 1969, John Wooden and Kareem Abdul-Jabbar, who was known then as Lew Alcindor, won three NCAA titles at UCLA. Abdul-Jabbar was named the tournament's Most Outstanding Player all three years and went on to become the leading scorer in NBA history. Wooden's teams won a record 10 NCAA championships.

than the head of the science department or the language department or the math department.

I guess I'm the only person that still calls Kareem Adbul-Jabbar Lewis. Not Lew—Lewis. Mostly I say Kareem, but sometimes I slip and call him Lewis. I was with him just the other day and I slipped a time or two. When I do that, I catch myself and say I'm sorry. But he's not critical of me for it. He knows I care for him.

Kareem was always a good student, very intelligent. You never had to worry about him not going to class or not being on time for practice. His biggest problem was migraine headaches. He'd come out to practice and say, "Coach, I've got the migraine," and he'd go in and lie down on the training table in a dark room. Then after a while he'd come back out and work as hard as anybody. He was unselfish and never was a problem.

Coaches don't like to hear me say this, but I don't believe a coach should be making more money than the president or chancellor of the college. And I'm not so sure that any coach should be making more than the head of the science department or the language department or the math department.

I learned more about man's inhumanity to man—how cruel people can be—from him than I ever did from any other individual. I learned just how rude some people can be. I remember once he had been signing some autographs and I said, "Lewis, the bus is waiting. We've got to go." And to the fans he said, "Sorry," and you'd hear, "Look at the big so-and-so," and "Too good to sign autographs." I heard a lot worse than that too.

Bill Walton was the same type of player as Lewis. Once practice started, he was just perfect—a hard worker, an unselfish player, always working to improve himself technically and to improve the other players too. Between practices I worried about him, though. He was antiestablishment. Once he was in a protest that stopped traffic on Wilshire Boulevard—I think he wanted the impeachment of President Nixon—and was involved with the people who were taking over the administration building and trying to get petitions signed.

I talked to my players every year before practice started and I'd always say, "I don't care what your religion is. I don't care what your politics are. You have a right to your own ideas. But all I ask is you please stay open-minded and listen to the other fellow. When your method of protesting denies other people their rights, in my opinion, you're defeating your whole purpose."

Bill would test me once in a while. He didn't think I had the right to make him cut his hair or to tell him he couldn't wear a mustache or a beard or goatee. I told him, "You're right, Bill. I don't have that right. I do have the right, however, to determine who is going to be on the team. We're going to miss you." And so he followed the rules. I'd have lost respect if I hadn't stuck with it. We get along wonderfully today. He calls me three or four times a week.

I always felt my job was done during the week, and if I'd done a good job I could go up in the stands and let the players handle the game. Except for a few instances, I think a coach should be able to do that. I don't think you have to be on the sideline walking up and down and yelling and giving signals. I think that promotes insecurity among the players, makes them feel you don't have confidence in them.

I never yelled at the players at halftime. I didn't see any point to it. I didn't want them to come charging out onto the floor. We'd come in and talk things over technically. I didn't want them to get too excited. I think that's artificial, like the difference between passion and love. Passion is temporary, while love is more enduring. I didn't want a lot of rah-rah stuff. I didn't want them to get tired. I wanted them to save their energy, not go running around bumping into people.

Sure, I barked at the officials. I'd heckle them. But I never used profanity and I tried not to be personal. I'd say "Hustle," or "Can't you see he's traveling?" or "Can you count to 10 seconds?" when we were using our press. Sometimes I'd say, "Call them the same at both ends," and "Don't be a homer." I'm sort of ashamed of that because it was implying an official wasn't being impartial. I'd say those were two of the worst things that I ever said to the officials.

I know you want to talk about the game we played against the University of Houston in the Astrodome. When J. D. Morgan first told me about it, I didn't like the idea at all. I didn't think that was any place to play a basketball game. We were way out in the middle of the place, and I told my players, "If you have to go to the bathroom, do it now because you've got a quarter of a mile back to the restrooms." And the people were so far away. They couldn't see the game. A lot of people go to places just to be a part of it, to be seen. Well, a lot of people go to church just to be seen too. (laughs)

When J.D. told me that the game would be good for college basketball, I didn't agree with him. But he was right and I was wrong. But it didn't change my feeling about the game. Playing there made it a farce, but it brought the most attention to intercollegiate basketball there had ever been up until that time. So that was a good thing.

I think it's harder to be a coach today because the athleticism of athletes has changed coaching quite a bit. Had team play improved to the degree that individual playing has improved—my, it would just be out of this world. Many of the European players who come over here are more fundamentally sound than our own players.

I have also said that the purest basketball played today is on the better women's college teams. They play below the rim rather than above the rim. It offends people when I say that, but I don't think I'm being tactless because I really believe it. They have to be careful too, though. When Lisa Leslie, who was playing for the Los Angeles women's pro team, first dunked the ball, I said, "Uh-oh, that's the worst thing that could happen to women's basketball. They're going to have everybody trying to dunk now. That's not part of their game, and it shouldn't be."

Bill would test me once in a while. He didn't think I had the right to make him cut his hair or to tell him he couldn't wear a mustache or a beard or goatee. I told him, "You're right, Bill. I don't have that right. I do have the right, however, to determine who is going to be on the team. We're going to miss you."

But I would still love coaching today because I love the young men. And I wouldn't change. I might have to make certain changes because of the way society has changed, but my basic philosophy would be the same and my players would know that I care for them more than just as athletes. When my book *Practical Modern Basketball* was published, I had a section titled "Handling Your Players." Then I heard Wilt Chamberlain say, "No one handles me. You handle things, not people." I thought he was absolutely right, so if you pick up that book today, you'll see "Working with Your Players," not handling them.

I think a coach who permits the media or the alumni or the parents or anyone else to affect his judgment is weak. The only type of pressure that amounts to a hill of beans is the pressure you put on yourself to do the very best you can. If you don't put pressure on yourself, you should be fired. If you put pressure on yourself to be the best, then you'll have that peace in your heart that we all need more than anything else.

I always took my wife along on basketball trips because we wanted to be together. That was my one stipulation: that she must go on every trip she was able to go on. I never went to a Final Four without her, up until the time when I lost her [Nell Wooden died in 1985], and then I didn't go again for 10 years. She kind of judged coaches on whether they brought their wives or not. She figured if they didn't, they must be out cutting around. (laughs)

Last year I received the Medal of Freedom Award from President George W. Bush in the White House, which is the highest honor given to anyone not in the military, and I'm very proud of that.

I'm 92 years old, and I've started a new career writing children's books. One of my granddaughters, who teaches kindergarten and elementary school, said I should adapt my Pyramid of Success for youngsters. I developed the pyramid years ago to show the building blocks that go into success, but some of the words were too difficult for children. So I went to work with Steve Jamison, a writer with whom I've worked

before, and we did things like change *industriousness* to *hard work* to come up with a book called *Inches and Miles*. The idea is to show that success isn't built on material things, but things they can't take away from you—like friendship and character.

I write poetry these days too. Here's one of the latest:

But there is no fear within my heart because I'm growing old.

I only wish I had more time to better serve my Lord.

When I've gone to Him in prayer He's brought me inner peace

And soon all cares and troubles and other problems cease.

He's helped me in so many ways, He's never let me down.

Why should I fear the future when soon I could be near His crown?

Though I know down here my time is short, there is endless time up there

And He will forgive and keep me within His loving stare.

I've been blessed in so many ways. My children, my grandchildren, and my great-grandchildren are all within 50 miles of me, and I see them all regularly. My extended family of players and fans are here in Southern California. And last year I received the Medal of Freedom Award from President George W. Bush in the White House, which is the highest honor given to anyone not in the military, and I'm very proud of that.

There was one thing I wanted to ask the president, but I didn't do it: "How come you let Sammy Sosa go for those two minor leaguers?" (laughs)

CHAPTER 3

Kareem Abdul-Jabbar Tells about Life at the Top

Los Angeles, California, January 2005

When I first met coach Wooden, he was working out of a Quonset hut on the UCLA campus, and he reminded me of somebody from a different era, the 1890s maybe. He was this very quaint midwestern gentleman who seemed as if he should be in a Thomas Hart Benton painting. You could almost see him fitting in perfectly driving a hay wagon. Everything about him said rural Indiana. The movie *Bonnie and Clyde* came out when I was in college, and when I saw it I thought about coach Wooden. He just epitomizes an earlier era to me.

When he started talking to us about his Pyramid of Success, it made me suspect he was a Mason. We got a lecture about it every day in practice. I was just glad we didn't have to memorize it. (laughs)

In high school, my coach was Jack Donohue, who was exactly the opposite from coach Wooden. Donohue was a New York Irishman who later went on to coach at Holy Cross. Coach Donohue was one of those guys who kissed the Blarney Stone—he had this absolutely great gift of gab and sense of humor.

He was always making fun of his players, and you had to keep your guard up because you didn't want him to start needling you.

He was this very quaint midwestern gentleman who seemed as if he should be in a Thomas Hart Benton painting. You could almost see him fitting in perfectly driving a hay wagon.

Coach Wooden was so different. He was a great communicator too, but he always had a very serious demeanor. People thought he was stern, but that was really just hype. He was a very sweet man, and he had a genuine desire for us to learn about basketball and how to be good human beings and to graduate from college. That was really important for him and is something you usually get only from your parents. Most basketball coaches just want you to play.

I had a serious commitment to getting my degree, and it meant a lot to my parents too, because they expected me to do well in school. They demanded it, really, and always rewarded me when I did. I'll always remember my mom pointing out how articulate Jackie Robinson, who went to UCLA, was, implying that he was someone I should pattern myself after. What impressed me most about Robinson, though, was how he had so much to say about things that had nothing to do with baseball. That had a real effect on me.

People always want to know how I ended up at UCLA. I grew up in New York and played at Power Memorial Academy, which was an all-boys Catholic school. I was heavily recruited by St. John's and NYU. And Michigan, which had good teams with Cazzie Russell then, was interested too.

I'll always remember my mom pointing out how articulate Jackie Robinson, who went to UCLA, was, implying that he was someone I should pattern myself after. What impressed me most about Robinson, though, was how he had so much to say about things that had nothing to do with baseball. That had a real effect on me.

But when I went out to UCLA in March, it was 70 degrees. There was snow on the ground in New York, and that was more or less it. I was torn somewhat about not going to school in New York because I'd won an academic scholarship that would have given me some cash every month that I couldn't get at UCLA. That was my biggest regret.

But there was more to it than just the weather. I had been following UCLA for some time, although I

did it by reading the box scores because the games weren't on TV. I really liked what I heard about the way they played the game, the way they used the full-court press to great advantage. People say our UCLA teams were the best they ever had—we had four high school All-Americans—but the team I enjoyed the most was one I didn't even play on, the 1964 team.

The tallest player was 6'6", and they just ran everybody off the court. By the second half, the other team was always calling time because they couldn't breathe, and then Kenny Washington would come off the bench and score 20 points and have 10 rebounds and four assists and be blocking shots. I thought, "These guys know how to play." They were such great athletes.

They won every game that year, and what I remember is how everybody said they were going to lose every major game they played because they didn't have a legitimate center. But that didn't seem to matter to them. They played Kansas early in the year, which I think had two seven-footers, and just ran them off the floor. I was so impressed with that.

That was my senior year in high school, and it really got my attention. What I liked was they played an up-tempo game that wasn't necessarily reliant on muscle. I was a skinny kid in high school, and I didn't think I was going to survive the muscle game. I liked the fact that UCLA really emphasized speed and agility and great defense. That's the way I wanted to play the game. It was the way the Celtics played—find the open man, everybody playing tight, pressing defense. It was what I thought I could be effective at as a professional player.

I did get homesick that first year at UCLA. I missed my friends and parents and the excitement of New York, but I realized it was good I was out here because I needed all the time I could get for school. And I did do pretty well. I ended up with a B average and I graduated on time. And it wasn't long before I was making friends on the team. I lived in the dorm with guys like Lucius Allen, Lynn Shackelford, Kenny

Abdul-Jabbar was all but unstoppable when he was close to the basket. Ineligible for varsity competition his freshman year, he led UCLA's freshman team to a win over the Bruins' varsity players, who were the defending NCAA champions. The freshman-varsity game was never played again. Photograph courtesy of ASUCLA Photography.

Heitz, and Bill Sweek. We all became fast and furious friends, and we're still in contact.

The fact that freshmen were ineligible to play then really helped me a lot. It gave me a year to deal with

I never regretted coming to UCLA. I couldn't have had a better college basketball career, and I got my degree. I did everything I was supposed to do. If there was a downside, it might have been that after we won the NCAA championship my sophomore year everybody just expected us to win it the next two years too.

academics, and though we played freshman ball, we didn't have as much pressure or scrutiny as the varsity did. It also helped us learn the coach's system, to understand the offense and defense and how to be patient. I think that made us better players. We beat the varsity that year, and they did away with the freshman-varsity game. I guess it was kind of hard for them to be No. 1 in the nation and No. 2 on campus.

I never regretted coming to UCLA. I couldn't have had a better college basketball career, and I got my degree. I did everything I was supposed to do. If there was a downside, it might have been that after we won the NCAA championship my sophomore year everybody just expected us to win it the next two years too. That robbed us of a sense of discovery because if we won, we were doing what everybody said we should be doing, and if we lost, we screwed up. So it was difficult for us to get in a positive mindset sometimes, but I guess it worked out OK, didn't it? Those expectations were something I had to put up with my entire career, actually. Because of my size and talent, people would try to minimize the effort and discipline it took to achieve success.

One of the things I learned from both coach Wooden and coach Donohue was that if you wanted to win you had to stay in shape. So I got used to training 12 months a year—I think I was ahead of the curve there.

The time when I was in college was horrible in terms of the way the country was being torn up: the 1968 Democratic National Convention, the Tet Offensive, Martin Luther King's assassination, Bobby Kennedy's assassination, and the shootings at Kent State. That all happened around the same time, and I found myself thinking, how can a country survive something like that? There were times when I felt that I should speak out, but I don't think that was any different from how a lot of people felt. A lot of people became activists because of the My Lai massacre and the bombing of Cambodia and Laos. Somebody had to say something. Remember when Fred Hampton got murdered in Chicago? A couple of friends of mine were living in the same building when it happened.

We lost only two games while I was at UCLA. One was against USC—it was my last regular-season game—when they stalled a lot and beat us 46–44. The other one, of course, is the game everybody remembers in the Astrodome.

Some people said I shouldn't have played in the game because of the eye injury I suffered in a game we played eight days earlier. But the way I looked at it, we couldn't win if I didn't play, and right down to the end I thought we were going to squeak it out.

The thing I remember about the Astrodome is how unreal it felt to be playing a basketball game there. It was the most uncomfortable place to play a game anyone could have imagined. The court was out at second base, so we were in this place with fifty-five thousand people, but there was nobody by the court at all. It was like we were playing a game out on a prairie. It was really weird.

The lights weren't very good that night, but lighting has never really bothered me that much. The big problem was I just didn't have any wind that day because

I hadn't played in so long—I'd missed two games with the eye injury—that and not being able to make a shot. The ball just would not go down. And Elvin Hayes had a great game. We just couldn't guard him.

What's funny about that is that as a pro Elvin couldn't guard *me*. When he played with the Bullets, they had Wes Unseld guard me because Elvin didn't like to do it. His whole thing was to step up and block the shot, but I'd just take a quick step away from him and shoot the hook shot. He could never time it. I always thought Elvin wasn't really a center anyway. On the best teams he played for he was a power forward.

The way Elvin told me the story, he was the number-one player in Louisiana, and he couldn't even apply to LSU. He had to go out of state to make his mark. Houston was considered liberal and cutting edge then because it recruited blacks. Did you know they recruited me? It's true: I got a letter from Lyndon B. Johnson telling me Houston was interested in me.

One thing about that game I didn't realize for another 10 years was its social implications. When the athletic directors in the South saw Houston with an integrated team beat the best team in the country, a light went on as far as understanding they were shunning tremendous talent in their home states because of the color of players' skin.

That's when those conferences started improving by using *all* the local talent, not just the white kids. The way Elvin told me the story, he was the number-

one player in Louisiana, and he couldn't even apply to LSU. He had to go out of state to make his mark. Houston was considered liberal and cutting edge then because it recruited blacks. Did you know they recruited me? It's true: I got a letter from Lyndon B. Johnson telling me Houston was interested in me.

Anyway, I was just glad we got a chance to play them again that season in the Final Four and to show the world who was really the better team. Then the next year everybody was waiting to see if UCLA was going to do it again, and we did. In fact, UCLA did it four more times after that—seven championships in a row. People talk about dynasties, but what college is going to win seven NCAA Tournaments in a row?

When I went to the NBA, the biggest thing as far as I was concerned was just to see if I could do it. A lot of people thought I was going to have a hard time because I wasn't a bruiser, and I have to admit I was wondering about that myself. But what I found was that being able to run is a great substitute for not being a bruiser. I made it so the big men had to run. They couldn't jog up and down the court so much anymore. I remember I ran past Walter Bellamy on the court once and he said, "Slow down, man. You're making me look bad." (laughs)

I'll tell you what my goal was—aside from winning, of course. I just wanted to have people respect me like I respected Wilt Chamberlain. When I was in high school, I saw what a physical specimen he was, and I never thought I could eclipse what he had done. But I thought maybe I could have people respect me the same way they respected him. I never thought I'd break any of his records. I never played against Bill Russell—his first year of retirement was my first year in the league—but I do think Wilt was the most tremendously gifted in that he was so strong.

What I learned from watching Russell was how to play a mobile, aggressive defense. I'd body my guy and then I'd go help elsewhere, try to block shots and cut off lanes for layups. Offensively, I always tried to stay in constant motion around the three points of the key to make it easy for my teammates to hit me while I was moving so I could get off a quick hook shot, which I shot pretty accurately. I tried to make people work at trying to figure out where I was going to be. What I wanted was always to be someplace else getting a shot off before they could react. That was how I made my bread and butter.

I tried to make people work at trying to figure out where I was going to be. What I wanted was always to be someplace else getting a shot off before they could react. That was how I made my bread and butter.

I've done a lot of things since I retired from the NBA. I just wrote a book titled *Brothers in Arms*, about a black tank unit that fought bravely in World War II but didn't get any recognition. I wanted to do my part to see that they got the recognition they deserved. I've always been interested in history.

The one place I can't get anything going is in basketball. People don't want to hire me. I think there's an underlying resentment because I was never gregarious as a player and people think I can't communicate. I was the head coach of a U.S. Basketball League team in Oklahoma City and we won the championship, but it didn't springboard into anything. The NBA is a closed door to me. It just doesn't look like I'm going to get to do any coaching.

I was always wary of the press, I guess. I didn't know who was a wolf and who was a sheep. But I think I'm dealing with the public a lot better now. I take time with them. When you're a young man, you don't really think about it, but now I realize that when I have some time, I should take time with people. But still, there are times when you don't know how to deal with it.

Coach Wooden and I are in touch a lot now—I just talked to him two weeks ago—and I think our relationship has become stronger over the years. My mom's dead and my father has to be taken care of, so, in a way, he's the only connection I have to that time in my life.

CHAPTER 4

Bill Walton: My Battles with John Wooden

San Antonio, Texas, January 2005

I was the easiest recruit UCLA ever had. I used to listen to their games on the radio in bed at night. Remember those little $9.95 transistors where you put the battery on your tongue to see if it was still good? I'd listen to Fred Hessler broadcast the UCLA games and Chick Hearn do the Lakers.

My dad refused to allow the *San Diego Union* in the house—he didn't like its politics—so we got the *Los Angeles Times*, which had all these stories about UCLA basketball and football. This was in the midsixties, when Gary Beban was the quarterback for UCLA and they went to the Rose Bowl. My brother Bruce and I both thought it was so unbelievable, and I fell in love with the 1964 and 1965 national championship basketball teams. We both had the sense we would go to UCLA. Bruce, who was a year ahead of me, went first and became an All-American tackle on the football team. Later, he played for the Dallas Cowboys in the Roger Staubach era. He was a perfect big brother except he was a bully. (laughs)

Denny Crum, who was John Wooden's chief assistant, started recruiting me, and in my junior year, I went to Pauley Pavilion for the first time. They were playing the NCAA Regionals there. It was Kareem Abdul-Jabbar's last game, and the place was going crazy. I'd never seen anything like it, and I told myself, "That's what I want."

It was the era of Vietnam, Watergate, the Beatles, the Rolling Stones, and I'm like, "Yeah! I'm going to UCLA! I'm free, free, free at last." Little did I realize that John Wooden was standing on the steps waiting for me.

We didn't have a TV when we were growing up. Bruce, my other brother Andy, my sister Cathy, and I bugged my parents relentlessly to get us one. But they said, "No, we can't afford one." But we kept hounding them. We said, "We'll eat less if we can have a TV." One night at the dinner table, my mom, who was a librarian, said, "OK, we've saved enough money to buy a TV," and we all went, "Yay!" But then she said, "But I've been doing a lot of research in the library, and I've decided that there's nothing on television worth watching, so we're not going to get one."

We were all just crestfallen, but in another year or so we got one and I was able to see the Houston-UCLA game in the Astrodome. Do you know that was the one game in Kareem's college career that he did not shoot 50 percent? He was 4 for 18. We paid attention to things like that. We were all such Bruins fans.

My mom and dad were the most unathletic people. I never shot a single basketball with my dad. One time I saw him run at a church picnic and I fell over laughing. But he taught me everything about life—about family and trust and confidence and love. Mostly what he taught me, though, was about hard work. He had three jobs, and we lived from paycheck to paycheck. He was a social worker in the daytime, an adult educator at night, and a music teacher on the weekends. I thought we had just the greatest life ever.

My parents were strict, though—we had so many rules and regulations. When I graduated from high school in 1970, I was really ready to leave home. It was the era of Vietnam, Watergate, the Beatles, the Rolling Stones, and I'm like, "Yeah! I'm going to UCLA! I'm free, free, free at last." Little did I realize that John Wooden was standing on the steps waiting for me.

Today our house is a shrine to coach Wooden. I took my sons to his house and had him show them how to put their shoes and socks on the way he taught us. We've got his Pyramids of Success all over our house and pictures of coach Wooden peering at us from different corners. I used to write some of his sayings on the kids' lunch bags: "Be quick but don't hurry." "Happiness begins when selfishness ends." "Failing to prepare is preparing to fail." "Never mistake activity for achievement." And I call him all the time.

But, I've got to say, when I think about some of the things we did back then, I feel so bad. I was John

Wooden's worst nightmare. He would give all these speeches, and the first time we heard them we'd think "Oh, wow! This is great!" The second year it was, "What is he talking about?" The third year, we knew the speeches backward and forward, and we would mouth them back to him. We'd throw in rock 'n' roll lyrics while we were doing it—something from Mick Jagger, John Lennon, Jerry Garcia, or Bob Dylan. One day we were all at the center of the court and Coach was giving his talk, and we were mouthing it right back to him, throwing in quotes from Dylan.

Coach Wooden and I fought about everything because no matter what he said, I always wanted to know why. "Why do we have to do it this way? Why? Why? Why?" When I got to UCLA, coach Wooden was this young, spry guy with jet-black hair and a fine step wherever he walked. Within 18 months, he had a heart attack, his hair turned white, and he was all bent over.

Well, he started to lose it, and in the sternest voice I've ever heard from him, he said, "Goodness gracious sakes alive, if I ever hear any more of this Bob *Dye*-lan song crap, I don't know what I'm going to do with you guys." We just fell over laughing. We couldn't believe he'd said *crap*. The only other time he got that mad was when we were in Tucson our senior year for the NCAA Regionals, and in the middle of the night we were all out in the Jacuzzi with the cheerleaders, making a lot of noise. He came out in his nightgown—no, really—and he was very upset.

Coach Wooden and I fought about everything because no matter what he said, I always wanted to know why. "Why do we have to do it this way? Why?

Bill Walton led UCLA to two more national championsips, including an 87–66 victory over Memphis State in 1973, in which he played a nearly perfect game. Walton scored on 21 of 22 field-goal attempts for 44 points.

Why? Why?" When I got to UCLA, coach Wooden was this young, spry guy with jet-black hair and a fine step wherever he walked. Within 18 months, he had a heart attack, his hair turned white, and he was all bent over.

The problem was that I was raised by my parents to think for myself, to question authority, and to be involved. So we argued about politics, religion, social issues, Vietnam, clothes, beards, hair length—you name it, we had an argument about it. And you know what? He won every single one. He would always finish every one with, "Bill, I really admire and respect your obviously heartfelt positions that you have elucidated so sharply and crisply. But you know what? I'm the coach here. I make the decisions, and if you want to be on the team you'll do what I say. But whatever you do, please rest assured that we've enjoyed having you." I was never willing to test him on that.

On our way home he said, "Come on, Walton, what is this all about? You're representing UCLA, you're the college Player of the Year, you're an Academic All-American, you're the team captain, and you get yourself *arrested*?"

One day I went into his office and said, "Coach, the basketball season is in the fall and winter quarters. I'd like to go to Berkeley in spring quarter." He just looked at me like I was crazy and said, "No, Bill. We're not going to do that."

I suppose you want to hear about the time I got arrested. The whole campus was protesting the Vietnam War. We moved down into Westwood Village, and the police came in from the other direction to meet us. They charged toward us and we backed up, then we charged them. The other guys on the team were there too, but you could see the police pointing at me and saying, "That big guy, we're going to get him." And they arrested me and took me to jail.

Dr. Charles Young, who was the chancellor of UCLA then, says that as I went by in the paddy wagon I gave him the finger.

It's true. I've done a lot of things I'm not proud of, Eddie. Coach Wooden had to come down to bail me out, and oh, was he mad. On our way home he said, "Come on, Walton, what is this all about? You're representing UCLA, you're the college Player of the Year, you're an Academic All-American, you're the team captain, and you get yourself *arrested*?"

I said, "Coach, this war is just the worst. We've got to stop it right now, and we're going to do it."

He said, "I agree that the war is wrong, but I think your protesting is the wrong way to go about it. What you should do is write letters."

I said, "Write letters? What are you talking about? My friends are coming home from Vietnam in body bags and wheelchairs, and you're telling me to write letters?" Finally, he dropped me off and I said, as if nothing had happened, "See you tomorrow at practice."

Then this flash of inspiration went off in my head like a lightning bolt. I went down to his office and asked his secretary for a piece of stationery. It had coach Wooden's picture on it, and basketballs representing all the championship teams, including ours. I wrote this incredible letter to Nixon outlining his crimes against humanity and demanding an immediate end to the war and his resignation. At the end, I thanked him in advance for his cooperation.

The next day at practice, I showed it to the guys and they all wanted to sign it. Then I took it to coach Wooden's locker and said, "Coach, remember yesterday when we had that talk and you told me to write letters?"

"Yes, Bill."

"Well, I wrote a letter, Coach, and I'd like you to take a look at it and sign it, please."

I handed him the letter and it's got his picture at the top and all our signatures at the bottom and you could just see the blood leave his fingers. You could tell he wanted to tear it up. But he handed it back and looked up at me with the sad, soft eyes of a father who's been let down and said, "Bill, I can't sign this."

"Are you sure, Coach?"

"Yes. Bill, you're not going to send this in, are you?"

"Oh, yes, Coach, I am."

He could have just crumpled it up and thrown it away—I'd have never gotten another piece of that stationery—but he handed it back to me and I mailed it in. Two months later, Nixon resigned. You know, Coach Wooden's got a letter from Nixon on the wall at one end of a room in his house. I always sit at the other end. (laughs)

"OK, men, gather round," he'd say, and we'd sit down and be ready for some unbelievable speech. But he'd just look at us and say, "Men, I've done my job. The rest is up to you. When the game starts, don't ever look over to me at the sideline. I can't do anything for you." And that was it. Every game. It was like, "I've taught you how to play, now go and play."

I'll tell you what really makes me sick about those days when I think about it: not going to China for that historic basketball game you broadcast. We were supposed to go—Nixon had called up Coach and J. D. Morgan and asked them to represent the country—but we didn't think it would be any fun. We wanted to go to the beach. We wanted to go to Yosemite. We wanted to chase girls. We wanted to tour with the Grateful Dead. Who wanted to go to China?

J.D. was so mad the day we told him we weren't going. And in retrospect, I totally agree with him. We should have gone to China. We should have won all our games. We should have done so many things. I just wish somebody had taken me aside and

said, "You know what, Bill? You're making a big mistake here."

But I probably wouldn't have listened anyway. We were 17, 18, 19 years old, and we thought we knew everything. I can never thank all of them—coach Wooden, J. D. Morgan, Charles Young, Ducky Drake, who was our trainer—for being so forgiving, so caring, and so loving. I thank them for their patience, because they should have washed their hands of me.

Here's why John Wooden was such a great coach: he let us play. He hardly ever called timeouts, which he thought were an admission of defeat that gave the other team a chance to regroup. And as fierce as he was in practice—he was like a caged tiger, barking, pushing, driving—he'd come into the locker room before games and be the calmest person in the world.

"OK, men, gather round," he'd say, and we'd sit down and be ready for some unbelievable speech. But he'd just look at us and say, "Men, I've done my job. The rest is up to you. When the game starts, don't ever look over to me at the sideline. I can't do anything for you." And that was it. Every game. It was like, "I've taught you how to play, now go and play."

People thought he was so quiet and composed during the games, but he'd be sitting there with that rolled-up program and be razzing the refs and taunting the other team. Once, I was sitting on the bench and a guy made a shot, and Coach jumped up and said, "You think you're really good. Let's see you do that on Walton." (laughs)

I was really lucky with all my coaches. From a guy named Rocky, who was the volunteer coach for every sport we played starting in the fourth grade, to coach Wooden and Lenny Wilkens, my first professional coach, and then Jack Ramsay, Paul Silas, Gene Shue, and at the end of my career, K. C. Jones and Red Auerbach. I never played for any of the gargoyles, the egomaniacs, the self-promoters. I'm glad about that because I probably would have quit basketball. Today players see coaches as interchangeable parts, but I played for six coaches who are in the Hall of Fame, and I know the difference. I know the value of a John Wooden and a Red Auerbach.

My first two years at UCLA we went undefeated and won the NCAA title. This was when teams liked to fast break all the time—that's what's wrong with today's game, no fast breaks—and that's the game I know. My favorite part of basketball was starting the fast break by blocking the shot, deflecting the pass, or getting the rebound, and then whipping the ball out and watching the other guys race down the floor. My sophomore year, we set an NCAA record for biggest winning percentage—more than 32 points per game—and it was nothing for us to score 110 points per game. But then the other teams started slowing it down, and by the time we were seniors, the scores were like 45–38.

The game everybody says was my best was the NCAA championship we won my junior year when we beat Memphis State 87–66. That was UCLA's seventh straight title, and I made 21 of 22 field goal attempts and set a record for the Finals with 44 points. But I've always thought I got too much credit for that game. Our guards had 23 assists between them: Greg Lee set a championship game record that still stands with 14, and Larry Hollyfield had a career high with 9. When Larry Hollyfield gets nine assists, you know it's a harmonic convergence.

Of course, I remember the shot I missed. It was in the first half, and I knew immediately that I missed it, so I just grabbed the rebound and put it right back in. Coach Wooden tells me to this day, "Walton, I used to think you were a good player until you missed that shot." (laughs)

Our senior year was when the trouble started. The game we lost at Notre Dame that broke our 88-game winning streak is the one people remember, but we had a losing weekend in Oregon where we lost to the University of Oregon and Oregon State too. And, of course, we lost in the semifinals of the NCAA Tournament to North Carolina State. We had a seven-point lead with a few minutes to go and we lost in double overtime. Oh, man.

What went wrong that season? Everything. Everything that made us a great team our first two years. We stopped listening to the coach—by then we thought everything he said was crazy—and we started beating ourselves. It was just terrible. If there's one thing I could redo, it would be my senior year. We were good enough to win them all.

Looking back, I really love the fact we were able to build such a great basketball rivalry between UCLA and Notre Dame. I love the animosity, the bitterness, the anger. Whenever my boys got mad at me when they were growing up, they'd say, "Dad, I hate you. I'm going to Notre Dame."

The trouble actually started 12 days before the Notre Dame game when I broke my back. We were playing at Washington State, and I was submarined while I was making a high play at the basket. A guy just cut my legs from underneath me, and I spent the next eight days in the hospital. Then they put me in a corset with steel rods, and I couldn't play in the game we had against Iowa in Chicago two days before we played Notre Dame. I played the whole game in South Bend, though. Every minute of it.

What did we have, an 11-point lead with about three minutes to go? And this predated the shot clock, predated the three-point shot. How could we *lose*? We just gave the game away, that's all. We beat them the next weekend at home—thank goodness we had another shot at them—and looking back, I really love the fact we were able to build such a great basketball rivalry between UCLA and Notre Dame. I love the animosity, the bitterness, the anger. Whenever my boys got mad at me when they were growing up, they'd say, "Dad, I hate you. I'm going to Notre Dame."

When I left UCLA, I became the highest-paid player in the history of team sports at that time. My agent started talking to me about what we should do with the money, and I said, "Look, I don't care about any of that stuff. The only thing I want is nobody telling me that I have to cut my hair or shave my beard. The sad thing about that is I've got the worst beard in the history of Western Civilization. I've got the only beard that makes Bob Dylan's beard look good.

Today I'm an NBA broadcaster, and who ever would have thought that would happen? I remember when I couldn't speak at all; I was so shy and stuttered so badly that I couldn't say hello, I couldn't say thank you. I was winning all those awards, and coach Wooden would say, "Bill, you need to go to these dinners and accept these awards."

I'd say, "Coach, I am not going to go up there to start stuttering and embarrass myself. The only way I'll go is if you accept the award and give the speech for me."

But he said, "Bill, you have to give these talks," and I did, even though it was one of the hardest things I ever did. Later, Marty Glickman, the great broadcaster, worked with me so I could get my first broadcasting job, but it was coach Wooden who first convinced me I could overcome my limitations.

John Wooden is a saint. He really is. I love that man.

PART III

January 20, 1968

UCLA's game against Houston in the Astrodome changed the face of college basketball and proved that my belief in the game as a national television attraction might not have been so crazy after all. The stars were all in alignment that night as we had the top two teams in the country—which were both undefeated—the top two players, the largest crowd ever to see a basketball game in the United States, and basketball's first prime-time television audience, which was its largest in history. And to top everything off, it turned out to be a great game, with Houston breaking UCLA's 47-game win streak with a 71–69 victory.

Here, from some of those people who played important roles on that magical night, is a behind-the-scenes look at a key moment in the evolution of March Madness.

Guy Lewis coached basketball at the University of Houston for 30 seasons, during which his teams posted a record of 502–279, made the NCAA Tournament 14 times, and went to the Final Four five times. I consider his exclusion from the Basketball Hall of Fame in Springfield, Massachusetts, to be scandalous.

Elvin Hayes was the star of Houston's first nationally ranked team and the college Player of the Year in 1968. He led the Cougars to the Final Four twice and scored 30 or more points 37 times during his career, including the 39 scored against UCLA in the Astrodome. After a 17-year NBA career, Hayes retired as the league's third-leading scorer and rebounder in history and the all-time leader in minutes played.

Dick Enberg was broadcasting UCLA's basketball games on television in Los Angeles when I hired him to do the play-by-play from the Astrodome. He went on to become one of the best—and best-known—broadcasters in the country. Enberg has broadcast the Final Four, baseball, the NFL, the Olympics, Wimbledon, major golf tournaments, and much more.

Ted Nance, who was the publicity director for the University of Houston, was among those primarily responsible for planning and promoting the game.

Gary Cunningham was an assistant to John Wooden for 10 seasons during UCLA's glory years. In 1977 he became the Bruins' head coach for two years before moving into the athletic administration. Today he is the athletic director at the University of California–Santa Barbara.

Jerry Norman played at UCLA in the fifties and was an assistant to John Wooden for nine years. UCLA went to five Final Fours and won four national championships during his coaching tenure. He then left the game and began a successful career in business.

Lynn Shackelford was, along with Lew Alcindor, Lucius Allen, and Kenny Heitz, one of four high school All-Americans who entered UCLA in 1965. A

6'5" forward known for his long rainbow jump shots, he starred for three years on Bruins teams that won 88 games and lost only 2. He later played professionally and became a basketball broadcaster.

Mike Warren was a guard on the UCLA team that played Houston in the Astrodome and went on to win the NCAA championship. After graduation he became a successful actor, playing in *Hill Street Blues* on television for seven years and a number of other shows.

Don Chaney played a key role in Houston's upset victory. He played 11 seasons in the NBA (and one in the rival ABA) and won two titles with the Boston Celtics. He later coached the Los Angeles Clippers, the Houston Rockets, the Detroit Pistons, and the New York Knicks.

Mickey Herskowitz, the veteran *Houston Chronicle* columnist and author, covered the game in the Astrodome and believes it played an important role in the development of the University of Houston and the city itself.

CHAPTER 5

Guy Lewis on His Big Idea

Houston, Texas, January 2004

I was born in Arp, Texas, about 200 miles east of Houston, and I still go back every two years for my class reunion. There are only about 900 people in the town, but the school district is pretty big, so we always have a good turnout. I went to the University of Nebraska for two years, but I hated it because Coach liked to kill us in practice. So one day I said, "I'm not coming back here."

My brother was at the University of Houston—there was hardly any school here at all then, it was really just starting—and he convinced me to give it a

The game with UCLA in the Astrodome is my favorite game of all time.

try. Nobody thought our basketball team would win anything—I think we were picked to finish last in our conference—but we won the first two years I played.

After that I was an assistant coach, but I also had a farm with some cattle, so I wasn't too anxious to

coach full time when they asked me if I was interested. Finally they called and said, "We've asked you before, and this is the last time we're going to ask." And I said, "Hold that job." It was a pretty good decision, I guess.

My first year as coach we won nine games, and the next year we won ten. Then I got on a roll and we started doing a little better. Twenty-seven straight winning seasons. That's not too bad, is it? And I never coached anywhere except at my alma mater.

The game with UCLA in the Astrodome is my favorite game of all time, but I really had trouble trying to talk our athletic director, Harry Fouke, into it. The first time I mentioned it to him was in his office, and he kept saying, "No, no, no, no. Just get out of here with that talk." About two weeks later, I went back again and it was the same thing: "Get out of here. Don't even talk about that."

When I came back the third time, I said, "Harry, now listen, dammit, we could have a good crowd, and I'm telling you we can beat them." This time he didn't throw me out of his office, so I stood at the door and asked, "How much has Houston ever gotten to host a basketball game?"

He said, "You know the answer to that. We've gotten $5,000 a couple of times."

I said, "All right, I'll pay the university $10,000, and I'll pay UCLA $10,000."

He just looked at me. Hell, he knew I couldn't raise $10,000. I probably couldn't have raised $500, but he said, "Dammit, if you believe in it that much, come in here and let's talk about it." I said we could sell thirty-five thousand tickets, and he said, "You're crazy," but I could tell he was starting to think about it.

Then Harry said, "Well, by God, if we do this, we've got to talk to the judge." I'll have to admit I hadn't really thought about the Astrodome. But the next thing I knew, we were up in that famous suite up high in the Astrodome where Judge Roy Hofheinz lived—he had about nine rooms up there—giving him our pitch. He listened to us for about 10 minutes, and then he said, "Where are you going to put the court?"

"In the middle of the field," I said.

"But people won't be able to see the ball or the players from that far away," he said.

"Look," I said, "is it a good field for baseball?"

"It's great," he said. "Everybody loves it."

"Well, damn," I said, "you have this little ball. Don't you think people could see our big one? And besides, most of the players on my team are bigger than the ones on your baseball team."

He just laughed and said, "Well, damn if you're not right there."

So we talked him into it, and I told him we'd get UCLA to come. We hadn't even *talked* to UCLA at that point, and quite frankly I wasn't sure they would come. We'd played them here once before, in 1961, in our gym, and beaten them 91–65, so I knew John Wooden's memories of Houston weren't so hot. But I never thought of playing anybody else. They were the No. 1 team in the country. They had Lew Alcindor, and we had Elvin Hayes, so I knew we were good too.

On the way home from seeing the judge, Harry said, "Are you going to talk to John Wooden?"

I said, "No, you are. I got the ball rolling. Now it's up to you."

The night of the game the players ran out onto the court and the Astrodome was packed. The noise was just overwhelming, and I told one of the players, "Just come back here a minute. Slow down. I want to enjoy this." He did, and we walked slowly out onto the floor.

I knew Harry was close to J. D. Morgan, who was UCLA's athletic director, and by then he was as excited about the game as I was. And he talked to J.D. and got it done. John Wooden didn't want to do it at first. He was worried about the setting and the lighting and the crowd—it really didn't appeal to him. But J.D. kept thinking about those thirty-five thousand people. The way he worked on John was to keep telling him it would be televised all over the country and it would help college basketball. Finally John had to agree he was right.

The two months leading up to the game were just crazy. I sat in my little office and the phone kept ringing and ringing with people wanting tickets or just to talk about the game. I didn't have a secretary, so my assistant and I would take turns answering the phone, which was sitting on my desk between us. He would pick up one call and I'd get the next until one of us got tired and walked out of the office. All anybody wanted to talk about was that damn game. It was the same thing when I got home. My wife would have 15 names for me to call, and I'd call them all. We didn't have an unlisted number in those days. We didn't even know we could get one.

The night of the game the players ran out onto the court and the Astrodome was packed. The noise was just overwhelming, and I told one of the players, "Just come back here a minute. Slow down. I want to enjoy this." He did, and we walked slowly out onto the floor. I looked around and saw two other coaches who were supposed to be playing games of their own that night. They had rescheduled them so they could come to our game.

We had only practiced in the Astrodome once, but I didn't think that was going to be a problem, and it wasn't. I went in there just knowing we were going to win. I may have been the only one who felt that way—me and the team, anyway—but I just knew we would. I knew Elvin was going to have a good game—I didn't know he'd score 39 points, of course—and I thought it would be close, but I was sure we were going to win.

Our game plan was to beat UCLA's press, for which they were famous. We knew if we could do that, we could win. The way you beat a press is by passing, so I told the players not to run down the court too fast, but to come back and meet the ball and then just keep passing it. George Reynolds was our ball handler and he brought the ball up for us, but the key was that we didn't put the ball on the floor much. That really made a big difference.

We put Ken Spain, our 6'9" center, on Alcindor, and he did a really good job. They said Alcindor had an eye injury, but there is no question that Ken had a lot to do with him scoring on only 4 of his 18 shots. That was the key defensively. I still think about Ken a lot. He died of cancer in 1990. He was only 44.

My son played in that game. Vern was a guard, and he played four minutes. Later he went into coaching, but when he won 31 games his first year, he said, "This is too easy. I'm getting out." And he went into business.

As for Elvin, he was just great that day. I honestly think he wasn't going to let anybody beat him. And when he ended up dribbling the ball with time run-

ning out at the end of the game, it didn't bother me at all. I knew we'd be all right. He wasn't going to lose the game for us then.

Elvin was the best dunker I ever had. Later, when Hakeem Olajuwon and Clyde Drexler were on the same team in the eighties, Tommy Bonk, a Houston writer, called us Phi Slama Jama, and that nickname stuck. But Elvin and his bunch could really dunk too.

Elvin was the best dunker I ever had. Later, when Hakeem Olajuwon and Clyde Drexler were on the same team in the eighties, Tommy Bonk, a Houston writer, called us Phi Slama Jama, and that nickname stuck. But Elvin and his bunch could really dunk too. We were Phi Slama Jama before anyone knew what to call it.

We were Phi Slama Jama before anyone knew what to call it.

The dunk was an important part of our game, and we worked on it. It's a high-percentage shot, and I think when a big man gets around the basket he ought to just explode up there and stick it in the hole. We practiced it over and over—a four-step movement where you catch the ball, check the defense, step to the basket, and then dunk. It wasn't for show. I would tell coaches who didn't like it, "You can't dunk without hustling." But a lot of people didn't like it, and they outlawed it for a while. Lew Alcindor thought it was because of him, but I read once where John Wooden told him, "It wasn't you that caused them to outlaw the dunk. It was that crazy bunch from Houston." And that's probably the truth.

Nobody lobbied for the dunk to come back like I did—every chance I got. I wore out Ed Steitz, who was the chairman of the NCAA Rules Committee, telling him what an injustice it was to take the dunk away. Finally he called me and said, "Guy, would you leave me alone if we put it back in but didn't let you dunk in warm-ups?" I said, "Ed, I don't give a damn about dunking in the warm-ups. I want to dunk in the game. Do that and you won't ever hear from me again." And finally they restored it.

After we beat UCLA, we didn't lose any games the rest of the season, right up until we played them again in the NCAA Tournament. What's funny is that we lost on the same floor we beat them on. The floor we used in the Astrodome originally came from the Sports Arena in Los Angeles. They just bundled it up and put it on a truck and brought it here.

After we beat UCLA, we didn't lose any games the rest of the season, right up until we played them again in the NCAA Tournament. What's funny is that we lost on the same floor we beat them on. The floor we used in the Astrodome originally came from the Sports Arena in Los Angeles. They just bundled it up and put it on a truck and brought it here.

A lot of people say the game did great things for college basketball, and some folks made a lot of money from it too. I don't mind that they got money and I didn't. It was just a different time. You say John Wooden made $32,500 his last year coaching? Well,

he beats me, then. I only made $30,000 up until the eighties, when they finally gave me a contract for $60,000 and then $75,000. The coach here now makes $300,000. He started out at $150,000, and he had never coached a day in his life. He'd always been an assistant.

I knew it was time to retire when all of a sudden the bad calls that are part of the game really started getting to me. I found myself just giving hell to the referees, and finally, when we lost a game on a shot that must have been taken three seconds after the gun went off, I said, "That's it. I'm going to quit."

I called my wife and she said, "You're just mad," and I said, "No, I mean it." Then I talked to our athletic director and told him what I was thinking, and he said, "Let's not tell anybody. We'll wait until the end of the season." Well, we had three games that week and we won them all, and I guess he thought I'd change my mind. But I went into his office and said, "I'm quitting." And I did. It's a good thing too. I'd probably still be out there.

My wife and I are enjoying retirement. I work in my yard a lot—I've got a lot of azaleas and camellias—and I play a lot of tennis and we do some traveling. I haven't missed a home basketball game at Houston since I retired, which is 15 seasons now, and this year I'm going to my 47th Final Four.

It's nice that people think I should be in the Basketball Hall of Fame, but I don't think I'm going to make it. I'm not the only coach with a pretty good record who hasn't gotten in, you know. Last year, they didn't take Eddie Sutton, and Lefty Driesell isn't in, either. As big as college basketball is today, maybe it should probably have its own Hall of Fame.

University of Houston coach Guy Lewis first came up with the idea of playing UCLA in the Astrodome, little dreaming that both teams would enter the game unbeaten and it would become one of the most eagerly anticipated contests in basketball history. During his 31 years at Houston, Lewis took the Cougars to the NCAA Tournament 14 times and to five Final Fours. Photograph courtesy of the University of Houston Sports Information Department.

CHAPTER 6

Elvin Hayes: Overcoming Hate and Winning Basketball's Biggest Game

Houston, Texas, January 2004

I grew up in Rayville, a small town of approximately five thousand people in northeast Louisiana. I always wanted to be a baseball player, but I couldn't because I didn't have any gym shoes. That's how poor we were. I went from the first grade all the way into the ninth grade and I never had a pair of shoes. I used to go barefoot winter and summer. If I had to go someplace, I had to borrow some shoes from one of my cousins.

I went to Little League practice once and the coach said, "Get off the field. You'll break your neck out here with no shoes on." The other players had spikes or at least gym shoes. So I couldn't play. I still love the game today. I know everything about it, all the trivia.

I played basketball barefoot on the playgrounds, and by the time I got to high school and had a pair of shoes, I was pretty good. We won 54 games in a row, and Guy Lewis came and recruited me to go to Houston. What appealed to me was the fact that Houston didn't have any good players, so there

would be nobody to compare me to. It seemed like a perfect situation. What I didn't know was that was the year they integrated the Houston athletic program. There weren't very many schools in the South recruiting black players back in the early sixties. Houston was one of the first.

I always wanted to be a baseball player, but I couldn't because I didn't have any gym shoes.

There was no question about my staying home and going to LSU, because blacks couldn't go there. But later my sister ended up being an English professor at LSU, my niece graduated from LSU and is now a lawyer in the Louisiana attorney general's office, and my nephew graduated from LSU and is now a heart specialist. And Shaquille O'Neal played basketball there later on. So things changed, didn't they?

When I got here, it was my first time out of Louisiana—I had never spent a night away from my mother—and adjusting to a big city was very difficult.

My first day here, I got on the bus and went back home. One of the Houston coaches came to get me, and my mother sent my brother to stay with me.

My biggest problem was that I had been in a black world. I had never been around whites, and I had to adjust to an all-white school with just a few blacks. It was totally new to me. When you were walking down the street back home, you had to put your head down and say, "Yes, sir," or "No, sir," and go in doors for blacks only and drink out of a black water fountain. And now I was around white people, and I had a white roommate. It was a big transformation in my life, getting rid of the mind-sets and stereotypes, everything I had been taught.

There were still places we couldn't go. If we played in Shreveport, Louisiana, for instance, there were restaurants where the white players could eat but we couldn't. And our parents couldn't come visit us in

When you were walking down the street back home, you had to put your head down and say, "Yes, sir," or "No, sir," and go in doors for blacks only and drink out of a black water fountain. And now I was around white people, and I had a white roommate. It was a big transformation in my life, getting rid of the mind-sets and stereotypes, everything I had been taught.

the hotel. I had to go outside and stand on the sidewalk to talk to my family. Then we'd play the games, and the kids would come in and cheer for us—white kids, black kids, big kids, little kids. They'd say, "Hey, man, give me your autograph," things like that. I think sports helped open some doors.

Coach Lewis was like a father to me. My father died when I was in the eighth grade, so my years at Houston were the development years I'd never had. Lewis just enhanced my life so much. I was going through this really rough transitional period, and I'll admit it, I had a real problem. I just had a lot of hate in me, a lot of junk. He helped me overcome 18 years of hate.

One time Coach called me into his office and he said, "Why do you hate me? What have I ever done to you? Just tell me one thing." I just sat there. I couldn't say anything because I realized he was right. He had only been trying to help me. He had me eating at his table, coming to his house, and being with his kids. He was treating me like part of his family, and I had been shutting him out. That conversation totally transformed me. He is just a tremendous man. All that I achieved in basketball and as a person has been through what I learned from coach Lewis.

Another good thing was that we never really had a racial problem here in Houston the way they did in other places. There was a huge difference between Louisiana and Texas at the time. I think the integration of the University of Houston and the success the basketball team had was one reason for that. It crossed over, not just on the campus but throughout the whole city, like a fire that kept spreading. It was great not only for the university but for everybody in town. I felt that way when we won the NBA championship in Washington in 1978 too. The whole city enjoyed it so much.

I remember the first time I heard about playing UCLA in the Astrodome. We had just lost to them in the Final Four in Louisville—they went on and beat Dayton to win the tournament—and Coach came in the locker room and asked us, "How would you like it if we played them in the Astrodome next year?" We thought it was great and began preparing for them from that moment.

And when the next season started, it just got bigger. Because we were an independent then, we played a

Elvin Hayes scored 39 points in Houston's 71–69 victory over UCLA in the Astrodome. College basketball's Player of the Year in 1968, Hayes led Houston to the Final Four twice, then went on to a 17-year career in the NBA. Photograph courtesy of the University of Houston Sports Information Department.

tough schedule and were on the road a lot. We beat some good teams and remained undefeated. They were No. 1 in the country and we were No. 2. Every morning the first thing we did was look at the paper to see if they'd won. We didn't want anybody to beat them. We didn't want anybody *touching* them. That's how psyched we were. Then we heard the game was going to be on national television at night, and we knew college basketball had never gone nationwide like that. Two undefeated teams, two All-Americans—you couldn't write a better script than that.

I remember the first time I heard about playing UCLA in the Astrodome. We had just lost to them in the Final Four in Louisville—they went on and beat Dayton to win the tournament—and Coach came in the locker room and asked us, "How would you like it if we played them in the Astrodome next year?" We thought it was great and began preparing for them from that moment.

We were still playing our games in the Rice Gym, which seated approximately twenty-five hundred people at that time, and when we got to the Astrodome I was thinking, "I wonder if anybody will be in here tonight." All I knew for sure was that my family had come in from Louisiana for the game.

We were always a very loose basketball team. We would have music blasting in the locker room before games, and everybody would be up dancing and moving around. But that night we were all silent. Each guy sat quietly in his cubicle like we were in

deep meditation. It was like something was wrong and we were waiting for something bad to happen to us.

Then Coach gave us his pregame speech and we all put our hands together and said, "One for all! One ball!" All of a sudden they opened the door and we saw all the people and heard all the noise, and I thought, "Oh, my God. What's happening?"

I guess you'd have to say that game made me. Out of all the things that I have accomplished as a professional basketball player, the thing I am most recognized and known for is the UCLA-Houston game in the Astrodome. Kareem Abdul-Jabbar's star was shining so brightly then: he was the most heralded player ever to come out of high school, he was an All-American, an all everything. So that night television gave me a chance to showcase my talent and display our team. And of course it was such a great game. It just made my career, and I know Dick Enberg says it made his too, and a lot of other people's careers, too.

UCLA was a great basketball team. They had so many weapons: Kareem, All-American; Lynn Shackelford, All-American; Lucius Allen, All-American; Mike Warren, All-American; Edgar Lacey. Practically that whole team was All-Americans. But there are certain times when everything falls right for you. And in that game it all fell right for us.

I knew Kareem pretty well by the time we played. I met him when he was a freshman and I was a sophomore and we played a game against Oregon State in Pauley Pavilion. We got together and talked a little bit. And then we got to know each other a little more when they beat us in Louisville. Even then we were pretty friendly.

But after we beat them, there was a strain between us and it was never the same. It was that competitive thing between us. He had something I wanted. His star was shining very brightly, and I wanted to take his star out of the sky and put mine there. I went into the game just determined that every chance I got I would try to go one-on-one with him. I would try to shoot on him, dominate him—embarrass him, really. They had Lacey guarding me, but I tried to put myself in a position so it would be Kareem and me the whole night.

In the first quarter, I could see he was coming down the court very slowly so I would make sure to get the rebound and release it very quickly and beat him down the court. After the game, *Sports Illustrated* had a shot on the cover where he was backing up and I was going up from the top of the key shooting over him. I tried to do that every time—get him down low, get the ball, turn around, and jump over him.

Defensively, Ken Spain would jump with Kareem and kind of beat up on him while I would come over and help try to block his shot. What we were trying to do was throw his rhythm and timing off. They said Kareem's eye was bothering him, but I have to wonder about that. He was 7 for 8 from the free-throw line, so his eye wasn't bothering him there.

It all came down to two free throws I made with 28 seconds left. So many times playing in my back-yard in Louisiana I would put myself in that situation: "Elvin Hayes goes to the line, no time on the clock. He's got two free throws. He makes one. The crowd goes crazy. The referee is giving him the ball. He makes the second one. Elvin Hayes wins the game!" You couldn't have had a better situation, could you? That is how you want it to end.

After I made the free throws, UCLA got the ball back, but they never got a shot away. They tipped the ball out of bounds and it came in to me. I started dribbling it, and I was thinking, "Why do you have the ball? Pass it. You shouldn't be dribbling the bas-ketball." Somebody could have stolen it from me. But there I was dribbling it with one hand running around all over the place. Finally I threw the ball to George Reynolds near the center-court line, and for the first time all night I was able to relax. The gun went off and we won the game.

Nobody knew then how historical the game would be, did they? It did so much for college basketball by showing it was a marketable product. I think a lot of what the game has become today is because of that night. They used to say Texas was a football state, but now we have three professional basketball teams, and two of them have won NBA championships. I think a lot of it has to do with TVS taking the chance and promoting that game, Eddie.

All of a sudden they opened the door and we saw all the people and heard all the noise, and I thought, "Oh, my God. What's happening?"

I've traveled all over the world since then, and there is no place—Germany, Portugal, Japan, China, Israel—where somebody doesn't come up to me and say, "I saw you in that UCLA-Houston game." There were fifty thousand people there, but by now the number must be up to one or two hundred thousand. Once a guy told me, "It was my wedding day and we had to get to the church, but I kept sneaking away to watch the game on television. People kept saying, 'Where are you going? It's your wedding.'" Those are the kinds of stories people tell me.

We played UCLA again in the NCAA Tournament, and they beat us. We had to play without George Reynolds, who was our starting point guard. We heard that someone had found out that he hadn't taken a math course in junior college his freshman year, so he could not play in California. He could play everywhere else, but not California. If we had had George, we could have broken their press the way we did in the Astrodome, but we just didn't play our best, and it showed.

I played 16 seasons in the NBA, and if you look at my career statistics, it says I played exactly fifty thou-sand minutes. It was a record then, but now Kareem and Karl Malone have surpassed it. That was how I

I've traveled all over the world since then, and there is no place—Germany, Portugal, Japan, China, Israel—where somebody doesn't come up to me and say, "I saw you in that UCLA-Houston game."

planned it. I said at the beginning of the season that whenever fifty thousand minutes came, I was going to walk off the floor.

We were playing the Kansas City Kings in the old Kemper Arena, and I played every minute of the game and it went into double overtime. And then they announced, "Elvin Hayes has just hit fifty thousand minutes," and I walked off the court. I told Bill Fitch, our coach, "Take me out of the game," and that was it. I thought it was a good round number, and I just felt I wanted to leave with fifty thousand minutes. Not 50,001, just 50,000.

I didn't regret retiring like that, but it did hit me afterward. You miss the camaraderie of the locker room, but I think that the most important thing is that from the eighth grade all the way through high school, college, and the pros, you never prepare for when it's going to end. One day I was sitting here in Houston and all of a sudden tears were running from my eyes and my heart was breaking because it was the first time I didn't have basketball in my life. You really do miss it. It's something that's a part of your life every day for so many years, and then all of a sudden you're not doing it anymore. That's very difficult.

I'm very proud of my family. One of my daughters is a speech therapist, and another one is a biology teacher. My oldest son is an assistant minister at a church, and my youngest son just finished college. He majored in public relations and radio communications, but now he's decided he wants to be a chef. I said, "I send you to college for four years, you graduate, and then you decide you always wanted to own a *restaurant?*" (laughs) So he's going to culinary school to become a chef.

I got totally away from basketball and went into the car business. I owned three dealerships, and then I sold them, thinking I was going to take some time off. But now I'm buying a General Motors dealership, so I guess my retirement lasted only a year. But I enjoy myself too. I go on a lot of cruises. Every couple of months I'm on another one. If you want me, that's where you'll find me—on a boat somewhere, just cruising.

CHAPTER 7

Dick Enberg on Broadcasting the Game That Made History

New York City, New York, December 2003

Alexander Graham Bell invented the telephone, and you invented college basketball on television, Eddie. We had no idea how popular it would become, did we?

I'll tell you one person who did understand—my old broadcast partner, Al McGuire. I remember when we were watching a game together back in the seventies and he said, "This is so big—college basketball and television. Big, big, big! Money, money, money." He was one of the first coaches I heard talk about it that way.

Al was such a special guy. We broadcast some of his games at Marquette in the 1976-1977 season, when he won the NCAA title, and then he worked with Billy Packer and me at NBC. The first month they were so afraid of what he might say they wouldn't even let him sit with Billy and me at courtside. They had him off in a room somewhere else in the arena—a locker room or an officials' room—and put a camera in with him and gave him a button to press when he wanted to talk. But by the time they

made all the switches, the moment was gone and Al was talking about something that was ancient history.

Finally, after six or seven games, Billy said, "You've got the best bench coach in the country sitting where he can't even see the game. Get him out here with us." So thanks to Billy, Al came out to join us, and he was every bit as good as we all thought he would be.

I started in radio when I was a junior at Central Michigan University. I applied for a custodial job at the only radio station in town—WCEN, the central spot on your radio dial. I wound up being the disk jockey and then the sports director for a dollar an hour.

One of the great things that happened in my career was broadcasting UCLA basketball for eight of

Dick Enberg was the announcer for UCLA basketball in Los Angeles when he called the play-by-play for the game in the Astrodome. Six years later, he broadcast Notre Dame's victory over UCLA in 1974 that broke the Bruins' 88-game winning streak. In 2004 Enberg returned to Notre Dame for the 30th anniversary celebration of that game.

Of all the things I've done in nearly 50 years of broadcasting, the UCLA-Houston game was the single most important.

John Wooden's ten NCAA championships. NBC was watching—a lot of those games were on TVS—and they said, "Let's hire this Enberg." That was the start of things for me.

I started in radio when I was a junior at Central Michigan University. I applied for a custodial job at the only radio station in town—WCEN, the central spot on your radio dial. I wound up being the disk jockey and then the sports director for a dollar an hour. When

I went to Indiana University to work on my masters and my doctorate, I auditioned for their new sports network and won, so I was the announcer for football and basketball during the four years I was earning my degrees.

I went out to California in 1961 and became a college professor and an assistant baseball coach at California State University, Northridge. To supplement a poor teacher's income, I worked during the summer in radio and television for anybody who would hire me. In 1965 Gene Autry's television station hired me full time for $18,000. That was three times what I was getting as a college professor with a doctorate.

Then J. D. Morgan hired me at UCLA. He was a very strong athletic director, and there was never any question that he was the boss. It was John Wooden's team, but you always had the sense that J.D. was really in charge. When they were in a room together, his seat was higher than coach Wooden's. Some people thought he got too much attention, but J.D. was a very shrewd man and very loyal to his people. I will always be indebted to him for his belief in me.

In 1966 they came up with this unique idea for televising UCLA basketball. They said, "Why don't we televise the road games live and the home games on tape delay at 11:00 PM?" I said, "That will never work. People aren't going to watch a game that's three hours old. They'll already know the score."

Well, I was wrong. It was immensely successful because UCLA was such a powerhouse. Kareem Abdul-Jabbar was on the team then, and everybody wanted to see him. People wouldn't turn on the news in the evening because they didn't want to know score. They wanted to watch it later. My father was living with me then, and when I'd call home, he wouldn't answer the phone. I had to say, "I'm not going to tell you the score, Dad. I just want to talk to you."

The UCLA-Houston game in the Astrodome was the next year, and I didn't learn until later how I happened to become the announcer. J. D. Morgan turned out to be a better friend than I knew because after all the details had been worked out for the TVS telecast, the last thing he said before you left his office was, "Oh, by the way, one other thing. I want you to use our announcer."

You were trapped, weren't you? It wouldn't have mattered if I couldn't have spoken a word of English, you had to use me. If J.D. hadn't said anything, maybe I would still have had my opportunity down the line, but that was a magical moment for me. Obviously you were good for my career. I hope I was good for yours.

You were, I promise you.

They tuned in looking for the upset, and they got it. That's why the game is so memorable. Had UCLA won, it would have been just another case of the Bruins beating everybody they played. But Houston winning made it a huge story.

Of all the things I've done in nearly 50 years of broadcasting, the UCLA-Houston game was the single most important. People ask me to name the biggest things I've ever done, and I talk about Nolan Ryan's no-hitters, a couple of Super Bowls, and Bjorn Borg and John McEnroe at Wimbledon. And I always mention the trip you and I made together to China in 1973, which was the first time a game ever had been broadcast to the United States from there. But in terms of historical significance, the UCLA-Houston game is number one because it was the start of something big. It was the most important college basketball game ever televised.

It just showed how far we had come. When I was at Indiana in 1961, I got a call from a television station in Columbus, Ohio, saying they wanted me to

telecast the NCAA championship game between Ohio State and the University of Cincinnati in Kansas City. Well, I was thrilled to death. It was the biggest thing that had ever happened to me, even though it was shown only in Ohio. But then seven years later UCLA-Houston was shown on 120 stations around the country and tens of millions of people watched. At the time I thought, "Well, maybe that's about as big as it's going to get." But of course it was only the beginning.

What I remember was that because the court was exactly in the middle of the Astrodome floor, nobody had a good seat. Everyone was a mile away from the action. And in order to protect the sight lines of the people in the box seats, which were far away and on the level of the floor, they dug holes in the floor of the Astrodome for the press and the broadcasters. We were sitting in foxholes with only our heads above the ground. When Houston won, we could hear the sound of the fans running. It was like the charge of the Alamo. They were leaping over our foxholes to get onto the floor to celebrate. That's one memory I'll always have of that game.

Here's the other thing I'll never forget. By the time the second half started, the telecast had become a huge hit around the country. It was a great game, and it looked as if Houston might pull off the upset. We were getting calls from all over from advertisers wanting to buy time. So while the game was progressing, you were passing me handwritten notes—you didn't have the best handwriting in the world—and I was trying to decipher those 10-second drop-in commercials. I was plugging cars and shaving cream and everything else, all from the handwritten notes you were giving me.

One thing I think is very important is that Houston won. UCLA fans wanted their team to win, of course, but for the great majority of the audience the big attraction of the game was, "Can anybody beat this John Wooden powerhouse?" They tuned in looking for the upset, and they got it. That's why the game is so memorable. Had UCLA won, it would have been just another case of the Bruins beating everybody they played. But Houston winning made it a huge story.

In the NBA—during the regular season at least—the fans don't really get into the game and cheer with any passion until the fourth quarter. In college basketball, they're cheering as soon as the players walk in the door. An hour and a half before tip-off they're cheering. There's a purity about that, a raw enthusiasm.

Coach Wooden, who is a dear friend, gets a little upset with me, I think, because when I talk about memorable UCLA games I always mention the ones they lost—the Houston game and the one in 1974 to Notre Dame that broke their 88-game winning streak. He says, "Don't you remember all the games we won?" But the truth is they lost so few games that it became a happening whenever they didn't win.

The year after the Houston-UCLA game, you hired me to do a weekly Saturday afternoon game in the Midwest. You had Loyola of Chicago, DePaul, Marquette, the University of Detroit, and Notre Dame—the five Catholic schools in the Midwest. And although the pay wasn't exactly overwhelming, it was a chance for me to go back to my roots in the Midwest and let everyone know that, hey, I was doing OK.

I'd do a UCLA game on Friday night at Pauley Pavilion, and as soon as it was over, I'd drive to the airport and catch an 11:00 or 11:30 red-eye to the Midwest. I learned very quickly that after flying all night, it didn't make any sense to go to a hotel and have to leave for the arena two hours later for a Saturday afternoon game. So I'd go right from the airport to the arena. But I had to make arrangements to have a guard let me in through a security door. I'd go to the first-aid room, where they always had a cot, and get a couple hours sleep, then I'd shave in the men's room before they opened the gates. I'd do the game, go back to the airport, fly back to L.A., and do the Saturday night UCLA game. So I would do Friday night and Saturday night UCLA games in Los Angeles and a game in Chicago or Detroit in between. No wonder I'm losing my mind. (laughs)

The series you arranged between Notre Dame and UCLA was extremely important to college basketball. They played each other twice during the season— UCLA would take a break from its conference schedule. John Wooden and Digger Phelps, who had started to make his mark, had large followings, and J. D. Morgan saw the advantage in having games that would draw a national audience.

What I remember about Notre Dame ending UCLA's 88-game winning streak is that they played again in Pauley Pavilion the very next weekend, and UCLA won. They played at 8:00 PM on the West Coast, which was 11:00 PM in New York, and it was the highest-rated basketball game ever at that time. It drew more than UCLA-Houston, and even the NCAA championship game had never reached that level at that time. The game was on the cover of *Sports Illustrated*, and the newspaper coverage was tremendous. And again, it was because UCLA had lost the week before.

In 1975 I went to NBC and was there for 25 years. I did NFL football with Merlin Olsen, and Wimbledon and golf. But college basketball was my entrée, and again, it was the exposure on TVS that was significant. After that, I wasn't just an announcer people knew only in L.A. You're the one who taught television how to do college basketball. Your experience showed what worked and what didn't work. I can honestly say that when I went to NBC to do the college game of the week it wasn't much of an adjustment. It was what you and I had been doing all along.

In the NBA—during the regular season at least—the fans don't really get into the game and cheer with any passion until the fourth quarter. In college basketball, they're cheering as soon as the players walk in the door. An hour and a half before tip-off they're cheering. There's a purity about that, a raw enthusiasm. And then television started adding to it. If TVS was in town, it meant it was a national broadcast, which made it even more intense for the fans.

I remember Al McGuire once told me, "I used to know who this Al McGuire was when I was a coach, but then I got into television and all of a sudden I became this guy people thought was clever and funny. I don't know who the real Al McGuire is anymore. Maybe I'm the one that I've created. I don't know."

There's no sport more emotional than college basketball. Football has these crescendos, and baseball is more cerebral, but with basketball, once the ball's in the air, it's an emotional exercise. And it's a great television game too. It all happens right in front of you, and you've got those nice little moments when someone is fouled, they go to the free-throw line, you get the camera right in their face, and you say, "Here's Eddie Einhorn, that 5'9" spark plug out of Philadelphia. He's averaging 13 points a game, and he played the cello until he was 12 years old." And of course my days as a college professor made it very dear to be back on the campus with the kids who are so enthusiastic about everything.

When I think about the growth of college basketball, I remember that the first year I broadcast UCLA games was their first year in Pauley Pavilion. Prior to that, John Wooden's national championship teams played in the UCLA gym, the Pan Pacific Auditorium, the Shrine Auditorium, and even a few games in the Sports Arena, which was brand-new back then. They didn't really have a permanent home. But within five years of the television era, new arenas were being built all over the country. Now just about every major university has one. The arenas themselves are testimony to the popularity of the game.

The coaches were always so fascinating to me. John Wooden, for instance, never wanted to call the first timeout. It didn't matter what happened, he felt that was a sign of weakness to call a timeout first. Even on the rare occasion when they got off to a bad start, he'd always wait for the opposing coach.

Then you had Digger Phelps, who was the first to understand what television meant. His attitude was, "Hey, if we're going to be on national television in prime time, I'm going to milk it for all it's worth." So he would wear the boutonniere in his lapel, and he would allow you to come into his locker room and show him giving his big pregame fight talk. And he would wait until the arena was full before he walked out onto the floor, because he knew the camera would be on him. Some coaches would come out with their team, but Digger always made the grand entrance.

Before long, the coaches were television stars, and some of them had trouble handling it. I remember Al McGuire once told me, "I used to know who this Al McGuire was when I was a coach, but then I got into television and all of a sudden I became this guy people thought was clever and funny. I don't know who the real Al McGuire is anymore. Maybe I'm the one that I've created. I don't know."

The trip to China in 1973 for TVS is one of my top five experiences. They'd had that table tennis competition the year before—remember Ping-Pong Diplomacy?—and Chou En-lai, the Chinese leader, asked for our college basketball champions to come over the following year. When you called and asked if I'd like to go, I said, "Are you kidding? Nobody's ever broadcast a basketball game from China before."

Then a couple of months later, you called back and said, "I've got some bad news. It looks like the trip is off. UCLA doesn't want to go." It was Bill Walton's team, and those were the burn-baby-burn days with all kinds of antiwar stuff going on. I still kid Walton about it. I say, "I can't believe someone as intelligent as you would turn down a trip to China." And he says, "Don't talk to me about that. I'm still sick to my stomach that I didn't go."

But then a couple of weeks later you called back and said the trip was on. I don't know how you did it, but you put together an all-star team and we went. We took a women's team too, and they played the Chinese women.

The game was in Beijing—they called it Peking then—and we stayed in what used to be an ambassador's residence. I remember I had a hole in my sock and I kept throwing it away, and every day I'd come back to my room and they'd taken it out of the trash can and folded it and put it back on the bed. When you looked out the window, you saw soldiers from the People's Liberation Army teaching elementary school children how to throw hand grenades. And in Canton, a city of 4 million people or so, the airport had three cars in the parking lot. Four million people, three cars!

We knew we were going to be greeted by some special dignitary, and we all were wondering if it might be Chou En-lai or even Mao Tse-Tung himself.

None of our equipment worked in their electrical system, so we brought our own, and it was the first time I ever saw small portable cameras. I'll never forget our opening—standing on the Great Wall of China saying, "Welcome to TVS." Amazing. There was no press box in the arena, so you just cleared four seats and put one camera on my right and one on the left. We knew we were going to be greeted by some special dignitary, and we all were wondering if it might be Chou En-lai or even Mao Tse-Tung himself. We were all lined up to see who it would be, and there came Madame Mao wearing an ugly, gray dress. It was the first time she had worn a dress since 1949 or something.

We had some fun, didn't we?

CHAPTER 8

Ted Nance on Putting the Game Together

Houston, Texas, January 2004

I enrolled at the University of Houston in 1953, and Guy Lewis was my physical education teacher. He was also the freshman basketball coach and assistant varsity coach. We had a gym that was about as big as a hotel room, and upstairs over the gym were the basketball offices.

The first time I heard anything about playing UCLA in the Astrodome was right after we got back from the Final Four in Louisville the previous spring. It was the first time we had ever gotten that far in the tournament, and we lost to UCLA in the semifinals, 73–58.

I went to work writing sports for the student paper, so I was at the gym a lot, and when I graduated I went to work for the *Houston Chronicle*. I

went back to the school in 1958 as an assistant in the sports information office, and in 1960 I became the sports information director. Harry Fouke was the athletic director then, and he and J. D. Morgan were the guys who made the Houston-UCLA game happen.

Harry first met J.D. when he was UCLA's tennis coach. They were coming in to play us, and J.D. called Harry up one day and he said, "The NCAA tennis tournament is going to be played on clay courts. Do you have any there in Houston?" We had a couple on the campus, but they weren't very good, so Harry said, "I'll get you fixed up out at the River Oaks Country Club which is *the* country club in Houston." What Harry didn't know was that Arthur Ashe was playing for UCLA then. Houston was still pretty segregated at that time, but there weren't any problems. UCLA practiced at River Oaks and nobody said a word. And because of that Harry and J.D. became good friends.

The first time I heard anything about playing UCLA in the Astrodome was right after we got back from the Final Four in Louisville the previous spring. It was the first time we had ever gotten that far in the tournament, and we lost to UCLA in the semifinals, 73–58. After that Guy Lewis went to four more Final Fours, and he lost to the eventual national champion every time. We always seemed to draw UCLA in the semifinal game, or a team like the University of North Carolina, which had Sam Perkins, James Worthy, and Michael Jordan. We lost to some great teams, I'll tell you that.

I put a full-page ad in our football program with a picture of Lew Alcindor and Elvin Hayes in the NCAA Tournament game from Louisville, and I started calling it the Game of the Century.

Well, we hadn't been back from Louisville very long when Guy said, "What do you think a rematch would be like?" I said, "That would be great. Where are we going to play, though?" He said, "What about the Astrodome?" The first thing I thought was where were you going to put the court, over by the third-base line? But Guy went to Harry with the idea and it just took off.

At the time, we played in the Rice University gym, which seated approximately twenty-five hundred people, because our own gym was so small. We also played some games in a high school gym approximately 15 miles from the campus, and the players had to get there on their own. We played some games at the Sam Houston Coliseum downtown too. Counting the Astrodome, we actually played on five different courts that we were never able to practice on, and we still had a 40-something home-game winning streak at one point. So Guy did a heck of a job.

Houston was a private school until 1964, when it became a university, and boom, the enrollment went from approximately twelve thousand to twenty-

one thousand just like that. In those days our entire athletic administrative staff numbered eight people, counting secretaries. Today most schools have 80 people, which is ridiculous.

We had a meeting about playing in the Astrodome, and Harry said, "We've got to get at least thirty thousand people there"—he didn't dare think of filling up the place—"so from now on, we're going to be talking about this game." So we started promoting it during football season. I put a full-page ad in our football program with a picture of Lew Alcindor and Elvin Hayes in the NCAA Tournament game from Louisville, and I started calling it the Game of the Century. It was hard to sell tickets at first because we had a good football team that year and everybody was interested in it. But Guy kept talking it up and we kept promoting it. We were always mentioning the game on the radio during halftime of our football games.

One thing that helped was we played a national football schedule because we weren't in a conference. We played Michigan State, Florida State, Wake Forest, and the University of Georgia, and sportswriters from around the country would come in to cover them. I found a life-sized picture of Lew Alcindor's head, and I placed it above the door of my office right where his head would be if he was standing there. Alcindor was 7'4", and the ceiling of my office was 8'. The writers would start to walk out of my office, see his head, and do a double-take. They couldn't believe how tall he was. I might have cheated a little bit, actually, and put his head at 7'6". They would say, "What's that doing up there?" I'd start talking about the game, and they'd say, "We'll be back."

I have to tell you about the football game we played at Michigan State that year. They had been the co-national champions the year before—that was when they played that famous 0–0 tie with Notre Dame—and we opened our season up there and beat them 37–7. When we got back to Houston there were five thousand people at the airport, and a lot of them were out there on the tarmac. The plane couldn't even pull up to the gate. We had to get off and walk, and the students were driving the baggage trucks around. Then a few months later we played UCLA at the Astrodome. We were definitely on the sports map after that. I even got a secretary out of it: I'd never had one before. (laughs)

"I'm going to take the seats at the very top of the stadium, the ones farthest away from the playing field, and call them skyboxes. We'll put in a TV set and a bar, and we can charge anything we want."

Ticket sales really started taking off when basketball practice started in November. Everybody could see we were going to be better than the year before even though we had lost one of our starters, Melvin Bell, who had broken all of Elvin's freshman records and was a really physical player. The first time I had a hint that the game might take off was when we went over to Hawaii and beat Marquette in the Rainbow Classic. I figured nobody else was going to be able to beat us, and I _knew_ nobody was going to beat UCLA. Both teams did keep winning, and by December I was convinced there was going to be a tremendous crowd.

A friend of mine, Charlie Miller, said, "You know, I think we ought to buy some tickets to this game ourselves." So we bought 50 tickets apiece, which really came in handy because at the last minute _everybody_ wanted to go to the game. I had so many people call me it was unbelievable. By the end, people were calling and saying, "I don't care where I am, just get me in the stadium." By then I knew we were going to have a sellout.

The press interest was amazing too. I could always judge by the number of media requests what kind of a crowd we'd have. I started getting requests from

Newsweek and _Time_ and publications that never covered sports, like the _Christian Science Monitor_. I'd been at the Final Four that year, and I knew we were going to have probably three times as much press as they'd had there.

One of the ways we handled the press was by putting a second row in the baseball dugouts, which at the Astrodome were three times as long as a typical dugout. When the stadium was built, Dick McDowell, who was the Houston Astros' ticket manager, asked Judge Hofheinz, "What's the deal on these long dugouts?" And the judge said, "Dick, everybody wants a seat behind the dugout." That was the way the judge thought. He was a master promoter.

One day he asked Harry, "How would you like to take the worst seat in the house and make it the most expensive?" Harry didn't know what he was talking about, but the judge pointed up high and said, "I'm going to take the seats at the very top of the stadium, the ones farthest away from the playing field, and call them skyboxes. We'll put in a TV set and a bar, and we can charge anything we want." Nowadays, of course, everybody has skyboxes. The judge's skybox was a suite that was completely furnished and even had a chapel with an altar that was on a swivel. On one side, there was a cross. You could press a button and the lectern turned around and there was a Star of David on the other side. (laughs)

Getting back to the press, we used the football press box too, and a lot of booths upstairs. We had reporters all over the stadium, including out by the basketball court, which was in the middle of the field. The center circle was right around second base. Everybody was filing by Western Union—nobody had faxes or cell phones in those days, of course—so I had this army of runners going back and forth with the copy to Western Union, which was set up at home plate.

We started thinking about the halftime show, and I said that because the game was going to be on national television we should try to do something special. Harry had never thought much beyond having bands, but I was talking to a local photographer, Evan Peskin, who was a music promoter on the side. He said he could get us a group called Jay and the Techniques. I told him Harry wouldn't pay anything, and Evan said, "I'll get them for nothing. We just want the exposure. We're doing an album, and I'll take a couple of pictures of the group with the Dome in the background and we'll put it on the cover."

Well, the month before the game, Jay and the Techniques had a hit record, *Apples, Peaches, and Pumpkin Pie*, and they were on the *Ed Sullivan Show*. So we got publicity out of that and had one of the first halftime shows ever to bring in outside entertainment. Jay and the Techniques are still going strong, by the way.

The NCAA made a terrible mistake in setting up the tournament. They came down and took a survey—checking the lighting and the seating—and they got this brilliant idea that they were going to raise the court up off the floor of the Astrodome like a boxing ring. What they didn't stop to consider is that a boxing ring is small, so you can see the action on the side opposite where you're sitting.

As for the game, it was sensational. Not long ago a columnist at the *Port Arthur* (Texas) *News*, picked the top events he'd ever covered at the Astrodome. He had Super Bowls, games between the Oilers and the Cowboys, the Astros and the Phillies in the

National League playoffs, and Billy Jean King playing tennis against Bobby Riggs. But his number one of all time was the Houston-UCLA basketball game. He said he'd never seen anything like it. And just about everybody I meet says they were either there or watching it on TV. I don't think we got a single complaint from anyone saying they couldn't see the game because they were so far away. They were just happy we won.

Right after the game, Guy started pushing to have the NCAA Tournament in the Astrodome, and in 1971 we got the first Final Four ever played in a domed stadium. By then the demand for tickets for the tournament was huge. The coaches were all in favor of playing in bigger arenas because they each got four tickets for the game, and by the time they gave those out, there were a lot fewer to sell. UCLA won in 1971 and we didn't make it to the Finals; we lost to Kansas in the Midwest Regionals by one point.

The NCAA made a terrible mistake in setting up the tournament. They came down and took a survey—checking the lighting and the seating—and they got this brilliant idea that they were going to raise the court up off the floor of the Astrodome like a boxing ring. What they didn't stop to consider is that a boxing ring is small, so you can see the action on the side opposite where you're sitting.

But a basketball court is so large that if you're sitting underneath you can't see what's happening at the other end. So the people in the front row—who had paid a lot of money to be up close—couldn't see a lot of the action. The NCAA was getting bombarded with complaints from the fans and the sportswriters. Then the photographers started climbing up to take their shots, and they were blocking off people who were really starting go nuts. It was a mess.

Here's a story about our game with UCLA that I've never told before, but I guess it's OK now. The Astrodome was located right in the middle of a big field and didn't have doors that fully closed. All they had were chains that came down over the entrances. So there was a real problem with rats that came in from the field and ran all through the stadium. I'd be up in the press box after a football game and look down at the stands after everybody was gone and see rats out on the field eating spilled popcorn. A friend of mine who was the head of Terminix in Houston would come in on a constant basis to exterminate them. He and his guys were picking up dead rats all the time.

Well, about 10 minutes before tip-off the night of the game, everything seemed to be under control, so I walked through the press area back under the home-plate stands where we'd had a pregame meal. They hadn't cleaned up yet, and the place was totally deserted. When I walked in, what did I see out on one of the tables but two gigantic rats. All I could think, was, "Oh my God, if any of the sportswriters see this, it will be all over." I started throwing stuff at them and chasing them away. (laughs)

CHAPTER 9

Gary Cunningham on Learning from the Master

St. Louis, Missouri, April 2005

I was a fairly highly recruited high school athlete at Inglewood High School near Los Angeles, and I committed to play for Pete Newell at California. But over the summer I changed my mind because I saw I had a chance to actually play at UCLA, whereas Cal was loaded and I thought I'd have to wait. That's pretty funny, isn't it? Going to UCLA because I didn't think they had as good a team as Cal did. I was really impressed with coach Wooden right from the start, of course. I thought he was just so honest. There was no show about him. He wasn't trying to impress you—what you saw was what you got. I came from a blue-collar family, and he was my kind of guy.

My senior year, 1962, was the first time UCLA went to the Final Four, although we lost in the semifinals to the University of Cincinnati. By then I had decided I wanted to be a college professor. I got my masters at UCLA, and when I started work on my doctorate in 1965, the education department offered me a job to teach full time. Well, two days later, I went up to the student union for breakfast and there was coach Wooden sitting there.

"I lost my freshman basketball coach yesterday," he said. "How would you like to coach?"

I was really impressed with Coach Wooden right from the start, of course. I thought he was just so honest.

Now anybody else would just jump at a chance like that, but all I could say was, "I'll have to talk to my department chairman." The chairman said it was OK as long as it didn't affect my teaching. So I went back to coach Wooden and he said, "Fine, you're an assistant coach." Every year I planned to get out of it and pursue this other dream, but I stayed with him for 10 years, became alumni director for two more years, and then head coach. I've been in intercollegiate athletics now my whole career—all because I had breakfast at the student union that day. (laughs)

Guess who was waiting for me when I got to my first practice with the freshman team? Lew Alcindor. He was a great player even then, but what I really liked about him was that he was so teachable and attentive. He played so effortlessly that it didn't look like he was working hard, but really he just did things efficiently.

Mostly, we worked on his skills. Because we needed a big guy to play against him in practice, we brought in Jay Carty, who had played at Oregon State and was in graduate school at UCLA. Jay was 6'8" and really helped us out practicing against Kareem [Lew], because the next tallest player on the freshman team was Lynn Shackelford at 6'5". Every day, there was Jay, out there trying to guard Kareem in practice. Talk about thankless tasks.

Kareem was very quiet then and a little aloof—certainly he's more articulate and outgoing now—and he was very protected. He insisted on not meeting with the news media and had a lot of barriers put up for

Guess who was waiting for me when I got to my first practice with the freshman team? Lew Alcindor. He was a great player even then, but what I really liked about him was that he was so teachable and attentive.

him. I don't think that helped him in his social development. What a lot of people don't know is how smart he is. He finished with high scores on his Regents Exam in New York and never had a problem in school. It's interesting that UCLA's two greatest players back then, Kareem and Bill Walton, were both very bright guys who were history majors and almost 4.0 students.

Kareem was never a follower, but a quiet leader, and very much a team player. Players could still dunk in college when he was a sophomore, and when, because of him, they put in the rule the next year that players couldn't dunk, I think it actually made him a better player. He had to develop other shots, rather than just turning and slamming the ball

through the basket, and he became much more versatile offensively. I remember once when he scored 56 points against USC and he probably had 15 dunks. Later he couldn't do that because they changed the rules. Kareem always got double- and triple-teamed, but we had the perfect complement for him in Shackelford, who was a great shooter. Kareem would just kick the ball out to Shackelford, who would score what would be a three-point shot today.

In contrast to Kareem, Bill Walton was one of the most animated players on the court, so enthusiastic about everything. And he was eager to learn and really quick at getting it. He was a guy you could throw into the pool and say, "OK, move your arms and kick your legs," and he'd be swimming in five minutes. Bill was a "cause" person—he was into a lot of things—but on the court he was a model player. You wouldn't want a better player than Bill. He did everything you asked him to do and more.

People always ask about the game where our freshman team beat the varsity. It was the dedication of Pauley Pavilion, and they turned it into coach Wooden's night. All his former players were there, and they formed a human tunnel. He came out and there was this huge ovation. And here was this 25-year-old guy coaching the first college game of his life—and we won by 15 points.

I was so embarrassed for coach Wooden that I would not even come out of the locker room to talk to the press. Afterward they had a reception at the student union with Coach and all his former players, and I thought I was going to get fired. My wife Barbara and I just sat in a corner. We were afraid to socialize with anyone. Well, I didn't get fired, but that was the last freshman-varsity game they ever played.

One unfortunate thing about that game was that it set the tone for the rest of the year, where the media focused on the freshmen instead of the varsity, which did not go to the NCAA Tournament that year. I think our game might have hurt their confidence. After that, though, we won seven straight NCAA Tournaments.

Who ever could have imagined something like that? The funny thing is I think the best team we ever had was that one that lost to North Carolina State in 1974 and broke the string. It had Bill Walton and Keith Wilkes, but we kept throwing the ball away, and North Carolina State kept making great plays.

In all the years I worked with John Wooden, he never talked about winning. Never. All he said was we'll do the best we can, and if things fall into place I think we'll have a good team.

In all the years I worked with John Wooden, he never talked about winning. Never. All he said was we'll do the best we can, and if things fall into place I think we'll have a good team. His great strength was organization and teaching. The coaching staff would meet with him every day to plan practice, and if we wanted to change something, we really had to fight to convince him. But in the game itself, he basically turned the way we ran the press and the adjustments with the big guys over to me and Jerry Norman. He really mentored us. He didn't want "yes" guys. He valued our input, and I think that made the team better.

He would let the assistants at least walk through the offense of other teams, showing where they set screens and so forth. But I'm not sure the players remembered that when they got on the court anyhow. Where I think coach Wooden was ahead of his time was in the drills he prepared for screens, and pick-and-rolls, and what have you. Whatever the other teams did, we were prepared because we had done all these drills.

The one thing I don't think a lot of people realized was that we were a very sound defensive team. Our scores were high because of the style of offense we played—we ran and took advantage of shots off the fast break—so the scores weren't down where those of a ball-control team would be. But we were very good on defense. Coach said that's what wins games,

because when your offense fails, your defense will win for you if you're consistent.

What can I tell you about the game in the Astrodome? It was such a bizarre place to play, with the floor in the middle of a big open area and the people a long way from the court. Kareem definitely was hurt. He had a corneal abrasion and he couldn't see. It's like closing one eye and trying to have good depth perception. I believe that if his eye had been healthy we would have won.

It wasn't my decision whether he should play or not, but I thought we were better with him with a bad eye than without him. Even if he didn't score, he's an intimidating force defensively. Elvin kept shooting those 18-footers all night. He was great.

We didn't appreciate it at the time, I guess, but that game was a tremendous boost for college basketball, and for television too. It was really the forerunner of what happened after that because it provided the basis for what was to come. Everybody was watching, weren't they? The ratings were tremendous. I think what television did, and what our winning so much did to some extent, was help popularize the game. All of a sudden, kids were playing basketball all over the place.

Of course, we got our revenge for what happened at the Astrodome at the end of the year in the NCAA Tournament in the Sports Arena. That was probably one of the finest games we ever played. We just took them apart in the first half. The best thing about our game was the press. We got layup after layup, and Mike Warren had a great game. But we also used the diamond-and-one defense, which is a kind of zone, and it really worked.

I'll tell you a story about that. One season when we were going up to Oregon State, we convinced coach Wooden to put in a two-three zone. Well, we just destroyed them because they couldn't shoot from the outside. But the next time we tried it, they shot the eyes out of the basket and beat us. I don't think coach Wooden ever let us use the zone again until we got to Houston.

I always thought J. D. Morgan was responsible for a lot of our success. J.D.'s big strength was the way he took a lot of things off coach Wooden's shoulders, like scheduling. It started when he walked into Coach's office and saw his desk piled with recruiting information and travel arrangements. J.D. pushed the stuff off his desk and said, "John, from now on you don't have to worry about this stuff. I'll do it. You just coach the team."

Sometimes he would do things Coach didn't want done, though, like schedule one nonconference game on the road at Notre Dame and all the rest at home. Coach wanted to play more road games so we'd be tougher at the end of the year, but we'd win another national championship and J.D. would say, "See, John, I know what I'm doing."

J.D. was ahead of his time in terms of promotion, television, and making money. But he was violently opposed to charging boosters for things. Today all of us need booster money to survive, but he never wanted to owe anything to anybody. And we always knew that, right or wrong, he was fighting for us and that he cared. He lifted the whole UCLA athletic department. You have to give J.D. a lot of the credit for what we did.

During games J.D. used to sit on the bench. Sometimes he'd even give advice. He'd tell Coach he ought to take a player out and things like that. Coach Wooden didn't like it, and I know it would have intimidated the heck out of me to have the athletic director sitting next to me. Well, at one of their meetings, the Pac-10 legislated J.D. off the bench. I guess he left to go to the restroom and they passed the rule that an athletic director can't sit on the bench and told him when he came back. So he started sitting in the first row *behind* the bench. (laughs)

When coach Wooden retired in 1975, Gene Bartow took over, and I became executive director of the Alumni Association. Gene had a great record—he went 52-9 in two seasons—but the pressure of following Wooden was just tremendous. I think a lot of the pressure was self-imposed, and it was very hard on him. I was honestly happy for him when he left, because I was fearful for his health. I thought he might have an emotional breakdown. He got a break when he went to the University of Alabama–Birmingham, which worked out great for him.

In 1977, after Gene left, J.D. asked me if I'd coach the team. I was enjoying my job in the alumni office and was not interested in coaching as a career, so I can't really explain the logic of it, but I said, "OK, I'll do it." We did all right, I guess, winning 50 games and losing 8. Even though we never got out of the NCAA Regionals we had a successful program. We won 101 games when I was a freshman coach and didn't lose very many—15 maybe. Is 101-15 good enough? Not at UCLA during that time, it wasn't. (laughs) But I never really felt any pressure. Maybe it's because I was family—I didn't know any better. I did learn it's better to be the second guy to follow a legend than the first.

I realized after my first year that what I really wanted to be was an athletic director. So I told J.D., "Keep your eyes open for a coach because I want to do something else." So I coached at UCLA for only two years, but they were two quality years, and I left a lot of good players in the program.

One of the things I learned is that when you're caught up in winning, it's hard to realize what you're achieving. When I left UCLA and was athletic director at Western Oregon State College, I saw how excited people got when a team like Oregon State just *made* the NCAA Tournament. That really made me realize that what we'd accomplished at UCLA was phenomenal.

I've had a lot of opportunities over the years to go to the really big programs, but I've always been happy where I was. So many of my colleagues, coaches and athletic directors, stay too long and things start going badly, and then they leave the profession bitter. But I've had a good life. When I hang it up I'm going to be happy.

CHAPTER 10

Jerry Norman on the Bruins' Revenge

Los Angeles, California, January 2005

People don't always remember that the UCLA dynasty began in the early sixties. We went to the Final Four in 1962, and two years later we were undefeated and won the national championship. And in 1965 we did it again. The biggest guys on those teams—Keith Erickson and Fred Slaughter—were only 6'5". But with Gail Goodrich and Walt Hazzard, those were wonderful teams.

The NCAA Tournament was really different when I played. My first year, there were only eight teams in the tournament. Four of them played in Kansas City and four in New York. It wasn't until my senior year that they held the first regional tournaments. I remember our regional was in Corvallis, Oregon.

I went into the navy after college—this was during the Korean War—and then I came back to UCLA, where I taught for a couple years before becoming an assistant coach. At first I just coached the freshman team, but then I became a full-time assistant. I did just about everything, I guess: recruiting, checking on what the players were up to, and working with coach Wooden to devise strategy.

Recruiting was really different back then. When I started, the recruiting budget for the entire basketball program was about $500, which was inadequate for going out to see the players you were interested in or having a player visit the campus. The NCAA allowed visits, but after you'd paid for travel there wasn't much money left over. So I created the freshman-varsity game, with the proceeds going to the recruiting budget. That resulted in enough funds to let us go out and do a reasonable job.

Those games ended when the freshmen beat the varsity during Kareem Abdul-Jabbar's first year. The team was embarrassed, but I never thought that was such a big deal. Anybody would have been drubbed by that team with four high school All-Americans. They were all outstanding players—Kenny Heitz, Lucius Allen, Lynn Shackelford—and when you put Kareem in there, it was a very dominant team.

The way we recruited Kareem shows you how different things were then too. We didn't even meet him until he came out to UCLA to visit. We got some help from some of our alumni. Dr. Ralph Bunche, who was the ambassador to the United Nations at that time and had played basketball at UCLA, wrote him a very nice letter. And Willie Naulls, who was in the NBA then, helped too. All these things added up, I think.

Kareem was on the quiet side, but he seemed to get along with two or three of the players he met when he was here. He spent more time with them than he did with us. The players would ask me, "What do you want me to tell him, Coach?" and I'd say, "What difference does it make what I tell you? You're going to tell him whatever you want anyway." (laughs)

Kareem was very coachable. He was undefeated as a freshman and lost one game his sophomore year. I remember one of our student assistants saying, "Maybe we can motivate him to do better." I said, "Motivate him? He's only looked up at the scoreboard twice in his life where his team hadn't won the game. You usually build motivation through fear you're not going to win."

> Kareem was on the quiet side, but he seemed to get along with two or three of the players he met when he was here. He spent more time with them than he did with us. The players would ask me, "What do you want me to tell him, Coach?" and I'd say, "What difference does it make what I tell you? You're going to tell him whatever you want anyway."

What we emphasized in those years was to keep up the tempo of the game, make sure we took the highest percentage shots we could. It was to our advantage to run the ball, but if we didn't get a good shot off the break, we had ways to set up our half-court offense.

We knew the game in the Astrodome would not be easy because we had to travel. It was the middle of the conference season, and at that time you had to be a conference champion to qualify for the NCAA Tournament. We were more focused on that. So maybe the players weren't as well prepared mentally as they could have been, which is a coaching error. We didn't turn it into a situation where they really had to win the game because of all the attention it was getting. And Kareem scratching his cornea the week before just added to the feeling that the game wasn't that important because we weren't at our best.

We knew that he had double vision and that offensively he probably wouldn't be able to do what he normally could. So we had to adjust offensively, keeping the ball out in the perimeter more and having other players take a lot more shots than they were used to. When you have an eye injury, it affects how you're going to run down the floor and how you're going to react.

I think Kareem is right when he says he had to play because we couldn't win without him. He was our only player with any substantial size, and without him in there, they were going to take advantage of their size offensively. They had some big kids—Elvin Hayes and Ken Spain were both 6'9"—and they would have taken advantage of that had Kareem not been in the game. They would have taken the ball inside because we didn't have anyone to defend inside.

And there comes a point where perception is more important than reality. If the perception is, "Oh, his eye is not really scratched that bad or he wouldn't be playing," go ahead and let them think that. Maybe they'll be afraid to do some of the things they could have done by taking advantage of the situation. Maybe we could have run more if he hadn't been in there, but whether the result would have been different we'll never know.

We never really talked about it after we lost, but all the players knew we were probably going to be playing Houston again that season. We had the two

Eight days before UCLA played Houston, Abdul-Jabbar's cornea was scratched in a game at California. He arrived in Houston wearing a patch over his eye and had one of the worst shooting games of his career.

best teams in the country by a substantial margin, so it seemed unlikely that we wouldn't meet in the NCAA Tournament. I was concerned about playing them again because I felt their confidence level had increased substantially after they beat us, and they had become a much better team. Elvin Hayes' scoring average jumped up substantially, and I thought he was playing even better toward the end of the season than he did against us.

So we had a decision to make: do we try to limit Elvin, or do we try to limit the players around him and let him get whatever number of points he's going to get? What I remembered about the game in the Astrodome was that Elvin had 29 points in the first half but only 10 in the second. We made the right adjustments and played well defensively, but offensively, we didn't play well at all in the second half.

So coming into our game against them in the semifinals of the tournament, I felt we could upset their balance if we could keep Hayes from getting the ball. They were so dependent upon him scoring that if we could keep the ball away from him . . . well, it's hard to score without the ball, isn't it? So we needed a defense that would try to deny him the ball.

I came up with the diamond-and-one, which we had never used before. The "one" was Lynn Shackelford, and basically he was told to stay in front of Hayes and keep him from getting the ball. When I told coach Wooden about the diamond-and-one, he said maybe we should use it against USC in our last regular-season game to see how it worked. But I felt it would be better not to use anything so dramatically different because Houston would be scouting us, and the surprise factor would be a major part of its success. Coach Wooden agreed it would be best not to use it until we played them.

> **We never really talked about it after we lost, but all the players knew we were probably going to be playing Houston again that season. We had the two best teams in the country by a substantial margin, so it seemed unlikely that we wouldn't meet in the NCAA Tournament.**

Obviously, it was very effective against Elvin because he got only five points in each half and we won easily. Houston had a difficult time making any adjustments and figuring out what to do. We never used the diamond-and-one again, although we didn't play against anybody like Hayes again, either. And I've never seen anybody else use it since then.

That was my last year at UCLA. I had a family, and I felt that the coaching profession was not really suited to young kids. I just felt it would be best to make a change, so I went into investment business and I've done OK. It's like coaching: it's better to be lucky than good. Over the years, people have come to me about coaching again, but I just told them I had no interest, that I didn't want to look back. It was an exciting time and I'm glad I did it, but I'm also glad I made the change.

CHAPTER 11

Lynn Shackelford's View from Beyond the Arc

Los Angeles, California, November 2004

I played high school basketball at John Burroughs High School in Burbank, California, which is in the San Fernando Valley just over the hill from UCLA, and I had a really high arc on my shot even then. When I was a little kid we had a basket in the patio, and there were telephone wires between me and the basket. So I could shoot under the wires, which was hard, or shoot over them, which wasn't. So that's where I got the arc. When I got to UCLA, teams would sag off on Kareem Abdul-Jabbar in the middle, and I would be left open on the outside. I would just set up in the corner and pretend I was still in the backyard shooting over telephone wires.

Freshmen were ineligible when we got to UCLA, which coach Wooden liked, even though it meant that Kareem and the rest of us couldn't play for a year. He felt players needed a year to adjust to living away from home for the first time, adapt to college life, and learn the fundamentals of the game the way he taught them.

Coach's methods were so different from anybody's we had ever known. The day before our first prac-

tice at UCLA, we sat in a classroom and he stood up front telling us to keep our fingernails short and our shirttails tucked in and our hair cut short. I sat there thinking, "This is how they win national championships? Talking about *this*?" But after a while we came

Keith Erickson, who played at UCLA before I did, always says, "What John Wooden has to teach is so brilliant that the problem is it's wasted on 19- and 20-year-old kids."

to see that good basketball comes from perfecting minor details, paying attention to small things: the little pass, the correct footwork.

Practices were really important to Coach, and he'd work all morning with his assistants on what we needed for various drills—five minutes on this one, ten minutes on that one. They all lasted two hours—you knew by the clock when you were going to finish—

and it was nonstop because it was so organized. At the end of the two hours, you'd go, "I'm not that tired," but three hours later you'd be sitting in your dorm room and you'd be dead. It was a cumulative thing.

But we just learned so much. Keith Erickson, who played at UCLA before I did, always says, "What John Wooden has to teach is so brilliant that the problem is it's wasted on 19- and 20-year-old kids." It's not until later that you realize you were getting great instruction on life that goes beyond basketball. I think we all have that moral compass John Wooden gave us.

We had a pretty good freshman team, and when Gary Cunningham devised a way for us to handle the varsity's full-court press, we beat them, which didn't make coach Wooden very happy. The rest of that sea-

But even though the game was a big deal, Coach Wooden didn't have us prepare any differently than for any other game. As far as he was concerned, the game was an interruption because it came right in the middle of our conference season.

son, there was always a double-header—the freshman team would play a junior college team and then the varsity would play. All the games were sold out, and by halftime of our games the stands were always full. So that was a pretty good deal for the spectators— they could see two great teams for the price of one.

Kareem was the big star, of course, but he was really homesick in the beginning. He kept telling us how great New York was and how much he missed his family. Then he went back home for Christmas and when he came back everything had changed. He was in a good mood and cheerful and happy to be back in L.A. I think the weather had a lot to do with

it. But I could understand how being three thousand miles from home was a tough adjustment for him. How do you adjust in college if you're a 7'2" black guy from New York and you're at UCLA?

He was pretty much a loner—he would stay in his room and listen to jazz. But let me tell you something, he was a very bright guy and he was good to play with. He was very fair and seldom lost his temper or got critical. I don't ever remember him saying anything bad about a teammate in college or the pros. There are not many players you can say that about. His big problem was he wasn't good with the media and never has been. You need to work the media in professional sports, and he couldn't do it. He's just not a phony guy.

Winning those three championships was a great experience, but you have to remember the expectation level was so high, especially with Kareem on the team. People just assumed we were going to win every game. We played 26 games during the regular season back then, and there were only 4 games in the NCAA Tournament, so people expected we would go 90–0. Coach Wooden didn't think that was realistic, but a lot of our fans did. Some of them were probably disappointed that we went 88–2. (laughs)

One of those losses was to Houston in the Astrodome, but I always thought that made winning the national championship later that season more dramatic than if we had beaten them. We beat them in the semifinals of the NCAA Tournament the year before, remember, with a lineup of four sophomores and a junior. Kareem had to play Elvin Hayes in that game too, and Elvin was certainly a force Kareem didn't have to face every night. They were a big, physical team, and we beat them by 15 points.

After the game somebody asked Elvin what he thought of Kareem, and he said something like, "He was OK, but I think he's a little overrated."

Well, the game in the Astrodome had already been arranged, and someone told Elvin, "You know, you're going to have to play them again in January."

One of four high school All-Americans who entered UCLA in 1965, Lynn Shackelford played on teams that won 88 games and lost only two while winning three straight NCAA titles. Shackelford was known for his high arcing jump shots that gave the Bruins an outside threat to complement Abdul-Jabbar's inside game. Photograph courtesy of ASUCLA Photography.

"Oh, we'll definitely beat them when we play them down in Texas," he said. That was a pretty brave thing for him to say. I always wondered if he said it just to motivate himself.

There was a huge buildup for the game in the Astrodome. We were cruising along with a win streak of 47 games—none of us had ever lost a game since we came to UCLA—and were ranked No. 1

People think of the game as a matchup of Kareem and Elvin Hayes, but that wasn't the way it was at all. You wouldn't put Kareem on Elvin one-on-one because Elvin could go outside with his jump shot and you didn't want Kareem 20 feet away from the basket.

in the country. Houston was also unbeaten and was playing great too.

But even though the game was a big deal, Coach Wooden didn't have us prepare any differently than for any other game. As far as he was concerned, the game was an interruption because it came right in the middle of our conference season. In those days only 16 teams made it to the NCAA Tournament, and you had to win your conference to get there. Houston was an independent team and was looking for any wins it could get against good teams, but we had to concentrate on winning our conference. So, in some respects, I don't think we were well prepared for Houston that night.

We never watched film of the other teams in those days, and, in fact, I don't ever remember even talking about who we were going to play next. We might have talked about what we had to do against Elvin Hayes, but we had a game at home against Portland two days before we played Houston, so we didn't have much time to prepare. Not that coach Wooden

would have had us prepare for a specific team anyway. He just didn't believe in it.

We couldn't wait to get down to Houston and practice so we could see how it was going to be set up. When we got there and saw that midcourt was at about second base, it seemed almost eerie. Basketball is played in a confined area where you're used to having the crowd right on top of you—that's one of the things that makes it fun—and here we were 150 or 200 feet away from the nearest fans.

For television purposes, they brought in some lights and put them directly above the basket. They weren't very high, so if you were shooting under the basket you would be looking up right into the lights and they might blind you momentarily, whereas if you were shooting 20 feet out they didn't bother you. They certainly didn't bother Elvin Hayes, who scored 39 points in the game and was shooting from the outside really well. And they didn't bother me when I was shooting from the outside. But I think for somebody like Kareem, with his little sky hook underneath, it was awkward compared to a standard basketball arena.

Even before we started playing there were some strange things about the game. It was a long way from the court to our locker room, which I think was under the left-field stands, and coach Wooden didn't want us out on the court for the playing of the national anthem. He was afraid there might be an incident where maybe Kareem wouldn't stand up or something. So we went from the stands to the court to warm up, all the way back to the locker room for the national anthem, and then all the way back out to the court again. And then we did it all over again at halftime. In those days, you ran onto the court— showing that old college spirit—and then back again.

People think of the game as a matchup of Kareem and Elvin Hayes, but that wasn't the way it was at all. You wouldn't put Kareem on Elvin one-on-one because Elvin could go outside with his jump shot and you didn't want Kareem 20 feet away from the basket. At the start of the game, Kareem guarded him in close to the basket for a while, but then Elvin went out and started drilling open jump shots. So after a few minutes Coach realized that wasn't going to work and had three other guys taking turns trying to guard Elvin. Nobody could stop him that night, though. He was just too good.

One of the things everybody remembers about that game is how Kareem was playing with an eye injury. Let me explain what happened. Eight days earlier, we played a game at Cal and he accidentally got a scratch on his eyeball. The next night, he did not play against Stanford and we won pretty easily anyhow. Then we went home and played Portland on Thursday, again without Kareem. He was in the hospital resting so his eye would heal. The next day he got on a plane with a patch over his eye after being in the hospital all week and went down to play in Houston. When he got there he played a terrible game, and why not? He had one eye, he was looking up into the lights, and he was out of shape.

At one point in the second half, Mike Warren came up to some of us and said, "I know we can run on these guys. They look tired. But we're having to wait for him. We're losing our chance to go down the court and score. I'm thinking maybe I should go to Coach and ask him if we should take him out."

I said, "No, no, no. You can't do that. You're not going to ask Coach to take the greatest college player of all time out of the game. You just can't do that."

So he didn't. Afterward in the locker room, it was very quiet. Here we'd lost our first game since we came to UCLA, and we didn't know quite how to react or what to do. And there were some whispers that maybe we would have been better in the second half had Kareem not played.

Mike was certainly right about one thing: Houston was tired, but so were we. It was a very fast-paced first half. Elvin had 29 of his 39 points, and I was 4-for-6 shooting from the floor. But I was 0-for-5 in

the second half. I was just dead tired. With about 10 seconds left in the game, I was in the corner—one of my favorite spots to shoot from—and Mike Warren threw the ball to me. But Lucius Allen thought the pass was for him and ran over to try to catch it, and the ball went out of bounds.

Afterward in the locker room, it was very quiet. Here we'd lost our first game since we came to UCLA, and we didn't know quite how to react or what to do.

Ever since then people have said to me, "If you would have made that shot we would have tied the game." I never say anything, but I know the truth. I was too tired. I don't think I would have made the shot. I'm not trying to take anything away from Houston. They played a fabulous game and they deserved to win. They had to play on the same court in front of the same crowd as we did. Of course, the crowd was all for them.

Here's one thing I'll always remember about that game: after it was over, coach Wooden was smiling. Everybody else was depressed and didn't know how to act, but he smiled. I think he knew in the long run that it was going to work out for the best. He was looking at the big picture—it's not how you do in the middle of the season, it's how you do at the end. He understood that, and he was able to communicate it to his players.

Looking back, I'm glad things went the way they did. It was great for college basketball, and it made the NCAA semifinal in the Sports Arena in March a fabulous opportunity for us. I remember at the team breakfast the day of that game Mike Warren said, "Anybody hungry?" and I said, "No, I'm not hungry." It was the first time we were so nervous we couldn't eat before a game. That's how much we wanted to play.

After what Elvin did to us in the Astrodome, we knew we had to do something different to stop him, so for one of the rare times, Coach abandoned the man-to-man defense he had always believed in and put in what he called a diamond-and-one. The diamond was a zone that was meant to contain the other four Houston players who were not good outside shooters, and I was the one who was supposed to chase Elvin and keep him from getting off his great jump shot.

We figured that if we zoned them tight we could stop them from scoring close to the basket while we tried to stop Elvin outside. We had played some zone a few times during the season—usually when teams stalled to keep us from getting the ball—but this is the only time we ever had a special defense for one particular opponent.

"I'm very concerned with how you act after the game," he said, "especially because Louisville is the fifth most immoral city in the United States."

In the beginning of the game, it seemed to be working pretty well. I remember with about eight minutes gone Elvin had not only not scored, but he was hardly even looking for the ball. So I thought, "Hey, I'm doing OK," and just then Elvin got the ball at the top of the key, threw a fake, and I lost him, and he drilled a jump shot.

Well, coach Wooden and coach Norman came right out of their seats and started screaming at me. I was just glad I wasn't within five feet of them or they might have hit me. "Whoa!" I thought, "these guys are serious about keeping Elvin from scoring." But the plan worked pretty well because Elvin scored only 10 points, and we won 101–69. Later, Coach said the closest we came to reaching our potential in the Lew Alcindor era was in that game.

Thinking about it, there was another benefit that came out of the game in the Astrodome: it helped UCLA's recruiting around the country. Before that game we didn't get a lot of players from outside California, but when they saw UCLA on national television, a lot of them started dreaming about going there. So it all worked out well, didn't it?

Here's a funny thing about our team. We were never that close off the court. We played well together, but there was no great camaraderie afterward, and it's still that way. Oh, we have reunions, and I get together with a couple of the guys and play golf once in a while, but it's not like it is down in North Carolina where the former players get together and hang around for a day or two. I'm told they do that all the time, but it's never occurred to us. Isn't that odd?

Maybe this came from Coach. He never put a lot of emphasis on camaraderie or what took place off the court. A big night for him on the road was a hot fudge sundae after a win. I'll never forget our pre-game talk before our first NCAA championship game in Freedom Hall in Kentucky. Coach was standing at a blackboard telling the starters where to line up so they'd face the TV camera just right, and then he said he was concerned with our conduct after the game. We were about to play for the national championship and he wasn't talking about the game at all, but how we were going to act *afterward*.

It turned out he was worried because North Carolina was staying in the same hotel we were, and when they got upset in the semifinals the night before, they partied all night and tore the place apart. Well, John Wooden was not going to have his team partying all night. He always wanted to avoid the highs and lows.

"I'm very concerned with how you act after the game," he said, "especially because Louisville is the fifth most immoral city in the United States."

So we went out for our pregame warm-ups before the NCAA championship game, and we were all thinking one thing: which cities are worse than Louisville? (laughs)

John Wooden comes with a stamp on him that says Made in the Midwest. Not only is he from the Midwest, he's from the heart of the Midwest—Indiana. And not only is he from Indiana, he's from a small town in Indiana. I can picture John Wooden feeding the chickens, but I could never picture him body surfing in the Pacific Ocean. He's been out here for almost 50 years now, but he's still a Hoosier and still doesn't understand California. He appreciates the good weather, though.

UCLA players Mike Lynn, Lucius Allen, Mike Warren, and Kareem Abdul-Jabbar celebrate along with John Wooden after the Bruins crush North Carolina 78–55 in the 1968 NCAA championship game.

CHAPTER 12

Mike Warren: The Role of a Lifetime

Los Angeles, California, January 2005

I grew up in South Bend and went to South Bend Central High, which was where John Wooden coached. You know how big high school basketball is in Indiana, of course. To win a state championship was the epitome of the game. One of the biggest disappointments of my career came in my junior year when we lost in the finals of the state tournament to Muncie Central. I've always said I would give back one of the championships I won at UCLA to have won a state championship in Indiana.

I'll tell you a funny story about that. When the movie *Hoosiers* came out, I complained about it to the director, who directed some of the *Hill Street Blues* episodes I acted in. In the movie, they had Milan, the little underdog school, beating my school, South Bend Central, whereas Milan actually beat Muncie Central. The director told me that one of the filmmakers went to school in Fort Wayne, and South Bend Central used to wipe them off the court. So he got his revenge that way. I thought it was a great movie, though. (laughs)

Even though I went to coach Wooden's school and even though he had coached my coach, Jimmy Powers, in high school and college, he didn't recruit me. I don't think he knew anything about me, and I didn't

Coach Wooden had no idea what he was getting because he hadn't seen me play. He just took the word of a guy he respected, and it turned out to be an amazing opportunity for me.

know much about him other than the fact that he was revered in Indiana. I knew UCLA was good, but they weren't on television then, and you got the scores from the West Coast a day later. It all seemed a little remote.

I was being recruited by a number of schools when I ran into Walt Kennedy, an old geometry professor of mine who had been our scorekeeper at South Bend Central. What I didn't know was that he had been one of the top coaches in the area. In fact, coach Wooden says to this day that Walt Kennedy knew more about basketball than he did. "Have you decided where you're going to college yet?" he asked me, and I said no, but I was thinking about Michigan, Kansas, and a few other schools.

"Well, John Wooden is a friend of mine," he said. "Let me call him for you."

Soon I was getting letters from coach Wooden and Jerry Norman, and we set up a date for me to visit UCLA. There was still snow on the ground when I left South Bend. As soon as I got there, I knew I was in the right place. I was just enamored of California. In fact, I came home thinking that if I didn't get into UCLA I'd go to USC.

But I did get in, even though coach Wooden had no idea what he was getting because he hadn't seen me play. He just took the word of a guy he respected, and it turned out to be an amazing opportunity for me. It still is, in fact. It's kind of hard to be an actor in Indiana. (laughs) And to this day coach Wooden is one of my closest friends.

When I got to college, I wanted to be a social worker and save the world. But I almost flunked out my freshman year. I was just so bored in class, and being in California made for too many distractions. One day coach Wooden called me into his office and said, "How are things going?"

I said, "Great, Coach. I'm having a great time."

He said, "You're having *too* good a time. I made a promise to your mom and dad you'd get an education, and you're out here playing around. You're going to be back home before you know it if you don't straighten up and fly right." That's just the way he talked.

That scared me, so I buckled down, and my sophomore year I was an Academic All-American. You hear coaches talking about being interested in you more than just as an athlete. Well, coach Wooden really was. Yes, I played well for him, but I think he genuinely cared about me.

Coach Wooden was a big believer in conditioning, in fundamentals, and not doing anything extraneous

I had broken all the guards' scoring records at UCLA my sophomore year—I averaged 16 or 17 points a game—and when Kareem Abdul-Jabbar started playing the next year, my average took a big hit.

on the court. Things like dribbling behind your back or between your legs, which Walt Hazzard liked to do, were not his style. He was a very simple man when it came to his practices. I'll bet to this day you could go to his house and find three-by-five index cards telling you to the minute what he was going to do in practice. He didn't believe in scrimmaging either. Initially, he would hold scrimmages just to get a feel for who was going to be on the team and to weed certain players out. But after he decided on his 12 or 14 players, practice was just drills: shooting drills, rebounding drills, free-throw drills, defensive drills. All very fundamental.

We never worked out in the weight room or ran cross-country prior to the season, which was popular back then. I think there are probably some benefits to lifting weights as long as you don't bulk up too much, but how many times do you run a cross-country course on a basketball court? To me, doing 20-yard sprints was more beneficial.

I started playing point guard a lot during my sophomore year—I guess I handled the ball 75 to 80 percent of the time—and that meant I had to pass the ball. I had to be able to score too. Coach Wooden always said, "I don't want anybody who can't score. I may not want you to score as much as you want to, but if you can't score I don't want you playing for me." So I became a playmaker who made plays for the other guys, but I made them for myself too.

I had broken all the guards' scoring records at UCLA my sophomore year—I averaged 16 or 17 points a game—and when Kareem Abdul-Jabbar started playing the next year, my average took a big hit. I had to recognize that he was a great player and that we were all going to have to sacrifice our individual games for the betterment of the team. But Kareem made it easy because he was so unselfish. Had he been the kind of player who hogged the ball or read his press clippings, it would have been an insufferable situation. But he was a joy to play with.

I've got to tell you about the first time I saw Kareem. When he came out on his recruiting visit, they asked Edgar Lacey and me to meet him at the

When I look back at the game against Houston in the Astrodome, I think it wasn't a game that allowed the teams to compete at the highest level. Where the game was played wouldn't really allow you to do that.

airport. The only specific instruction we were given was not to gawk, not to make a big deal about how big he was because he was going to be bigger than anyone we'd ever seen. That was like telling a kid not to take a piece of candy—it became an invitation.

Well, Kareem got off the plane—he had to duck his head just to get into the terminal—and we were walking down the corridor at the airport where there was some artwork by elementary school students displayed in glass frames on the wall. I was thinking, "Don't stare," but we were walking right next to each other, and I had to see what the difference in our height was. So I looked in the glass and I could see my head, but I couldn't see anything beyond Kareem's upper torso. It was amazing. I just said to myself, "I don't know what it's going to take, but we've got to get this guy." Edgar had a Volkswagen, and Kareem rode in the front seat with

his knees up against his chest. That's how he made his first trip to UCLA.

I was dating an Asian girl at that time—she was about 4'11"—and Kareem was very enamored of her. After his visit, he wrote her letters and she showed me one. I said, "I don't care what you say to him as long as you tell him to come out here and play for us." (laughs)

We didn't practice against Kareem his freshman year, or even see him much. We practiced on the main floor at Pauley, and they were on what they called the freshman court. They had a curtain rigged up so we couldn't see very much. The first time we really saw him was in the freshman-varsity game, and he made us all look ridiculous. If he didn't block you, he made you change your shot. And he ran like a gazelle. He was just so graceful. You had to be Ray Charles or Stevie Wonder not to see that he was an incredibly gifted player. He just destroyed us that night. Actually, I have the distinction at UCLA of losing two freshman-varsity games. My freshman year the varsity creamed us, and my sophomore year we got creamed by Kareem's team.

When I look back at the game against Houston in the Astrodome, I think it wasn't a game that allowed the teams to compete at the highest level. Where the game was played wouldn't really allow you to do that. The atmosphere was not college-like, and the conditions were not the best in which to play. But in terms of the impact it had on college basketball, it created a furor, didn't it? I had guys coming back from Vietnam tell me they had heard the game on the radio. It created a tremendous interest that hadn't been there before because the game had been so regional, and that one game made it national beyond anyone's dreams.

It proved that if you can turn the games into an event, it's like *Field of Dreams*: if you build it, they will come. And now you have these spectacular events every year. That's what the game has become—a spectacle.

Don Chaney, with Guy Lewis and Elvin Hayes, played a key role in the University of Houston's victory in the Astrodome. Chaney appeared in two Final Fours with the Cougars. He later won two NBA championships with the Boston Celtics before going on to coach the Los Angeles Clippers, Houston Rockets, Detroit Pistons, and New York Knicks. Photograph courtesy of the University of Houston Sports Information Department.

CHAPTER 13

Don Chaney on the Roar of the Crowd

Katy, Texas, June 2005

I grew up in Baton Rouge, a block and a half from the Louisiana State University campus. I could sit on my back porch and listen to the crowds at the football games, but I couldn't go to school there because it wasn't integrated. I went to Houston because Guy Lewis came along and sweet-talked my mom and my high school coach at the same time.

Guy had the gift of gab. I'll tell you that. And wherever he went, he always rented a red convertible. It had to be red, and it had to be a convertible. No hard top for Guy. And his clothes were always perfectly tailored so they would fit just right. He was really something. He impressed my mom and my coach by telling them I had an opportunity to be one of the first black players at the University of Houston. I was interested in UCLA or Loyola of Chicago, which had won the NCAA Tournament the year before, but one day I came home and there were my mom and my coach sitting in the living room.

"Coach Lewis from Houston was just here," they said. "That's where you're going." I never had a choice. (laughs) My mom's always been a pioneer, and she wanted me to be one, too, I guess.

I had already met Elvin Hayes at a high school all-star game, and you have to give Guy Lewis a lot of credit for bringing in two black athletes at the same time, don't you? That was a bold move at the time, especially

There was a big buildup about Elvin and me coming to Houston, and people wanted to see us play. They'd fill the gym and even stand up when there weren't enough seats.

in Texas. It was an adjustment because I lived in an all-black neighborhood and went to an all-black high school, so I had to get used to playing and rooming with white guys. That was one thing coach Lewis didn't tell my mother, that the transition wasn't going to be easy.

Maybe the most ingenious move coach Lewis made was not having Elvin and me room together, which would have been comfortable for us. Instead, he made sure we roomed with white guys. That helped smooth the transition for me. But it was harder on Elvin. Baton Rouge is a small town, but it was the state capital, so I was exposed to a lot of different things he didn't see in the small Louisiana town where he grew up. He came in with a chip on his shoulder. For instance, he would throw his roommate out of their room all the time. Just throw him down the hallway. Guy Lewis would call me in and say, "You've got to talk to Elvin," and I guess I had a little bit of a calming effect. Somehow we got through it.

Kareem had this intimidating air about him. And he was just *huge*. It was like seeing King Kong for the first time. We were just the country bumpkins going, "Wow, look at that guy!" like everybody else.

One problem we had right off the bat was that our freshman team was so good. There was a big buildup about Elvin and me coming to Houston, and people wanted to see us play. They'd fill the gym and even stand up when there weren't enough seats. Then when the varsity came out to play they would leave. That created some animosity, and when we killed the varsity in the freshman-varsity game, the varsity players wouldn't even speak to us. There was some turmoil for a while because we all lived in the same athletic dormitory, and the football players and the basketball players wouldn't talk to us or even look at us. There was some racism there, no question about it.

Things changed quickly, though. Three years after Elvin and I got there, Houston had its first black homecoming queen. That was amazing to me, that a school that had been all white could have something like that happen in so short a time. The only word for it, I think, is righteous.

Playing with Elvin forced me to make adjustments to my game that really helped me later in the NBA. He was our big scorer, so I made a commitment to play defense, and because Guy Lewis ran a number of different defenses, we were very effective. I don't think Guy gets enough credit for orchestrating the defenses the way he did. Everybody thought he just had great players and let them play. Now that I've been a coach, I understand how important what he did was.

In our junior year, we became a powerhouse. We went to the 1967 Final Four in Louisville and lost to UCLA in the semifinals, and it was really some experience. Both teams ended up in the same hotel—I don't know how that happened—and it was the strangest thing. In walked Kareem Abdul-Jabbar, Mike Warren, and Lucius Allen with reporters, cameramen, and fans all around them. It was as if they had an entourage. I was thinking, "I wonder if they have to pay these people." (laughs)

Kareem had this intimidating air about him. And he was just *huge*. It was like seeing King Kong for the first time. We were just the country bumpkins going, "Wow, look at that guy!" like everybody else. People were calling out questions as if Kareem was a movie star, and the whole team walked around with an air about them that was frightening. I got the feeling that they were so confident that they would just step right over us—which they did when they beat us by 15 points.

Before the game, coach Lewis said we should have respect for them, but not be afraid to play them, not be intimidated by the media and the size of the arena and so on. He said they were undefeated but they had to lose sometime, and it might as well be now. That helped a little, but at the same time in the back of our heads, we were saying, "We can't beat that team."

We were overmatched in that game. Our team was very young and Elvin was still kind of raw. They pressed us out of our game, and because of who they were, their experience and notoriety, they dominated the game. I was embarrassed because I knew we had a much better team than that.

I can't remember when I heard we were going to play them again in Houston the next season, but I was overjoyed. I just assumed it would be on our home court at the Delmar Fieldhouse, and I was looking forward to competing against them again because we were all more relaxed and mature. I knew we had a better team.

I had no idea what the game would become—the Astrodome and national television, bringing in the baskets and the floor from somewhere else, all that

The noise, the roar of the crowd, was unbelievable. I'll be honest, I could feel my knees give out when we walked out on the floor.

stuff. And it was all so weird. When we practiced in the Astrodome for the first time, we could hear an echo every time the ball bounced. It was almost as if we were playing outside and had to calculate the wind. And the background was so far away instead of having the stands on top of you. I thought it was an ugly place to play basketball and didn't feel very comfortable at all.

But on the day of the game, it was totally different. The noise, the roar of the crowd, was unbelievable. I'll be honest, I could feel my knees give out when we walked out on the floor. I really felt nervous and started shaking. I don't think any of us anticipated the crowd, the colors people were wearing all over the arena, and the noise. To look up and see all that was frightening.

Before the game, Guy Lewis said, "You guys are making history tonight. This is one of the biggest games of your lives." But he didn't really have to motivate us. One comforting thing to me was the feeling that, win or lose, we were part of history. It was like a championship fight or playing in the Super Bowl. The losing team doesn't have to hang its head because they have made it to the Super Bowl. That calmed me down and took some of the pressure off. And besides,

we were undefeated too. We weren't cream puffs. We could stick our chests out too and feel good going into the game. No, we hadn't played well the last time we met, but we were ready this time.

When the game started, my nervousness went away, but it was still pretty strange. For instance, I would be bringing the ball up the court and I couldn't hear it bounce. Because of the noise from the crowd, I couldn't hear the ball hit the floor. All my life, I was used to that sound and it wasn't there. We couldn't hear what Guy Lewis was saying from the bench either. We'd get bits and pieces, but the noise level kept us from understanding him.

In the first minute of play, we started getting the ball in to Elvin just to get him going, and I could see right away how focused he was. His eyes were as big as basketballs. And when he hit his first couple of shots it reminded me of high school because of how easy he made it look. He nailed his turnaround jumper every time. He hit some shots when Kareem was right on him—just knocked them down—so in just the first two or three minutes we became a very composed team and felt we could beat them.

We had heard that Kareem had an eye injury, but on that particular night I don't care if he had four eyes, he could not have stopped Elvin Hayes. I have never seen a guy shoot that well. You know how they use the term in a zone? Well, Elvin was in a zone, because he was making shots when I know he couldn't even have seen the basket. They were all just going down for him.

The game was close right down to the end, and I was really concerned about them getting the ball for one last shot. But on one of the last plays of the game, I deflected a pass and knocked the ball out of bounds, and all I could think was now they didn't have enough time to win.

I'll never forget the adrenaline rush when it was over. I was stunned and almost lost consciousness. It was a feeling like I've never had before. I skydive a little bit, but this was even more of a rush. The next day the phone rang and rang and rang. Everybody I knew wanted to talk about the game. And we kept reliving it because they showed it over and over again on television for a week and a half. Every time you turned to a certain channel, they were running it again.

I always thought Kareem was a little bitter about that game. They asked us to be on a television panel about it in Los Angeles, and Guy Lewis, John Wooden, Elvin, myself, Mike Warren, and Lucius Allen all participated. But Kareem didn't show up. Later we became good friends, but we don't talk about that game much. Only when we're sitting and having a beer.

We met UCLA again that season in the NCAA Tournament, and one reason we lost was that George Reynolds, who played in the backcourt with me, couldn't play. George was a big part of our success, and we heard through the grapevine that UCLA did some research and discovered that George was a junior-college transfer and didn't have enough credits or something. So he was disqualified from the game and Guy Lewis' son, Vern, had to start in a big game for the first time.

Without George there, they were able to press us all over the court for the entire game and pack in the defense on Elvin. It was a great strategy because it threw us off our game. We were a run-and-gun team, and they just stopped us cold. Once we got across the time line, we couldn't get the ball in to Elvin, and because our offense was designed to work through him, it really threw us off. It wouldn't have bothered us nearly as much had George played. We might still have lost, but we would have been better. It was a pitiful game for us.

I've had a great life in basketball: 12 years playing in the NBA, 26 years as an assistant and head coach. But I have to tell you, even winning two championships with the Celtics wasn't quite the same as beating UCLA in the Astrodome. To me, that was the most amazing thing ever.

CHAPTER 14

Mickey Herskowitz: How Houston Became a Basketball Town

Houston, Texas, June 2005

If you really want to understand the impact of the Houston-UCLA game in the Astrodome, you have to know a little something about the University of Houston. It was founded during World War II as a night school, and even in the late fifties it still had Quonset huts on the campus that had been built as

Houston's teams were viewed as outsiders. In fact, the Southwestern Conference schools looked on them as outlaws in the early years. But the other schools wouldn't recruit black athletes, and that gave Houston a big edge.

GI housing. These Quonset huts had one big room, no bathroom, and no air-conditioning. It took years to get rid of those things. There was also a stockyard across the street, and when the wind shifted you'd get the stench of the slaughter. So the university

wasn't exactly a garden spot, and there was very little reason to go there. They tried for years to improve the image of the school and to get the buildings and the facilities they needed.

When it came to getting good athletes, it could be kind of embarrassing. In the late fifties, Houston tried to recruit Don Meredith, who was from Texas and was one of the top high school quarterbacks in the country. Jack Scott, who was the public relations man, and his assistant walked through the athletic department parking lot before Meredith's arrival, sweeping up cigarette butts and used condoms. I'm serious. The students would park in that lot at night and make out and throw stuff out the window. Meredith went to SMU, of course.

Houston's teams were viewed as outsiders. In fact, the Southwestern Conference schools looked on them as outlaws in the early years. But the other schools wouldn't recruit black athletes, and that gave Houston a big edge. It's funny because a lot of coaches who never thought of themselves as racist fell into a psychological trap. I can remember a very prominent coach telling me he would love to have some great black athletes, but he put a higher premium on chemistry and team harmony. It was just an excuse for not really going after them. But that's how Houston was able to get Elvin Hayes and Don Chaney and Warren McVea, who was an All-American running back. And they were followed very closely by others, who also had great careers.

The Astrodome took over the marketing and the promotion and built it up in a way no basketball game had ever been built up before. You almost thought it was too big for the city at the time.

The university started playing football in the Astrodome in 1965, and though that did very little to improve the campus itself, it improved the image of the school tremendously. It was a great recruiting tool because instead of taking kids to the campus, they'd take them to the Astrodome and their eyeballs would just fall right out of their heads. And the Astrodome immediately became the identity of the whole city. People all over the world were just fascinated by it. The idea of playing baseball or football indoors was something they couldn't conceive of.

Judge Hofheinz got the idea for the Astrodome when he saw the Roman Colosseum. He got Buckminster Fuller to design it, and then Hofheinz asked him if he could put in a baseball stadium with sixty thousand seats. So Fuller redesigned it. After it was built, the judge brought in writers from around the state—every columnist from any paper with any influence or any circulation—and we all sat in one of the box seats. He showed us the colored seats in the different sections, which nobody had ever done before. Then he started talking about the plumbing,

how forty thousand people could flush the toilet at the same time, and the water pressure wouldn't go down. And about how the air-conditioning moved 570,000 pounds of air or whatever it was an hour. And somebody said, "Gee, that's as much air as Hofheinz moves when he's giving a speech." (laughs)

But the judge was a great showman and a real visionary. It was crazy all the things he did in the Astrodome—Bobby Riggs versus Billie Jean King, a Muhammad Ali fight, midget auto races, polo, rodeos, demolition derbies. They even had a bullfight, although after they booked it they found out they couldn't actually kill the bull because it was against the law. So they had what they called a bloodless bullfight, although it wasn't really bloodless. Judge Hofheinz and the other promoters shed a lot of blood. (laughs) All these events put Houston on the map because suddenly writers who never came to town to cover anything were coming for one event after another.

Do you know how the judge came up with the concept of skyboxes? When they designed the stadium, there was a good deal of room left over between the highest level of seats and the roof, and the judge thought it was wasted space. So he filled it up with custom-designed skyboxes and added bars, color television sets, waiter service, and seats in front so you could watch the game and entertain customers. Who cared if you needed binoculars to see the floor?

I know the Houston-UCLA game was Guy Lewis' idea, but as soon as the judge bought into it, it became *his* idea. And in a way, it was because he added the showmanship elements that made it memorable. The Astrodome took over the marketing and the promotion and built it up in a way no basketball game had ever been built up before. You almost thought it was too big for the city at the time. The game itself was secondary to the promotion.

What you have to understand is basketball just wasn't a big deal in Texas. The old joke was that it was the third-leading sport in Texas behind football and spring football. And there was never a glimmer of interest in attracting pro basketball to Houston. But this game really captured people's imagination. They couldn't wait to see what basketball would be like inside that enormous cavern of a stadium. And of course everything fell into place with UCLA being the best team in the country and having a huge winning streak, Houston being No. 2, and both teams being undefeated.

The night of the game people just kept pouring into the stadium. I don't know what the walkup sale was, but it was huge. The thing I remember—and this was typical of the judge—is that he also had the National Boat Show in the Astrohall across the street the same night. I was walking in with my typewriter and press credential, and I heard a guy asking a ticket taker, "Where are the boats?" The usher said they were across the street, and the guy said, "Well, why the hell didn't somebody tell me that? I didn't come all this way to watch a bunch of guys in short pants run up and down the floor." (laughs) I couldn't believe anybody would go to a different event that night, but they filled up the boat show too.

At first, the game itself was really disconcerting. You had the feeling you could see under the floor, and during the warm-ups it all seemed so artificial. The noise of the crowd rebounded off the ceiling, and the bouncing of the ball—thump, thump—was like hearing a dentist's drill. For a brief moment, I had the feeling that it was a mistake, that it was going to be a circus not a basketball game.

But then the game started and I realized that it was going to be close and both teams were playing like hell, so I got over that. And I didn't hear anyone after the game, no matter how bad their seats were, say they weren't thrilled being there. Every time there is a big anniversary—the 10th or the 20th or the 25th—the people who were there love reading about it all over again.

The other thing about the game I remember is that it was the most partisan crowd I'd ever seen for any game—including football and baseball—in Houston. The first two or three years that the Astros played in the Astrodome, people sat there like zombies. They actually had to be given cues on the scoreboard to cheer and applaud. And the football crowds dressed like they were going to the opera—suits and ties for the men, dresses for the women, and fancy hairdos and hats. The Astrodome might have been the first sports stadium in the country where the women wore hats as if they were at the Kentucky Derby.

There was something about being indoors that made people think they had to dress up. And people would miss entire innings or quarters because they would be sitting there talking. They acted like they were at a party, not a sports event. Also, Houston was a city that would not boo. You never went to a game and heard anyone boo the opposing team. They didn't cheer much either, but the Houston-UCLA game gave the fans a chance to see how much fun it could be to be totally partisan and rambunctious and rowdy. That night, they all went nuts.

You can't overestimate what that game did for the University of Houston. It wasn't like other universities that had alumni all over the country who donated money and drove hundreds of miles to see a game. But the UCLA game literally gave the school an image transplant. It put it in the big leagues and made people think about it in a new way. It did wonders for the city too.

Even if you didn't care about basketball, if you were a sports fan in Houston you knew this was a once-in-a-lifetime event and you had to be there. It also gave the city a whole new appetite for basketball. The NBA came to Houston directly because of that game, and now it's very strongly entrenched in a city where you couldn't have found basketball with the Mount Palomar telescope before.

It all began with that game at the Astrodome. It was an amazing night.

PART IV

The Bluegrass State of Mind

The image most people have of sports in Kentucky is of horse farms, bourbon, and the Kentucky Derby. But the people who live in the state know there is something bigger—basketball.

The University of Kentucky led the way, starting with Adolph Rupp, who won four national titles in the forties and fifties, and followed by Joe B. Hall, Rick Pitino, and Tubby Smith, who won one championship each. And the University of Louisville won two more titles under Denny Crum.

I have had a special feeling for Kentucky ever since I announced the first Wildcats game on television and went on to produce a number of its most important games on TVS. I also made many good friends with whom it was great fun to talk again after all this time.

Of all John Wooden's assistants, Crum had the most success as a head coach. When he retired from Louisville in 2001, he had coached the Cardinals for 30 seasons, been to six Final Fours, and won two national championships. In 1994 he was inducted into the Basketball Hall of Fame.

Hall, who played for Rupp at Kentucky, assumed the unenviable task of succeeding him as coach and, in 1978, led the Wildcats to their fifth national title. In 13 seasons he compiled a record of 297–100. He and Crum now do a radio show that is heard around the state.

Pitino, who began his coaching career at Providence College, took Kentucky to a national championship in 1996 and reached the title game again the following year. He left the state to become president and coach of the Boston Celtics, then returned three years later to coach archrival Louisville. When the Cardinals went to the 2005 Final Four, Pitino became the first coach to take three different teams to the Final Four.

Smith, who had been Pitino's assistant at Kentucky for two years, became the Wildcats' coach in 1997 and led them to the national championship in his first season. In all, Smith's Kentucky teams have made the Sweet 16 six times and won five SEC titles. Smith also coached at the Universities of Tulsa and Georgia and has an overall coaching record of 343–120.

Billy Reed was, for many years, one of the most popular newspaper columnists in Kentucky and has a unique knowledge of college basketball in his home state. In 2003 he was appointed director of communications for Kentucky's Commerce Cabinet.

CHAPTER 15

Denny Crum: Pulling Up Stakes and Putting Down Roots

San Antonio, Texas, April 2004

I was born in Los Angeles and lived there all my life, 33 years, before I came to Louisville. But I just love it here—the hunting and fishing and golf, and the fact that Louisville basketball is always the main attraction. In Los Angeles there are hundreds of things to do, so even when I had the opportunity to go back to UCLA after John Wooden retired, I stayed in Louisville.

I tell people that I was the luckiest guy who ever lived because I got to play for coach Wooden and coach under him. He was like a father to me. I told my minister that he was my God coach, but coach Wooden was my coach. I don't know how you could put a value on the things I learned from him.

Coach Wooden asked me to be his assistant in 1969, which was Kareem Abdul-Jabbar's senior year. We won the national championship that season in Freedom Hall, where I coached for so many years after I went to Louisville. I'll never forget my first day of practice at UCLA. Coach Wooden and I got to Pauley Pavilion early and Kareem was one of the first players there. He walked over to a basket on the side

and started shooting, and I told Coach, "I think I'm going to go talk to him," and he said, "Good."

When Kareem left, there were all these articles saying, "That's the end of the UCLA dynasty." Everybody assumed that because he was gone it would be some other team's turn. But we just went from Kareem to Sidney Wicks, Curtis Rowe, and Steve Patterson, and we won the NCAA championship two more years in a row.

So I walked over and I said, "Lew (that's what we called him then, of course), I'd like to show you a couple of things that, added to what you can already do, will really help make you a better-rounded player."

He said, "Great, Coach, show me," and I showed him a couple of pivot moves. Well, here he was a senior and the greatest player in college basketball and he didn't know me from a load of coal, but he said, "Thank you," and came in early every day and worked on pivots. That was his attitude about wanting to learn.

I'll tell you a funny story about coach Wooden. He was always getting letters from people wanting him to diagram his offenses and explain how they worked. Well, after a while he didn't want to do it, so he'd say, "Write Denny Crum. He knows more about those offenses than I remember." That wasn't true, of course, but all of a sudden I was getting the letters and I had to respond to them because he told them to write me. (laughs)

When Kareem left, there were all these articles saying, "That's the end of the UCLA dynasty." Everybody assumed that because he was gone it would be some other team's turn. But we just went from Kareem to Sidney Wicks, Curtis Rowe, and Steve Patterson, and we won the NCAA championship two more years in a row. And then came the Walton era: I recruited Bill and Greg Lee and Jamaal Wilkes. When I took my first Louisville team to a Final Four, we played UCLA in the semifinals, and who was waiting for us? The guys I had recruited. We lost, of course. (laughs)

Let me tell you about how we recruited Bill Walton. We only found out about him because his brother, Bruce, who was a year ahead of him, was a tackle on our football team. This was before they had any high school all-star games, and nobody recruited in San Diego much because there never seemed to be any good players. But I went down to see him and I was really impressed.

Bill could block shots, rebound, and he was just a great passer. And in his senior year in high school, his shooting average from the floor was 82 percent. Most guys can't shoot free throws that well. And because he was the last guy down the court much of the time, he was shooting from the outside a lot. Bill's team was averaging 90 points a game, while their opponents were averaging 40. Sometimes you see a team win by 50 points, but to win by an average of 50 points for a whole season? I never saw anything like it.

After I'd seen Bill play, coach Wooden asked me what I thought of him.

"There's no redheaded freckle-faced kid from San Diego who is the best high school player you've ever seen. People will think you're an idiot if you say things like that. It just isn't logical."

I said, "Coach, I think he's the best high school player I've ever seen. He's so much better than Tom McMillen it isn't even funny." McMillen was a great high school player in the Philadelphia area at that time, and his picture had been on the cover of *Sports Illustrated*.

Well, Coach got up from his chair, walked around his desk, and closed the door to his office so nobody could hear what we were saying.

"Don't ever make a stupid statement like that," he said. "There's no redheaded freckle-faced kid from San Diego who is the best high school player you've ever seen. People will think you're an idiot if you say things like that. It just isn't logical."

But eventually I convinced coach Wooden to go to his home. I think the only home I ever got him to was Bill Walton's. His mother fed all of us, including Bill, and I can't even begin to tell you how much food this kid consumed. It was more than any human being I've ever seen, just unbelievable. (laughs) Then we went and saw him play. We sat up in the corner of the gym hoping nobody would notice, but soon everybody realized John Wooden was there and they all wanted his autograph. He kept signing them during the timeouts and at halftime. Bill played just a great game, and as soon as it was over we left.

We were in the rental car driving back to the airport and I was really curious to know what Coach thought, but I didn't say a word and neither did he. Then we got on the airplane and sat right next to each other, and again, not a word. Finally, just before we got off the plane, I couldn't stand it any longer and I said, "Well, Coach, what do you think of him?"

"He is pretty good, isn't he?" he said.

And that was it, John Wooden's highest accolade: "He is pretty good, isn't he?" (laughs)

Bill decided to come to UCLA, and it was common practice in those days to get jobs for players who were enrolling in the fall, so I called and asked him if he wanted a summer job.

"Thanks," he said, "but my brother and a couple of other guys have rented a house on the beach, and I'm just going to go down there to lie on the beach and read."

"OK, Bill," I said. "If you change your mind, give me a call."

Well, about halfway through the summer he called and said, "Coach, I need to take you up on that summer job."

"What's the matter?" I said "Did you run out of money?"

"Yes, I did," he said. "My brother and his friends are making me pay for my share of the food, and I don't have any money."

"Fine," I said. "I'll take care of it."

So I drove over to the alumni office and found a guy who owned a construction company in the San Diego area and called him. He said he'd give Bill a job for $3.75 an hour, which wasn't bad for construction labor back then. I called Bill and told him he could go to work on Monday. Late Thursday afternoon the next week, the contractor called and said, "Coach, what's going on? Bill didn't show up for work today. He didn't call or anything."

So I called him and said, "Bill, did something happen on the job? Are you upset about something or sick?"

"No, Coach, I'm fine. I just needed enough money to last me the rest of the summer."

He had half a summer to go and he earned $3.75 an hour for three days and he had enough money! That could only be Bill Walton. (laughs)

On the first day of practice, Bill came in wearing a beard and coach Wooden told the manager to send him over. "Bill, I notice you have facial hair," he said.

"Yes, I do, Coach."

"You know we have a rule that none of our players can wear facial hair."

"Well, Coach, I'm not just a member of the team, I'm an individual too, and I have a right to my own way and I like having a beard."

"It sounds like you believe strongly in that."

"I really do, Coach."

"Well, you certainly have that right, but I just want you to know we're going to miss you."

Bill ran out of practice, shaved, and came back. And he never said another word about it.

That's the way coach Wooden was. You did things his way. I remember when Curtis Rowe and Sidney Wicks were late to the training table meal a couple of times before a game and Coach warned them about it, but the next game they were two or three minutes late again. So he told them they weren't going to start. I forget who we were playing—Stanford or Oregon, I think—and at halftime Wicks and Rowe hadn't been in the game and we were getting beat by six or eight points. We were walking off the court to the locker room when somebody grabbed me from behind. I turned around and it was J. D. Morgan.

"What the goddam hell does he think he's doing?" J.D. said. "Thirteen thousand people paid to watch those two play and he doesn't even put them in the game? You go in there and tell him to get them in the game."

I said, "J.D., *you* tell him. I'm not telling him anything. He's already mad because they didn't do what they were supposed to do."

Coach put Wicks and Rowe in for the second half and we won the game, but he did what he thought was right. The way he looked at it, discipline was part of the deal. If you don't have discipline, then he can't rely on you. So J.D. was the boss, but coach Wooden was my boss, and I wasn't going to tell him anything. J.D. didn't go into that locker room, I guarantee you. And Wicks and Rowe were never late for training table again.

Bill's greatest game at UCLA was the 1973 NCAA championship game in which we beat Memphis State, 87–66. He was 21 of 22 from the floor, just about perfect.

But back to Bill. He did all kinds of things at UCLA outside of basketball—he led protests and was very active politically—but when it came to practicing and the games he was all business, and of course he was a great player. It was a shame his NBA career was hampered by his foot injuries. He had multiple operations on his foot, and I always told him it was because he was a vegetarian, that it was because he wouldn't eat meat that he had all those problems with his foot. (laughs)

Bill's greatest game at UCLA was the 1973 NCAA championship game in which we beat Memphis State, 87–66. He was 21 of 22 from the floor, just about perfect. Greg Lee would throw these high line-drive passes up to him, and he'd just catch them and lay them in the basket. His timing, his great hands, and his understanding and feel for the game made him just an awesome player.

Memphis State had a great team that year. Gene Bartow was the coach, and I think the fact that they got to the championship game is how Gene got the UCLA job when coach Wooden retired a few years later. I knew Gene was going to have a tough job

taking over for coach Wooden simply because he was following a legend. I was probably the one who was best suited to take that job at that time, but I had gone to Louisville and we hadn't won there yet.

I guess I could have waited, but I was 33 years old and I felt I was ready. I thought I should take advantage of the opportunity because I believed I could recruit all over the South, which was an untapped source for great athletes. We would get kids up to a game at Freedom Hall and they'd see eighteen thousand people and they'd go back home wanting to come play for us. We made a living for years with kids out of the South.

It was tough recruiting in Kentucky, though, because the whole state was for the University of Kentucky. They had fifty thousand-watt clear-channel radio stations, and in every community you went to they were all Kentucky fans. It was an uphill battle until finally we got the state's high school Mr. Basketball to come to Louisville five years in a row. That showed we had arrived. Every year it seemed that recruiting against Kentucky was as tough as playing against them, but somehow we managed.

When I first got here, the University of Kentucky wouldn't play us or any other school in the state. But then we played them in the Mideast Regional of the NCAA Tournament in 1983, won in overtime, and went to the Final Four. John Y. Brown, who was the governor then, was a Kentucky graduate, and he told the Kentucky people that it was about time they recognized that Louisville was on their level and that they needed to start playing each other. So now they play once a year and it's a huge game for both schools.

Now that I'm retired, I don't miss the hours or the coaching. I do miss the relationships with young people, though. You work with them all your life and then all of a sudden they're not there. It's like when your children go away to college and you realize there's no noise in the house. But I certainly have no regrets. I was fortunate to stay in one place for so long, which doesn't happen much anymore. I've had

Denny Crum went to six Final Fours and won two NCAA championships during his 30 years at the University of Louisville. He was John Wooden's chief assistant during a number of its championship seasons and played a key role in recruiting Bill Walton.

a number of coaches tell me the only way they were ever able to get a good raise was to change schools. There always seemed to be somebody else out there willing to pay you more than the people you've already done it for are willing to pay to keep you.

Now that I'm retired, I don't miss the hours or the coaching. I do miss the relationships with young people, though.

One of the things Joe B. Hall and I do on our radio show is have people call in, and they always ask about certain players or teams or eras and that brings things back. It may be something you haven't thought about in a long time, but all of a sudden it will bring back a particular game and you realize the fans out there went through it with you. It makes you understand how much they love it.

Another great thing is that most of the kids who played for us live in Louisville. Even the ones who didn't come from here stayed here, and we see them all the time. They come to the games and attend different charity events. You go to a Triple A baseball game and you'll see some of your ex-players. I have a great relationship with most of them. In fact, I've had a lot of them tell me how much more they appreciate me now than they did when I was coaching them. (laughs)

For instance, I had a player named Everick Sullivan, and if I had to list which of my players over the years I thought would go into coaching, I'd have put him at the very bottom because you couldn't coach him in practice. Well, he did become a coach—he's now the head coach at Vincennes University in Indiana—and one day he came up to me and said, "Coach, I owe you a big apology. I can honestly tell you that I didn't like you very much when I played for you. But now I understand why you did the things you did. I just want you to know I owe you a lot."

That makes you feel good when somebody recognizes down the road that you were trying to help him.

CHAPTER 16

Joe B. Hall on the Mad Genius of Adolph Rupp

Lexington, Kentucky, September 2004

Growing up in Kentucky, my dream was to play football at Notre Dame. Notre Dame quarterbacks were the heroes of every high school kid, and I would have crawled from here to South Bend to make the football team. I would have been the original Rudy. But the next best thing that could happen to a young man in Kentucky was to play for Adolph Rupp.

What you have to understand about Kentucky basketball is that it started in the high schools in the rural communities. The schools were so small they couldn't field football teams, but they could all support a basketball team. Often the kids had to travel a long way to get to school, and what with staying late after classes to practice they might miss the bus, so sometimes they lived in their coaches' houses. Just so they could play basketball.

Back in the late twenties and thirties, the smaller schools didn't even have uniforms. The kids played in cut-off jeans, or the fans would get together and buy them uniforms. Going to the games was a social function in these towns, and basketball became a way

of life. So there was a love for the game at the high school level and it carried over to the university. The players sensed this, of course—how important it was to the people of the state, how meaningful it was to their lives—and I think they got a lot of motivation from that.

Going to the games was a social function in these towns, and basketball became a way of life. So there was a love for the game at the high school level and it carried over to the university.

In those days Kentucky didn't recruit you; you recruited Kentucky. You'd come in for a weekend and there would be 75 of you. Guys would come in from the bus from all over, you'd scrimmage for two days, and then coach Rupp would have the manager come down and read off 10 names. They would come back the next weekend and there would be 75 more of you and you'd scrimmage again.

The big thing in those days was just getting a scholarship. My parents didn't have the money, and I would have had to work my way through college and not

I made the team, and the greatest thrill I've ever had in my life was that first night, coming out of the dressing room and through the stands onto the floor with the band playing the fight song, "On! On! U of K!" with Kentucky written across my chest.

had time for basketball. But getting a scholarship took the pressure off and allowed players to get a college education. Nobody thought about the pros. It was enough just to get four years of college.

I made the team, and the greatest thrill I've ever had in my life was that first night, coming out of the dressing room and through the stands onto the floor with the band playing the fight song, "On! On! U of K!" with Kentucky written across my chest. I was a freshman in 1948 when the greatest Kentucky team of all time was on the floor: Kenny Rollins, Alex Groza, Ralph Beard, Wallace Jones, and Cliff Barker. They won Kentucky's first national championship, and Kenny Rollins was the only one to graduate, so the other four came back and won the championship again the next year.

There seemed to be no limit to the interest in the team back then. I remember when they started talking about doubling the size of the Memorial Coliseum from 11,500 seats to almost 24,000. People said, "You'll have a white elephant. You'll ruin the demand for tickets." And I said, "No, sir, the first year you'll sell that facility out." Well, not only did they sell it out,

there were four thousand letters requesting tickets that were never even opened.

When tickets do become available, they're snatched right up, and there are so many stories about when a couple gets divorced and their biggest fight is over who gets the tickets. Sometimes the two divorced people remarry, but they still sit together at basketball games. It's probably the only time they ever see each other. (laughs)

Later on, Eddie, when you started televising Kentucky basketball for the first time, that did two things: it confirmed its greatness all over the country, and it gave the people in Kentucky the opportunity to see the games. A lot of them were seeing them for the first time, and to have our games in their living rooms just enhanced their support and their love for the sport and helped it grow.

I remember when you made a presentation at a Southeastern Conference coaches' meeting to produce a *Game of the Week* on Saturday afternoon and promised to have every team on at least once. Of course, you were going to have Kentucky on four or five times. (laughs)

I would have if I could. (laughs)

You went out of the room and we voted to let you have the franchise. It didn't cost much—about $1,500 a game—but it wasn't the money we were interested in, it was the exposure. It was just so beneficial to our program and our recruiting to be on television that I never objected to adjusting our schedule for TV.

Anyway, about coach Rupp, the players were just in awe of him. He was such a presence on the floor, so demanding. He had a way of correcting you that made you feel like you had just committed about the worst sin you could ever make in your life. It made you feel so small that you never wanted to mess up in practice again. The practices were tougher than the games.

He had a way getting the most out of you. A lot of it had to do with how organized he was, but some of it was through fear too. He was just so intimidating and relentless in his criticism. You could never achieve so much greatness that you could withstand his wrath when you made a mistake. I did something he didn't like one day, and he said, "Hall, if you ever did that in a game I'd take you down to the dressing room and I'd shoot you. . . . No I wouldn't. I'd shoot you right here before all the fans." (laughs)

"Cease! Cease this despicable display! Never have these hallowed halls seen such a poor effort at practice." Then he got down on one knee and picked something off the floor with his finger. "By George," he said, "a drop of sweat. One of the janitors must have dropped it while he was sweeping."

One afternoon late in the season, we were having just a horrendous practice—nobody hustling, no enthusiasm—and finally coach Rupp had all that he could stand. He walked out on the floor and stretched his hands up over his head and said, "Cease! Cease this despicable display! Never have these hallowed halls seen such a poor effort at practice." Then he got down on one knee and picked something off the floor with his finger. "By George," he said, "a drop of sweat. One of the janitors must have dropped it while he was sweeping." (laughs)

Do you know how superstitious coach Rupp was? He wanted to wear a blue suit at games because the color of Kentucky was blue, but the first time he did he got beat, so he never wore one again. He became known as the man in the brown suit.

Every morning, he dressed in the same manner, putting on the right sock first and then the left sock, then the right shoe, then the left shoe. He wore the same clothes every game day. He drove to the Coliseum the same way, parked in the same spot,

went to the student union for lunch with the players, and ate the same thing.

When he came back after lunch, there was a manhole cover on the sidewalk across from the Coliseum and he had to step on it with his right foot before he crossed the street. On game night, the first thing he did was go into the locker room, walk down to the third locker on the right, get a tissue, and wipe his glasses off. Then he threw the tissue down beside the trash can—always beside it, never in it. Then the managers came in and offered him three kinds of gum, and they had to be in order: Beechnut, Juicy Fruit, and Spearmint. He always took Spearmint and folded up the papers and threw them down beside the trash can. When he went out on the floor, there was an usher in a white coat who would meet him at the bottom of the steps and shake hands with him. The guy got sick once and they had to bring him to the game in an ambulance so he could shake hands with coach Rupp before the game.

On game day, wherever he was, he would walk through the parking lot looking for hairpins. If he found one on his walk, it meant a sure victory. If the open end of the hairpin was pointed toward him, it meant a blowout win. The next-to-last year he coached, he had an ulcerated foot and couldn't get around very well, so it became the job of the assistant manager to throw hairpins on the ground from his motel door to the bus. They'd have to go to the five-and-dime to buy a box of hairpins then dump them like an anthill right outside his motel door. He'd come out and say, "By George, Joe, look what I've found," and he'd drop down on one knee and scoop up that whole handful of hairpins and put them in his pocket.

When I replaced coach Rupp, I was out in the parking lot of the Coliseum, leaning up against the fender of my car talking to my assistant, Dick Parsons, and I looked down and there was one of the biggest hairpins I ever saw. I picked it up and said, "Dick, we're not going to start this foolishness, are we?"

"I hope not," he said.

Well, I pitched the hairpin up on the hood of the car and drove home. I got out and as I walked around the car to go into the house, that hairpin was still on the hood of the car. I picked it up and put it in my pocket, and from then on you'd find me out in those parking lots on game day looking for hairpins, rain or shine. I wasn't superstitious, but I didn't want to take any chances either. (laughs)

After I graduated, I coached at Regis College in Denver and Central Missouri State, and then I came back to Kentucky and spent seven years as coach Rupp's assistant before I took over in 1972. I figured if that didn't prepare me, nothing would. I felt like I had learned from the master, and I had confidence not only in the *X*s and *O*s of the game, but also in running a good, clean program.

It never bothered me being in coach Rupp's shadow because no one had more respect for him than I did. A lot of people would have been compared negatively. What people were saying at the time was, "I don't want to be the coach who follows Adolph Rupp. I want to be the coach who *follows* the coach who follows Adolph Rupp. Maybe when John Wooden retired at UCLA they should have hired me instead of Gene Bartow because I had experience as a legend-follower. (laughs)

It took me six years to win a national championship, but in my third year we took our team to the NCAA championship game that was John Wooden's last game. So that got the monkey off my back a little, even though we lost. The next year we won the National Invitation Tournament, and in 1977 we were in the top five in the country but lost in the regional finals to North Carolina. Then we won the national championship in 1978 and I was Coach of the Year. So that was a pretty good run. I felt the pressure was off by then.

In all the time I was at Kentucky I never negotiated a contract. I never asked for a raise, never asked for more money than I was offered. I was never worried about money. I made a good living. I got my chil-

dren's teeth straightened and got them all a college education. What more is a parent responsible for? I've seen money spoil more kids than it helped.

I never had a shoe contract either. I was offered one by all the major shoe companies, but I didn't think it was proper to ask my players to wear a particular shoe because I was getting paid. We always wore Converse, and finally I agreed to do $25,000 worth of clinics each year, so I traveled all over the world for two years for them. That's all the pay I ever got from shoes.

One of the things I inherited from coach Rupp was the unwritten policy that Kentucky would not play any in-state schools. We had an 18-game conference schedule, and we had traditional rivals like Indiana, Kansas, North Carolina, and Notre Dame that gave us a national presence. So if we started playing in-state schools, there would be no limit. Western Kentucky had a great basketball tradition, and Eastern Kentucky had some good teams, but we felt that if we played one, we would have to play them all and we'd be sacrificing our national schedule.

Anywhere you went in Kentucky, there were people who were fans of their school and also fans of Kentucky.

I also thought that Kentucky had border-to-border support and that to play another state school would polarize the fans. It would make them choose between Kentucky and their school, and we would lose some of that support. And if we beat them we were the bad guys, which we never had been in the state. Anywhere you went in Kentucky, there were people who were fans of their school and also fans of Kentucky.

But as Louisville grew in population, gained prestige, and built its program nationally, it got more support politically. People started demanding that

Kentucky play Louisville. There was a feeling that we had the whole pie and had to start sharing it. The pressure just grew and grew, and it was like we were avoiding them.

But once we started playing them, it turned into a good rivalry. There's been respect on both sides and it's been very competitive. The series started with me coaching against Denny Crum, and we split four games. And now we're splitting a radio show, except when he's out fishing or doing something else. (laughs) But we've developed a good rapport and have a lot of fun with the fans on both sides.

Rick Pitino, who began his coaching career at Providence College, won an NCAA championship at the University of Kentucky in 1996. After three years as president and coach of the Boston Celtics, Pitino returned to the state to coach the Wildcats' archrival Louisville. He is the only coach ever to take three different teams to the Final Four.

CHAPTER 17

Rick Pitino on Moving from the Hatfields to the McCoys

Milwaukee, Wisconsin, February 2005

A lot of people were surprised when I came back to coach at Louisville after having coached at Kentucky, and I was a little skeptical myself. In fact, the first time I talked to Tom Jurich, the Louisville athletic director, I told him, "A Kentucky coach could never coach at Louisville. It's the Hatfields and the McCoys."

There are fifty thousand Kentucky alumni in Louisville, so wherever you're pumping gas there's always a big blue van with a bumper sticker saying something that gets under your skin.

But then I started getting calls from friends in Kentucky who said, "We want you back. There are a lot of people who will not root for you one game a year, but they appreciate what you've done for

the state, so come back." Well, they miscalculated because there are a lot of people who will never look at me as anything except the enemy.

The one big trepidation I had was going back to Rupp Arena to coach against Kentucky. My friends said 70 percent of the people would give me a standing ovation, 20 percent would be silent, and 10 percent would boo. But when I came out on the floor, there were twenty-four thousand people booing me so loudly that you would have thought I'd kidnapped their families. (laughs) I was caught off guard. Fortunately the game started or the booing might never have stopped.

I'm very pleased with where I am now, but the one thing I don't like is that there are fifty thousand Kentucky alumni in Louisville, so wherever you're pumping gas there's always a big blue van with a bumper sticker saying something that gets under your skin. (laughs)

I was hired for my first head coaching job at Providence at 3:30 in the morning. I was an assistant at Boston University, and Lou Lamoriello—he's the general manager of the New Jersey Devils now—was the athletic director. He didn't want anybody to know he was talking to me. (laughs) It was a great start for me because it was a school with a long tradition, but they had been at the bottom of the Big East Conference for seven straight years, so there was nowhere to go but up. I was there for only two years, but they were magical, and the second year we went to the Final Four.

They eat, sleep, and drink the game of basketball. They grew up on Adolph Rupp and Cawood Ledford, the great announcer. They valued God and family . . . and, well, maybe Kentucky ranked up there with family for a lot of them.

This was in 1987, the first year of the three-point line, which was just the gimmick we needed. None of the other coaches in the league—Lou Carnesecca at St. John's, John Thompson at Georgetown, or Rollie Massimino at Villanova—would even *attempt* a three, and we made seven or eight each game. We led the nation in threes, and it propelled us to the Final Four.

After that I coached the New York Knicks for two years, and we were one of the top-scoring teams in the league, averaging 117 points per game. But the general manager, Al Bianchi, wanted a slower, more deliberate game, and I feel that any time the general manager doesn't like your style, you're probably better off elsewhere. So when C. M. Newton, the Kentucky athletic director, called and said, "Can I speak to you after the playoffs?" I said yes. Then I took the job.

When I came to Kentucky in 1989, it was foreign to anything I'd ever experienced culturally. I'd traveled extensively in the pros, but I'd never seen anything like Kentucky. There's a very small Jewish population, a very small Catholic population, very few Irish, very few Polish, and *no* Italians. (laughs) The one thing there that I *had* experienced before was their love for the game of basketball, which equaled mine. They eat, sleep, and drink the game of basketball. They grew up on Adolph Rupp and Cawood Ledford, the great announcer. They valued God and family . . . and, well, maybe Kentucky ranked up there with family for a lot of them. But to show you what a great place Kentucky is, Denny Crum could have had any job he wanted and he stayed 30 years.

At the press conference the day I took the Kentucky job, somebody handed me a *Sports Illustrated* titled, "Shame," with a little boy on the cover. We had just been put on probation for three years, and the article recounted everything Kentucky had done wrong and all the good players who had transferred. Only the short, slow kids stayed behind. More than anything else, people had lost hope. They felt humiliated and disgraced.

I had to be like a traveling salesman selling magic elixir and saying the dark time will pass one day and everything will be great again. Well, we used those slow kids who stayed behind—Richie Farmer, Deron Feldhaus, and John Pelphrey—and they all had their jerseys retired to the rafters ahead of some All-Americans because of the turnaround they represented. They became legends when they played in that tournament game we lost to Duke in 1992, 104–103, in overtime, on Christian Laettner's shot at the buzzer.

It was our first time back in the tournament after being on probation, and I've always wondered what would have happened if we'd won that game and then been beaten by Indiana by 20 points in the Final Four. Maybe it was better to lose the way we did. To me, that was the game that meant Kentucky basketball was back where it belonged. I know it helped with our recruiting, because four years later, when we won the NCAA title, we had eight players on that team who went to the NBA, which could never happen again. And then we went to two more Final Fours.

The one big problem we had in recruiting at Kentucky was a bitterness about race. Once, when we were trying to get Dwayne Morton, who was born in Louisville, I went to talk to his family and gave this big speech about why he should play for us. His grandmother was listening and she said, "Coach Pitino, I'm a big fan of yours." I smiled, thinking we were in, and then she said, "But every time I see those boys go on the court and step on that man's name, we applaud in this household."

But after you've coached the Celtics, which is the greatest franchise in pro basketball, and after you've coached Kentucky, one of the two or three best college franchises, then you can stop climbing and realize everything really should boil down to the pursuit of happiness.

She meant Adolph Rupp—the arena was named for him by then—and that was when I really understood the opinion of African Americans locally about Kentucky. Rupp might have been a legendary coach, but he sure wasn't legendary in the African-American community. The University of Louisville was viewed as the place where African Americans could excel, and Kentucky was a white-bread university. We lost Morton to Louisville.

C. M. Newton and I wanted to stop that type of talk. We felt it was the last thing we had to accomplish. Naming Tubby Smith the coach at Kentucky after me drove a stake through it, I think, and today the rivalry between the two schools is no longer based on race. Both teams have a high percentage of African Americans.

One big change in college basketball today is all the coaching that goes on during the games. TV time-outs are so long now, and a lot of coaches are huddling up, talking to the kids the whole time. This is what the other team is going to run next, this is what we're going to do—I don't think the kids can retain it. They're trying to get some water, to rest a minute. So I try to get everybody relaxed and then we talk a little bit.

Then there are all the assistant coaches we have now. You have your video coordinator who stays up all night putting the film together. You have your graduate assistants who deal with academics. You have your travel person, what they call a nonbasketball assistant. *And* you have your three full-time assistants. It's too much, but it's necessary too, because you're recruiting ninth and tenth graders today.

The other thing that bothers me is how vicious recruiting has become. No one trusts anyone anymore. If you learn one thing in the pros, it's not to have animosity toward another coach because you're both just trying to survive. But college is not that way. If you do a good job recruiting, you're going to win, and if you don't, you're not. It's not like in the pros where if the ping-pong ball doesn't come up your way you don't win the lottery. Every year I'm in it I realize that as the significance of the team's talent becomes bigger, the significance of my brilliance becomes less. (laughs)

Why did I leave Kentucky to become president and coach of the Celtics? I gave a lot of excuses: that I'd gone to school in New England, that I'd lived there most of my life, that I'd coached at Boston University for five years, that restoring the Celtics to their great tradition would be an unbelievable thing. But they were just an excuse for the $50 million they were offering me. In hindsight, maybe it shouldn't have been, because I made more than enough money to be happy in Kentucky.

One problem I've always had is that I've never been able to stay put to enjoy the fruits of my labor, so to speak. To say, "Look at the beautiful painting. Boy, am I proud of that." It was not necessary to take on a new challenge, to move up the ladder of success. But after you've coached the Celtics, which is the greatest franchise in pro basketball, and after you've coached Kentucky, one of the two or three best college franchises, then you can stop climbing and realize everything really should boil down to the pursuit of happiness.

I learned one very important thing coaching in the pros, and that was to take the losses and move on. When you play 82 games, it helps you realize that sometimes the other team is just better, that you should give them their due and forget it. Move forward and win the next game. I could never do that in college. When we lost, I'd be up all night, just devastated.

It wasn't until 9/11 that my attitude finally changed for good. I lost my best friend in life, my brother-in-law Billy Minardi, in the attacks. He used to console me after a tough loss. He would always be there, and he could never understand why I took the losses so hard. After he died, I said, "You know what—that's it." So now I just say my team had a bad night, so what? Let's move on. The way I look at coaching now is the way I look at life. You coach for today because you have no idea what's going to happen tomorrow. Cherish the victories, forget the defeats, and treasure what you have because you could be hot one day and gone the next.

I'll always remember something Jim Valvano told me. I was talking to the New Jersey Nets about taking their coaching job, and it didn't work out. I told them Jim was just the guy they needed. So they met and agreed on a deal, and then a week later Jim changed his mind. I called him and said, "Jim, what happened?" And he said, "I'm really happy where I am, and I don't want to mess with it." I'll always remember that. You don't mess with happiness.

CHAPTER 18

Tubby Smith: Breaking the Final Barrier

Lexington, Kentucky, September 2004

Let me tell you how I came to Kentucky. I was an assistant coach for Rick Pitino his first two years, from 1989 to 1991, and when Rick left, C. M. Newton, the athletic director, called and wanted to meet with me. Coach Newton had kind of guided me to Tulsa and to Georgia—I can see now he was mentoring me—and I talked to him as well as the president of the university. Jim Host, who runs the Kentucky sports television network, was also an important part of it. The fact that I already knew these people helped a lot.

I say all the time that I'm just the steward, the guardian, of the program.

I also knew the fervor and how basketball is a way a life in Kentucky—a religion, really—so I knew the expectations were going to be high. Following Rick, in fact, they were going to be off the chart because he really rejuvenated the program. But I also knew that Kentucky is one place where the program is bigger than the coach.

There are lots of schools where the coach makes the program. Look at what John Thompson did at Georgetown, Mike Krzyzewski at Duke, and Jerry Tarkanian at Nevada-Las Vegas. But at Kentucky the program belongs to everyone, from the president of the university down to the guy digging in the coal mine in eastern Kentucky or on the boat in the Kentucky River. I say all the time that I'm just the steward, the guardian, of the program.

We won the national championship my first year—some of the guys had been part of the 1996 championship team two years earlier—and since that time we've had some teams that were pretty talented, but not as talented as in those first three years. Let's face it, the rules have changed since then. The good players may leave early, there are new requirements about the retention of the student-athlete, and the scheduling is much tougher than it was then.

In my seven years here, I'll bet we played seven of the toughest schedules in the history of the program. With the new TV contract, there's a lot of pressure on us to play Duke, UCLA, Indiana, and North Carolina. There is also a lot of pressure because of the money from television. The administration wants you to generate a winning program to put people in the stands, but also to bring in money so you can support all the other sports at the university. So there is a lot of pressure on a coach today that wasn't there before.

The one thing I hate to see in college basketball today is a young man wasting his opportunities. I come from a family of 17. My dad scraped and saved and did all he could to help us out, but if I didn't get a scholarship I wasn't going to college.

The biggest thing that happened to college basketball in a long time was integration. I was a 10th grader growing up in southern Maryland and I remember watching Don Haskins' 1966 Texas Western team beat Adolph Rupp and Kentucky to win the NCAA Tournament with an all-black starting five. That game was played in Cole Field House at the University of Maryland, and watching it on TV had a real impact on me. It's the same thing that happened when Sam Cunningham of Southern California ran wild against Alabama in 1970 and Bear Bryant started recruiting black athletes. I think it elevated the game. And now here I am, coaching at the University of Kentucky.

My youngest son, Brian, is playing basketball now at Mississippi—times really have changed, haven't they?—for Rod Barnes, who is a great friend. I couldn't have found a better person for him to play for. All three of my sons played for Southeastern Conference schools, in fact. I coached against my oldest son, G.G., when he was at Georgia, and at the same time his brother, Solomon, was playing for me. It was the first time anything like that ever happened in college basketball. My wife wore a multicolored jacket that night, with red and blue in it. (laughs)

The one thing I hate to see in college basketball today is a young man wasting his opportunities. I come from a family of 17. My dad scraped and saved and did all he could to help us out, but if I didn't get a scholarship I wasn't going to college. I think when you recruit players it's a double-edged sword. You go into their homes and you tell them, "You're so talented. You're good enough to play at Kentucky." But very few of them will make it to the NBA, so you also want to tell them, "Don't waste this opportunity to get a quality education." A lot of them don't grasp that until later.

I've been coaching for 30 years now—6 in high school, 12 as an assistant in college, and now 12 as a head coach—and I tell people all the time that there's not another venue where you can teach the things you can in sports. It's the things you learn in church: the values, the integrity, the giving, the self-sacrificing, the commitment, the perseverance. That's why we need young kids to stay involved in athletics. I really believe that.

After coaching at Tulsa and Georgia, Tubby Smith arrived at Kentucky in 1997 and led the Wildcats to the NCAA championship in his first season. By 2005, Smith's teams had made the Sweet 16 six times and won five Southeastern Conference titles.

CHAPTER 19

Billy Reed on the Best Seat in the House

Lexington, Kentucky, September 2004

Basketball has always been huge in Kentucky, a lot bigger in some ways than it should be. When I started covering the University of Kentucky, they played in Alumni Gym, and it was the biggest arena in the South. Then they moved into Memorial Coliseum, and *it* was the biggest gym in the South. And then they went to Rupp Arena, and it was one of the biggest.

In many ways, I think Rupp was really misunderstood. He had a very dry wit, and he was one of the funniest after-dinner speakers I've ever heard. But *sarcastic!*

My theory is that a lot of this has to do with the fact that Kentucky is such a poor state. We're last in a lot of economic indicators—per-capita income, education—but everybody has to be number one in something, and Kentucky basketball gave our state something to be proud of. An airplane pilot

was flying across Kentucky late one night when he looked down and saw bright lights coming from one building in just about every town, the high school gym. "What's that?" he asked, and his copilot said, "Kentucky's playing basketball." That's the way it is in every small town from border to border.

Let me tell you about Adolph Rupp. I don't think he got as much credit as he deserves for revolutionizing the way the game was played. Back in the forties, everybody was playing Hank Iba's style of basketball. It was a slower game and low scoring. But coach Rupp believed in getting the best athletes and turning them loose. He popularized the fast break, and his teams were always entertaining. He would take them to New York and Chicago, to all the big-city arenas, and they were always very popular. And of course they were winning championships, which is how Kentucky basketball grew.

In many ways, I think Rupp was really misunderstood. He had a very dry wit, and he was one of the funniest after-dinner speakers I've ever heard.

But *sarcastic!* I guess my favorite story about him personally goes back to when I was working at the *Louisville Courier-Journal* in the late sixties and a player named Bob Tallent mouthed off to him during a game. Tallent came to practice the next day and his locker had been cleaned out. Rupp had kicked him off the team. In those days the press was so afraid of Rupp that nobody dared question him, but me being a young stupid kid, I got Bob Tallent on the phone and got his side of the story. The paper ran it on page one, and Rupp was furious because *nobody* questioned his decisions.

The next day, a writer from another paper said, "Well, Coach, what about the Louisville newspaper story?" and Rupp said, "Let me tell you about the media in Louisville. They've got one guy who is a goddam liar, and another who is an SOB, and Billy Reed is nothing but a little turd." I've always said that's what I want on my gravestone: "Here lies a little turd." (laughs)

Rupp never forgot it either. I'd go to his office and tell his secretary I wanted to see him, and I'd hear from inside his office, "What does that little turd want now? Well, send him in." And then he'd give me a great interview.

He could be that way to his players too. Once he took his team to New York and Ralph Beard, who was an All-American, wasn't playing too well. So Rupp came in at halftime and said, "Beard, I want you to go back in there and take a crap so that when you go back home you can tell the folks you did *something* in Madison Square Garden." (laughs)

Now that so much time has passed, a lot of people think coach Rupp was a racist, but I can make the case that he was no better or worse than anybody else coaching in the South in those days. I could not say what was in his heart about race, but I do know that he offered scholarships to Wes Unseld and Butch Beard, who turned him down and went to Louisville. And when the team came back from Maryland after losing that NCAA championship game to Texas Western, I rode in the motorcade with Rupp to the Coliseum for a pep rally. He talked a lot about the game, about how Texas Western was just too quick for his team, and he did not say a word about race.

After coach Rupp retired, Joe B. Hall coached for 13 seasons and then Eddie Sutton coached for four years, but Rick Pitino is the guy who saved Kentucky basketball. The program when Sutton left was as low as it's ever been. The cupboard was bare in terms of talent, and the recruiting sanctions looked really grim.

I think the eight years Pitino was at Kentucky were as good a coaching job as I've ever seen. He turned back to the Kentucky style of basketball. Joe B. Hall was known for the Twin Towers kind of talent that played inside, and then Eddie Sutton brought in Hank Iba basketball, but under Pitino it was back to the up-tempo game the fans had loved under coach Rupp. And of course after he won the national title he became wildly loved by the Kentucky fans and put the state back on the cutting edge of basketball after it had been shoved aside for a while.

When Pitino left to go to the Celtics, there was a little disappointment and animosity, but not too much. But when he left the Celtics to come back and take the Louisville job, my God, the Kentucky fans were furious, and many of them are to this day. It was like a slap in the face. I think it's silly myself. It was the best job available. Pitino wants to be in a place where basketball is important. He liked living in Kentucky. He's got a lot of friends. But feelings between the Louisville fans and the Kentucky fans run very deep.

Louisville has beaten Kentucky two years in a row now—at Freedom Hall and in Rupp Arena—and I'm surprised people weren't jumping off bridges all over the state. But both those losses helped Kentucky. They responded, and at the end of both those seasons they were better than Louisville.

I think Tubby Smith is just an excellent coach and a great guy. There was a lot of talk that because of Kentucky's alleged racism it wouldn't work, and I can't tell you there aren't people who don't judge Tubby by a different standard. But by and large he's been accepted. Racial considerations aside, he's a lot like a lot of people in this state. He comes from a blue-collar, rural background. He's very down-to-earth, very modest. I think he has done a great job and become very popular.

For many years Louisville had good basketball, but they weren't on the same level as Kentucky. Things

I was sitting at the press table, and before I knew it Digger was in my face, jabbing a finger at me and screaming, "This one was for you! For you! For you!" And he stormed off.

began to change when Denny Crum came here. They hired him because he was John Wooden's top recruiter, but he didn't really want to stay. He thought Louisville would be his stepping stone back to UCLA. Well, in his first year, 1972, he had a really good team that went to the semifinals of the NCAA Tournament against UCLA in Los Angeles. I was standing in the corridor before the game, with UCLA on one side and Louisville on the other, and Bill Walton came over, bouncing up and down.

"Hey, coach Crum," he said out of the side of his mouth, laughing, "what happened to the car you promised me when you were recruiting me?" Crum didn't crack a smile, didn't even look at Walton, just kept staring straight ahead. But I knew then that UCLA was pretty confident they could beat Louisville, and of course they did.

Crum had a chance to go back to UCLA at least three times—when coach Wooden retired, when Gene Bartow left, and sometime in the early eighties, probably when they hired Larry Brown. But by then he knew he wanted to stay. He said he wanted to coach in a place where basketball is really important. So that was a good thing for Louisville, wasn't it?

I've always loved covering college basketball. Over the years, Bobby Knight and I became very close friends. Once when I was covering a game in

Bloomington, Indiana, a call went against Indiana and the student body started chanting, "Bullshit, bullshit." Bobby went running over to the scorer's table, grabbed the microphone, and screamed, "Hey, this is Indiana! We don't do that here! Show some class!" Everybody applauded him and they stopped the chant.

After the game I went into the locker room and I said, "Bobby, I've got to ask you one thing. Why did you do that?" And he said, "Because it was a goddamn disgrace, that's why." (laughs)

Digger Phelps was another coach I always liked. Notre Dame used to play Kentucky in Freedom Hall every year—usually between Christmas and New Year's—and Kentucky would regularly skunk them. It got so Digger just hated to come to Louisville to play Kentucky. Well, in the early eighties, Notre Dame finally won. I was sitting at the press table, and before I knew it Digger was in my face, jabbing a finger at me and screaming, "This one was for you! For you! For you!" And he stormed off.

"What the hell was that all about?" I thought. I guess he just associated me with all his bad memories in Kentucky. So I wrote a column and said, "Digger said this one was for me. Well, if they won the game for me, I think I should get the game ball."

Four or five days later a box came in the mail from South Bend and inside was the oldest, most decrepit, beat-up basketball you ever saw. And sure enough, Digger had inscribed "To Billy Reed" and the score of the game. So naturally I got another column out of it, thanking Digger and all my teammates. (laughs)

I'll tell you one thing that bothers me now about the way the game has changed. It's that the ticket prices, and the donations you have to make to even *buy* tickets, have gotten to be so exorbitant. The middle-class fan is being priced out, and I think that's a shame. I remember one of my big thrills as a young kid was to go to Freedom Hall to see Louisville play or to go to Memorial Coliseum to see Kentucky. It's become such a huge business that a lot of whatever caused us to love it as young men unfortunately is kind of gone now.

PART V

The Brotherhood

I have always believed that the real stars of college basketball are not the players, but the coaches. They gave the game its continuity as many of them stayed at their schools for decades while the players were gone in three years or less.

When broadcasting games, I always longed for rock-star coaches, those distinctive and flamboyant personalities who loved the cameras, which loved them back. Whenever we broadcast a game that featured Al McGuire, Bob Knight, Digger Phelps, or Rick Pitino, my instructions to the producers were to get a shot of the coaches after a big basket as well as of the player who made it.

After reacting suspiciously at first, the coaches came to learn that television was not an intruder but a friend. I'll always remember the first time McGuire, who was desperate for a timeout but didn't want to use one of his own, ran up to me on the sideline and asked me, "Eddie, are you going to call a TV timeout?" I knew then that we had become part of the game.

Bob Knight is the only coach who was around when TVS began and is still active. Long considered to be the best tactician in the game, he had a colorful and controversial 30-year career at Indiana, where he won three NCAA titles before moving on to Texas Tech. When he picked me up at the airport in Lubbock, he was not many victories away from becoming the winningest college coach of all time, and I had a present for him: a small marble sign that said, "Winning is the best revenge."

Basketball was low on the Notre Dame totem pole until the school built a new arena and hired a dynamic young coach, Richard "Digger" Phelps, to fill it. A television producer's dream, Digger talked the talk—and dressed the part—but more important, he backed it up by winning some of college basketball's biggest games. He is now a college basketball analyst for ESPN.

At 6'10", John Thompson is the tallest coach in the Basketball Hall of Fame and has long been one of the game's most formidable presences. In his 27 years at Georgetown, his teams made the NCAA Tournament 20 times and went to the Final Four three times, winning the national championship in 1984. During our interview, Thompson spoke passionately and sensitively about the issues facing the game today.

The Atlantic Coast Conference was the only major conference whose rights TVS never acquired—thank goodness it only reached 7 percent of the country—but it has long been considered America's top basketball conference. At its heart are three schools separated by only approximately 30 miles—Duke, North Carolina, and North Carolina State—that have won nine NCAA titles.

Dean Smith is currently college basketball's winningest coach with 879 victories, 11 appearances in the Final Four, and two national championships. Mike Krzyzewski has won three national championships at Duke and made 10 trips to the Final Four. After a long career at Kansas, where his Jayhawks teams went to consecutive Final Fours, Roy Williams moved to his alma mater, North Carolina, where he won the 2005 NCAA title in his second year.

Al McGuire was a true coaching original, and no one knew him better than Hank Raymonds. After a lengthy career as McGuire's assistant at Marquette, Raymonds became the head coach when McGuire began his celebrated broadcasting career. Raymonds compiled an enviable record of his own before he became the school's athletic director, and I found his recollections of his years with Al to be priceless.

In the eighties and nineties, a ticket to a University of Nevada–Las Vegas basketball game was as hard to get as a seat at Frank Sinatra's craps table. UNLV won the NCAA title in 1990, and after finishing his coaching career at Fresno State, Jerry Tarkanian retired with a record of 778–202, which gave him the highest winning percentage in college history.

One final note that indicates the continuity of college basketball through its coaches: When Roy Williams played freshman basketball at North Carolina, Dean Smith coached the varsity. When Smith played at the University of Kansas (where one of his teammates was Adolph Rupp), his coach was Phog Allen. And when Allen played at Kansas, his coach was none other than James Naismith, who invented the game of basketball.

CHAPTER 20

Bob Knight Sets the Record Straight

Lubbock, Texas, June 2005

I really should have been a baseball player, but I wasn't smart enough to realize it. I liked basketball and I played it all the time, but I was just an average player, especially compared to my teammates Jerry Lucas and John Havlicek at Ohio State. I was a smart player and I had some abilities, I guess, but I was not a good jumper and wasn't good enough handling the ball to be a guard. So I was a 6'4" forward, which is pretty small for basketball, but a good size for baseball, where I could run and throw and field. I was a pretty good hitter too, and I developed a real feeling for the game. I've always wished I'd tried to do more with it.

I was a huge Cleveland Indians fan growing up in Orrville, Ohio, which is 50 miles south of Cleveland. Later, when I was coaching at West Point, I would drive down to the Jerome Avenue elevated, park the car, jump on the train, get off at left field, and go in to watch the Yankees. And now I'm friends with Sparky Anderson and Tony LaRussa, and of course I was a great friend of Ted Williams.

We'll talk about basketball in a minute, but first I want to tell my baseball story. Tony LaRussa was managing the Oakland A's in a spring-training game against the San Diego Padres in Yuma, Arizona, so my wife, Karen, and I drove up from San Diego for a couple of days. We went out to dinner and I was really getting on Tony about hitting, saying, "Damn, we need some hits. We need some runs."

The next morning I went to his coaches' meeting, and I started needling him again. Tony got pissed off, and he flipped his scorecard at me. It hit me right in the throat. "Goddam it," he said, "you make out the lineup." So I did, and I was sitting on the bench next to Tony. About the fourth inning somebody behind us starts saying, "One guy doesn't know anything about basketball and the other doesn't know anything about baseball."

Tony said, "Don't turn around. Don't get into a hassle," but finally curiosity got the best of me, and I turned around. It was Dick Enberg needling us from behind. Well, we got to the fifth inning and I had guys stealing and bunting and all kinds of stuff, and we were winning 3–0. So I said, "I quit. This is too easy. This isn't like basketball. You just sit here and win the game." (laughs) And that's my baseball story.

I was recruited by Wisconsin and Ohio State, where I was the sixth man on the team. Lucas, who is still the best player I ever saw in the Big Ten, and Havlicek were the stars. We went to three Final Fours and won the championship in 1960 when we were sophomores. We should have won the next one too, because we were better than Cincinnati. We just lost. But the third time they deserved to win. They were better than we were. I enjoyed playing, but I wasn't good enough to play at a higher level, and at that time you couldn't go to Europe the way you can today.

When I got to college, I majored in physical education, but I thought it was a waste of time. After the first year I switched to history and government, and then I got into the school of education. My last semester in college I started thinking about going to law school—I went to one of the assistant deans and asked him about it—but I decided I'd coach for a year and then go back to school. We had a sophomore on our team who had played for the best high school coach in the state, Harold Andreas, at Cuyahoga Falls, a suburb of Akron, and he hired me to coach his junior varsity team.

I made $4,600 to teach four classes and two study halls and $450 to coach. That's $5,050. The next year I was supposed to move up to assistant varsity coach and the teachers got an increase in pay, so then I was going to be making $6,300. Man, I thought that was all the money in the world. Plus, working with Andy was great. He was as good a coach as I've ever seen.

Then Dave Scott, a good friend who had been a hell of a player at Ohio University, called and said the Cleveland Browns had a basketball team to supplement their income during the winter. All the NFL teams had basketball teams then. Can you imagine that today? They'd go to these little towns to play pickup teams, and a lot of times they would lose because they were really awful. Vince Costello, the Browns' middle linebacker, was the captain, and they needed a few more guys, so Dave and I were going to join them. We would play approximately 50 games all over Ohio, so my income for the year was going to be $8,800—a fortune.

But that spring I went to the NCAA finals in Louisville, and I asked Fred Taylor, my coach at Ohio State, if he would talk to John Wooden for me about a job at UCLA. Wooden told him that Gary Cunningham was coming back from playing in the Philippines and was going to coach the UCLA freshman team. But he said if I wanted to go to UCLA law school, maybe I could do some scouting and help Gary with the freshmen.

Well, I'd only been to L.A. once—we beat UCLA in the L.A. Classic—and I decided to stay in Ohio with Andy. But as I was talking to Fred Taylor about going to law school, George Hunter, the Army coach, walked up and out of the clear blue he said, "If you're ever going to get drafted, call me and I'll bring you to West Point and you can coach our plebe team."

I just looked at him and said, "What if I just joined the army?" I wasn't married, and I thought going into the army might be a neat experience.

George said, "Well, if you do that you can come to West Point, but you'll have to go through basic training first."

I said, "Well, that's something else." (laughs)

I went home and told my dad what I was thinking, and I thought he was going to go into cardiac arrest. He had nine sisters and three brothers, and my older sister Carol and I were the first college graduates in the whole family. He was really upset I wasn't going to continue on in school, and he didn't think very much of me coaching, either.

But I thought it would be interesting, so I joined the army and went to Fort Leonard Wood, where I was on the regimental baseball team. I finished basic training and was making $91 per month instead of the $8,800

I was going to get coaching and playing basketball with the Browns. But the money never meant anything to me. It was the experience that intrigued me.

By then George Hunter had gotten out of coaching and Tates Locke took over at West Point. Tates had gone to school at Ohio Wesleyan University, which is just up the road from Ohio State, and he hired me. It might never have happened if Tates didn't know me. So I started basic training in June, and by Labor Day I was at West Point coaching the Army freshmen.

I got to know Pete Newell, Henry Iba, Clair Bee, Joe Lapchick, Red Auerbach, and Everett Dean. Pete was the one I was closest to over the years, but I learned different things from each of them.

So here I was a private first class, coaching and recruiting and playing on one of the six teams on the post. Some of the officers didn't like that because I'd played in college, but I said, "What the hell has that got to do with it? If basketball is available to Army personnel it has to be available to me."

They had to agree, but some of the company commanders kept bitching about it. I didn't say much because I was a PFC and they were captains or majors. I had a locker in the officers' locker room, and I never said a word all the time I was there. I'd just duck my head in and change my clothes. I didn't even shower there. I'd go home for that.

One of the great things about being around New York and Madison Square Garden at that time was the legendary coaches I met. I got to know Pete Newell, Henry Iba, Clair Bee, Joe Lapchick, Red Auerbach, and Everett Dean. Pete was the one I was closest to over the years, but I learned different things from each of them. I guess I was close to Clair too. He was a great defensive strategist who made

Long Island University a national power and wrote the Chip Hilton books.

In 1968 Clair was inducted into the Basketball Hall of Fame, and he asked me to drive him to the induction ceremony. Clair was a great speaker but he drank a lot, and when he drank he went on and on. There were four inductees that night and he was speaking for all of them, and I didn't want him to embarrass himself. So I told him, "I'm not going to go if you're going to drink." He said he wouldn't, so we went to Springfield and we sat at a table with famous coaches—Adolph Rupp and Frank McGuire and Harry Litwack. The girl came around to take drink orders. She stopped at Clair's spot and I said, "He'll have a Coke and so will I." Then later she came around again and I said, "We'll have a Coke again."

At that point Rupp said, "Goddamn, Clair, are you going to let that boy tell you whether you can drink or not?"

Well, it turned out that Clair didn't like Rupp, and I'm telling you, Clair was 75 years old and weighed about 140 pounds, but he went right over the table after Rupp. Frank McGuire had to grab him and say, "Dammit, Clair, get back there and sit down." (laughs)

After two years at West Point, Tates left to go to Miami of Ohio, and Colonel Ray Murphy, the athletic director and just a great guy, called me in and said, "We have decided to make you our next head coach." Well, I didn't want them to think I'd take the job under just any conditions, so I said, "I'll let you know on Monday." But then I thought maybe I'd overplayed my hand a little, so I went back and took the job. I was 24 then, which made me the youngest varsity coach in major-college history.

A year later, I was talking to the University of Florida and I told Ray Murphy I was going to go there. But then I thought things through and decided he had given me my first chance to coach, and I felt I had an obligation to stay at West Point. I thought he was going to jump over the desk and hug me or something, but he just kept signing papers, not even looking at me, until finally he stopped, looked up, and said, "I knew you would." That was a great humbling experience for me. We went to the NIT four times in my six years and we led the nation in scoring defense three times, so I guess we did all right.

The military environment at West Point was good for me. I liked the discipline and the toughness. But what I really enjoyed there was that wherever we played basketball, whether we won or lost, people were thinking that if the future of our country was in the hands of those kids we were in good shape. That was my whole objective with the Army basketball team.

Let me tell you about Mike Krzyzewski. I recruited him at lunch in the cafeteria at Weber High School in Chicago. He was the leading scorer in the Chicago Catholic League for two years, although he was really not a very good shooter. But Mike did more to adjust to the way I wanted a kid to play than anybody else I've ever coached. He played defense and ran our offense better than any kid who's ever played for me.

The military environment at West Point was good for me. I liked the discipline and the toughness.

There was a general at West Point who had been one of General Patton's corps commanders, and his son, who was the commentator on our broadcasts, was just a monumental pain in the ass. I didn't like him, and he didn't like me. So finally I'd had enough of the guy and decided to leave. I didn't even have another job—although I'd had some offers over the years; Jerry Colangelo wanted me to coach the Phoenix Suns—and I started thinking about law school again.

When I left West Point I had nothing to do with who replaced me. They didn't even ask me. But later I virtually named the coach, and it was Mike. He had spent a year with me at Indiana, and Army was reluctant to hire someone who had left the military. The

Army is funny about things like that. Just recently Mike got an award as an honored graduate of West Point, which really pleased and surprised me because he's not a career guy.

They had a great basketball tradition at Indiana, and it was intriguing to me to find out whether I was capable of coaching a team to the national championship.

I was staying in the Concourse Plaza Hotel behind Yankee Stadium, and I was lying in bed when I read in the *New York Post* that Indiana was looking for a coach. I knew I was going to have a chance to win the national championship at Indiana. I was going to be able to recruit from all over the Midwest, where they had a lot of good high school players who knew all about Indiana basketball.

I could have gone back to Ohio State—they asked me about four times—but I never did because I didn't like the way they were treating Fred Taylor. Woody Hayes called me once and said they wanted me, but I said, "Coach, I just can't do it." I wouldn't even go to our 25th reunion of winning the NCAA championship. Fred called me and gave me hell, but I said, "Coach, I don't like the way they handled your situation, and this is my way of showing it."

They had a great basketball tradition at Indiana, and it was intriguing to me to find out whether I was capable of coaching a team to the national championship. And after we did it, I'll tell you, nothing ever intrigued me like that afterward. Not even when I had a chance to coach an NBA team.

Red Auerbach called me once and said, "I want to talk to you about coaching the Celtics."

I said, "I don't want to do that."

He said, "Why not?"

I said, "Because if I did, I might lose one of the best friends I ever had in the process."

He said, "And who would that be?"

I said, "You."

He laughed and said, "I get you." He never pursued it. So I just stayed and stayed at Indiana. Pete Newell and Curt Gowdy once pleaded with me to go somewhere else, saying I'd been there too long. And in the end, they were right.

I never had to shoot at anybody, jump out of an airplane, or defend an island, so the most significant thing I ever did on America's behalf was coach the team that won the gold medal, because it showed the rest of the world something about American competitiveness.

Do I remember what happened in Puerto Rico? Like it was yesterday. More than anything, I remember it because it was so unfairly portrayed in the American press.

It was the Pan American Games in 1979, and we were practicing in a little Catholic school gym. The Brazilian women's team came in during our practice, although we had been told to stay outside when the Canadian women's team was practicing. I knew the coach of the Brazilian women, and I asked her to just have the girls quiet down a little or go on through to their locker room. Well, they kept making noise, and Mike Krzyzewski got into an argument with a Puerto Rican cop. I walked over, brushed Mike aside, and said, "Hey, you know, we were told to stay outside. Now you let them in."

The cop started shaking his finger in my face and hit me in the eye. I placed my hand—*placed* it—on his cheek and shoved him away from me. I didn't hit him. I didn't slap him. Then he hit me in the left eye, my head went down, and I was seeing out of one eye. So I shoved the guy away from me. His version

was that I'd swung a roundhouse punch at him and that I'd called the Brazilian women niggers.

Now, it's important to remember that I had eight black players out of twelve on the Pan American team sitting 25 feet from what happened, and three of them were going to play for me at Indiana the next year. I had never had a racial problem in my life, and if I was the worst racist in the world, why did I have eight black kids playing for me? The superintendent of the Puerto Rican police was sorry about what happened, and some of the players refuted everything that was said, but none of it was really refuted in the American press. So that's when I started to resent the press. It really ended any great relationship I was ever going to have with reporters.

I had to go to a hearing the next day. The cop took three steps and then took a roundhouse swing to demonstrate what I had done. I told the judge, "This is ridiculous. Look at him and look and me. Does he have a mark on his face? Does he have a broken bone?" I must have been the weakest puncher ever not to have left a mark or to have moved him from the spot where he was standing.

They had a trial later and they expected me to come back, but I told them to shove it. They said they would arrest me and I said, "On what?" I found out later there was no way they were going to make an issue out of it. I've never been to Puerto Rico since, and I never intend to go back.

Maybe the highlight of my career was coaching the U.S. Olympic basketball team in 1984. Henry Iba told me it's important the way you represent your university and your state, but now it's really important because you're representing your country. I never had to shoot at anybody, jump out of an airplane, or defend an island, so the most significant thing I ever did on America's behalf was coach the team that won the gold medal, because it showed the rest of the world something about American competitiveness. I'd have far rather been on the beach at Normandy, though.

I was really upset when politics kept us from going to the 1980 Olympics in Moscow, because our best ambassadors are our athletes. They show the world what America is all about. For Jimmy Carter to turn that down was one of the dumbest things I've ever seen, and Carter is a smart man. Then when the Russians wouldn't come to the 1984 Games in Los Angeles, that just proved they were dumber than we were.

You look at the broadcasters, and particularly the writers—you can't find a writer who was an athlete in any sport. My contention has always been that they had something against sports. They didn't have a girlfriend; the football players had girlfriends.

I spent 10 days in France in the spring of 1983 at the European championships to see some of the teams we would be playing against in the Olympics. I didn't like the French—when they wouldn't let us fly over their country to bomb Qaddafi. I said, "Bomb France." Don Donaher, who was one of my assistants, hated the French from the days when he was stationed in the army in Europe. Well, the next year we played France in the Olympics, and we were ahead by 40 points with 12 minutes to go when Don walked over to me with a note pad.

"I figured it out," he said. "If you don't substitute for five more minutes, just five more minutes, we can beat the SOBs by 70 points."

I said, "*That's* the Olympic spirit." We only beat them by 58, though.

What really interests me, all these years later, is how much you pioneered college basketball on television, Eddie. I've said it before—you were the absolute forerunner. Nobody did more to popularize college basketball than you did. It was enormous.

I'm just being honest. You took basketball to areas around the country where it had never been on television before. It was the foundation for all that's happening today. You can see hundreds of games during a season, and I think that's been huge for college basketball. Also, you've got integrity, and that really appeals to me. You're like Bob Hammel, the writer from Bloomington, Indiana, I've always been close to, in that neither one of you were athletes, but you don't have a grudge against sports. You have a genuine love for sports, and you want to do what you can for them.

You look at the broadcasters, and particularly the writers—you can't find a writer who was an athlete in any sport. My contention has always been that they had something against sports. They didn't have a girlfriend; the football players had girlfriends. They didn't get any attention; the athletes got all the attention. But they can write so they get to meet athletes, which I think is their purpose in life.

You know that movie ESPN made about me? After it was over I got a call from the actor who played me, Brian Dennehy, asking me if I was going to watch it. I said, "No, because I don't think it will even come close to portraying what I'm all about."

He said, "I don't disagree with you. They were the worst people I've ever worked with, and you may not have noticed, but I have done nothing to advertise that film. I told them I wouldn't."

These people who make sports films can't duplicate sports events. The technical aspects of most sports movies have been horrendous. Take that Robert Redford film, *The Natural*, based on Eddie Waitkus' life. No team ever dressed as badly as the team in that movie, and the pitchers looked like girls throwing the ball.

Why did I come to Texas Tech? Intrigue. I didn't have any idea I would stay in coaching after what happened at Indiana. I only went to three games the first season I was out of coaching, and I didn't miss it a bit. But then Gerald Myers, the athletic director

One of the winningest and most controversial coaches in college basketball history, Bob Knight won three NCAA titles during his 30-year career at Indiana University before moving to Texas Tech. Knight began his coaching career at West Point, where the star of some of his best teams was a young point guard named Mike Krzyzewski.

at Texas Tech, called me, and I could see what a challenge it was.

It's been great here. It's remote, but it's wonderful. I can play golf anytime I want, go fishing. I've been very happy, and my health is pretty damn good. I can't throw a chair as far as I used to, but other than that I'm in great shape.

They had won only nine conference games in the previous three years, it was a totally different part of the country, a different league, a different approach in what was a strong football state. I'd proven I could win national championships, but I was asking myself, "Can I take this program to a respectable position in a very good league?" With Indiana I knew I could do that, so maybe this was even a bigger challenge.

I had never thought much about having the most victories of any college coach—it never entered my mind until I left Indiana—but then I got to thinking about it, how close I was, and I thought, well, if I did that all those jerks would have to look at my name first on the list forever. (laughs)

At Texas Tech we've been very pleased that in four years we've been in the NCAA Tournament three times and the NIT the other year. I still enjoy figuring out how to put a team together and how to play against another team. It's been great here. It's remote, but it's wonderful. I can play golf anytime I want, go fishing. I've been very happy, and my health is pretty damn good. I can't throw a chair as far as I used to, but other than that I'm in great shape. (laughs)

I've had to say things and do things in coaching I wouldn't think of doing to somebody who came to me for help. But there are certain things that you have to do if you're going to be successful in your profession that don't carry over into your personal relations with people. I've been in touch with a lot of my players over the years, including some who didn't like what I did, who thought it was too intense and left. But they have told other people they made a mistake. I've gotten that a lot. So with one or two exceptions, I've never had anybody who played for me really bad-mouth me.

I'll tell you what I think the biggest difference is in the way kids are today. It's the parents. They're not as demanding today, not as upset when their kids screw up. They're more upset with the teacher or the coach. It's always somebody else's fault. They don't hold the kids responsible. So when people ask me, I say, "Hey, a 4-year-old kid is the same, but an 18-year-old kid is different because he's had 14 years with his parents." (laughs)

America needs sports. We're a competitively driven country and there are a lot of stressful jobs, so I think that sports are great because they help ease the stress. Look at the number of people whose major

I'll tell you what I think the biggest difference is in the way kids are today. It's the parents. They're not as demanding today, not as upset when their kids screw up.

hobby is following the White Sox or the Yankees or the Cardinals, or basketball. I think a lot of it has to do with the outdoors, the pioneer spirit that settled this country and the sports that developed from that. We developed baseball; we developed basketball; football is unique to contact sports. And the Canadians developed hockey, a North American sport. The people here were a hardy, rugged people who had to survive extreme weather conditions, had to shoot things to eat.

What would I like to have as my epitaph? Those who don't know me I don't care about, but I would hope that those who knew me would say, "He was honest, he worked hard, and he tried to make us better than we were." And from a personal standpoint, I would hope the people that I've known would say, "If there's a friend I knew I could count on, it was him."

Somebody asked me that question once, and, just in a humorous way, I said it would be sufficient for me if my epitaph read, "He was honest and he didn't kiss anybody's ass."

Basketball at Notre Dame was an afterthought compared to football until Digger Phelps arrived in 1972. The highlight of Phelps' career came in 1974, when Notre Dame ended UCLA's 88-game winning streak in South Bend. Phelps later became a college basketball broadcaster for ESPN. Photograph courtesy of Joe Raymond, *South Bend Tribune*.

CHAPTER 21

Digger Phelps on the Start of Something Big in South Bend

San Antonio, Texas, April 2004

How did I get my nickname? That's easy—my dad was an undertaker, and there was a radio character when I was a kid named Digger O'Dell, the friendly undertaker. So I was always Digger.

I grew up in the Hudson Valley in New York, near West Point, and when I was in the seventh grade I was the batboy for the high school baseball team. We'd go on road trips to places like Peekskill, Ossining, and Poughkeepsie, and when the guys were taking batting practice, I'd sneak back on the bus to eat the cookies and cupcakes in their lunch bags. I was so dumb that I'd go back out on the field with chocolate all over my face, so the players knew who did it, and they'd beat me up in the back of the bus on the way home. The coach said, "Phelps, if you don't stop taking those cupcakes and cookies, we're going to put you in one of your old man's boxes."

I laugh about it, but one thing you learn as an undertaker's son is to value life. I remember one night at dinner when I was 10 or 12 years old my mom and dad told me and my younger sisters that

we had to understand the role we played. All religions are our religions, all cultures are our cultures, and all skin colors are our colors, because when people lose a loved one they come to us, trusting us to get them through an emotional crisis they might never have faced before. I never forgot that.

I played basketball at Rider College in Trenton, New Jersey, and I was never more than a bench-warmer. One night I guarded Nick Workman, who was an All-American at Seton Hall University. He scored 42 points, and I fouled out in about eight minutes. (laughs) After college I wanted to go to embalming school in Syracuse so I could go into business with my dad, but my high school coach, Tom Winterbottom, was starting a summer league and he asked me to coach one of his teams.

I said, "OK, but you're going to have to teach me what to do." So he gave me a book by Ed Jucker, the basketball coach at Cincinnati, and in between funerals I'd go to the playground where Tom would teach me. Right away I was hooked, and I told my dad I didn't think I wanted to be an undertaker. So I got a job as a graduate assistant at Rider and after a while I said, "I can do this stuff." I never looked back.

Later, Dick Harter hired me to be his assistant at Penn and put me in charge of recruiting. I had one suit to my name when I went there, but Dick said if I got 75 applications from high school prospects before Christmas he'd buy me a new suit. Well, I got 90, and he took me downtown and bought me a new suit, which I wore at Fordham my entire first year there. That's how intense I was when it came to recruiting.

Everybody would put a dollar in and bet on who would get the first technical—Al or me—and when it would happen. We always gave them a winner, too.

We were 26–3 my one year coaching at Fordham, and that's when I met Al McGuire. Marquette came to New York, and Al and I went to a writers' luncheon at Mamma Leone's across from the old Madison Square Garden at Forty-eighth Street and Eighth. Al sat down next to me, and the first thing he said was, "You've got to get out of this school."

"Why?" I asked.

"Kid, you're hot," he said. "Trust me, I work with the Jesuits. Fordham's a Jesuit school. You've got to get away from them. You've got to leave after this year."

The next day, I faced Al's team for the first time—the Garden was packed with 19,500 people—and it was a real war. We were up two, down four, up three—it was like that all night. With six minutes to go in the first half, Al called timeout, pointed to the referee, and told his son, who was an assistant coach, "Allie, go tell Charlie Beale that he's a son of a bitch."

So Allie went over to Charlie and said, "Mr. Beale, my dad says you're a son of a bitch."

Al got a technical, we shot the free throws, and I was thinking, "What the hell is this?"

In the last minute of the game we were up by two, and Marquette knocked the ball out of bounds in front of their bench. It was our ball, but Al looked at Charlie Beale, who didn't have a good view, and pointed at his basket. All his players did the same thing. They got the ball, and we lost in overtime. What Al did was get a call against himself in the first half, thinking he'd have one go his way in the second half. All I could think was, "Boy, did I learn something tonight." Nobody could orchestrate the referees, the crowd, the team, and the students better than Al could. He was the master.

What I didn't know was that the people from Notre Dame were watching that game too, and that Al was responsible for it. Roger Valdiserri, who was the Notre Dame sports information director and an assistant athletic director for many years, told me Johnny Dee was leaving and he had asked Al for some names. Al said they ought to take a look at me. So I got the job partly thanks to Al, I guess. I stayed at Notre Dame for 20 years.

Anyway, a few years later, Notre Dame was playing Marquette in South Bend and I called a timeout. But the referee didn't see it, and when he asked who called time, I said, "Television." So the referee signaled a TV timeout and Al went bonkers and got a technical. I just looked over at him and said, "Fordham. We're even."

It was like that the rest of the time we coached against each other. The media guys would come to Milwaukee or South Bend and start a pool. Everybody would put a dollar in and bet on who would get the first technical—Al or me—and when it would happen. We always gave them a winner, too.

There was the time we went up to play Marquette and Al knew I'd be all dressed up for the game, which I had started doing, so he came out in tuxedo pants with a white shirt, black vest, and matching black-and-white tie. We were talking before the game, and I pretended not to notice until he turned around to walk away and I said, "Oh, Al, you don't button the top button on the vest." (laughs)

We were all broken up when he died so young. I'll never forget how I was in your box at the ballpark, Eddie, and we called him in the hospice and talked about the old days for 20 minutes. He died two weeks later.

You wanted more action to spice the game up, so you sent me a note saying, "Digger, get a technical." I wrote back, "Hell, no."

Nobody lived his life the way Al did. I remember asking him once what he was going to do after the season was over, and he said, "I'm taking my motorbike and I'm going to New Zealand for a month." That's the picture I'll always have of him—riding around on his motorbike all over the countryside with the wind in his hair. Al had the best hair, you know—long and black and wavy. I can just see it blowing in the breeze.

Do you remember when we first met, Eddie? You came into Dick Harter's office at Penn—this was the midsixties—and said you were the head of TVS. I said, "What's TVS?" and you said it was the network that was doing our game that week. That was the first I'd heard of it. You were probably only televising an Ivy League game because it was your alma mater. (laughs) We met again my first year at Notre Dame. We went 6–20—a great way to start, huh?—and one of the six we won was a TVS game, against Tulane in New Orleans during Super Bowl week. You and I went out to dinner and I said, "What do I have to do to market Notre Dame basketball?" because we didn't count for much next to football then. And you said, "Start playing a national schedule, and we'll take care of the rest."

So we started scheduling UCLA, Kentucky, Maryland, and South Carolina. And then my third year at Notre Dame, 1974, we knocked off UCLA and

ended their 88-game winning streak. That made us, and we were on TVS just about every weekend. We were traveling all over the country and our kids were treated like rock stars, everybody asking for their autographs and taking pictures. And it really helped our recruiting too. I always said either I'd recruit you or I'd beat you. The other schools were jealous, but I just said, "Hey, *you* go play UCLA twice every year, or one of Frank McGuire's great South Carolina teams."

Those were crazy times. We were playing Davidson at home once and we were winning by about 30 points. You wanted more action to spice the game up, so you sent me a note saying, "Digger, get a technical." I wrote back, "Hell, no." What did I want to get a technical for when we were up by 30? Or how about the time at UCLA where we were up by 15 points at halftime and you grabbed me before we went into the locker room and said, "What the hell are you doing to me? You're killing my New York audience. They're all going to turn the game off."

I said, "Geez, Eddie, there's another half yet," and sure enough we ended up *losing* by 15. So we're coming out of the tunnel at Pauley Pavilion and heading for the bus to catch the red-eye back to Chicago, and I saw you standing there. I yelled, "Are you happy now? You got your audience."

TVS was good for Notre Dame, no question about that, but I think we were good for TVS too. I remember when you bought the White Sox I told people I was half owner because without me you wouldn't have had the money to buy them. Or I would call Jerry Reinsdorf and say I wanted your suite for a game because I knew you weren't coming in from New Jersey. I figured I had earned it. I came each year to see my son-in-law, Jamie Moyer, pitch for the Mariners. You told me I was the only one you ever let in the box who was allowed to root for the other team. (laughs)

To me, TVS is the whole story about the growth of college basketball in a nutshell. People don't understand that there was no network television back then. But you had the vision to see what it could become—what ESPN would be, for instance—and what television would mean to the game.

Our rivalry with UCLA was heated even before we broke their 88-game winning streak in 1974. We played them in South Bend the year before, and John Wooden gave me a big lecture during the game. We had John Shumate guarding Bill Walton, and Shumate was all over Walton, so Wooden came over to our bench and said, "Digger, if you don't tell Shumate to leave Bill Walton alone, I'm going to put Swen Nater in the game, and you know what I'm going to have him do."

Nater was Walton's backup and a real rough player, but I just said, "John, I've got two football players sitting on the end of the bench and they'll kick the hell out of your whole basketball team, so let's just let it go, all right?"

Oh, man, how those UCLA fans used to get on me. The minute I showed my face in the arena they started booing and they never let up. I figured out a way to get them to stop for a few minutes, though. I'd wait until I saw John Wooden getting ready to walk out onto the court, and I'd put my arm around him and walk out with him. I knew they weren't going to boo *him*. (laughs)

So then they brought their winning streak to South Bend, and do you know what the last thing I did at the end of practice the day before the game was? I had the team practice cutting down the nets. True story. Our captains were John Shumate and Gary Novak, and I said, "Shumate, you take six guys to that end, and Novak, you take six guys to that end, and cut down the nets. Someday, you're going to tell your grandchildren about this." One of the players didn't get it. He said, "We can't cut down the nets. We need them tomorrow." But Gary Brokaw told me years later that when we did that before the game he knew we could beat them.

Here's an interesting thing about us breaking their streak. A UCLA graduate student wrote a book that had a lot of good stuff in it. He knew the players very well—Bill Walton, Greg Lee, Keith Wilkes—and he wrote how John Wooden would never call a timeout when things were getting tense. Well, we were down by 11 points with 3:28 to go, but then Shumate scored and stole an in-bounds pass and we scored again. We were down to 7 points. Then the crowd started to get into it, and Adrian Dantley stole a pass and scored and the place turned into a frenzy.

When we cut the gap down to 3, Walton looked over at the bench and Wooden was just sitting there with his program rolled up—nothing. They missed another shot, we scored again, and the difference was just 1 point. Walton looked over to Wooden again and signaled a timeout, but Wooden said no, just play. They missed another shot—they didn't score one point in the final 3:28—and Dwight Clay scored with 29 seconds left to put us ahead.

"John, I've got two football players sitting on the end of the bench and they'll kick the hell out of your whole basketball team, so let's just let it go, all right?"

They got a couple more shots off—one by Walton that just missed—but then Shumate got the rebound and threw the ball high in the air. The buzzer went off and the place went nuts because it was the end of the longest winning streak in the history of college basketball. Clay's shot was huge, of course, but what I remember is John Shumate holding Bill Walton without a point for the last 3:28 and Gary Brokaw shutting out Keith Wilkes.

I'll always wonder what would have happened if Wooden had called a timeout, but I knew he wouldn't. Remember the scene in *Patton* where Patton beats Rommel in North Africa and he yells, "I read your book, you magnificent son of a bitch!"? That's what I felt like.

John Wooden never changed his philosophy, though. He once said, "If you run your practices right, you should be able to just sit and enjoy the game and not be up and down on the sidelines like some coaches I know." I always thought that was a shot at me.

Rick Pitino *was* Louisville, Jim Boeheim *was* Syracuse, and so on. All of a sudden we weren't just coaches anymore—we were show business, entertainment.

When I went to Fordham I had a wife and three kids and I was making $14,000. Then I went to Notre Dame and they paid me $18,300. It was the shoe contracts that changed everything. Reebok and Adidas and Nike saw that basketball had an advantage over football. Kids don't wear cleats, but every kid in America owns a pair of sneakers. So they were the first to say, "We are going to pump money into college basketball."

That led to the NBA shoe contracts, of course—Air Jordans and all the rest—but it started in college, and pretty soon all the coaches had shoe contracts. Then we started appearing in ads and on our own television shows, and we became the face of our programs. Rick Pitino *was* Louisville, Jim Boeheim *was* Syracuse, and so on. All of a sudden we weren't just coaches anymore—we were show business, entertainment.

My last year at Notre Dame, 1991, I was getting $150,000 from Reebok, $100,000 from a television show, and $50,000 from Bike and Champion sporting goods. I was only making approximately $80,000 from Notre Dame—nothing like the huge salaries they pay now—but I was getting $400,000 or $500,000 overall. Father Joyce, the Notre Dame vice president who ran the athletic department, was great about it. He just said, "Anything Digger can make outside the university is fine with us."

I had a chance to go to the pros when Mike Burke wanted me to coach the Knicks after Red Holzman retired. He offered me $1 million spread out over four or five years. "You're New York, you're Fordham," he said. But my wife had just gotten her doctorate and been offered a job in the English department at Notre Dame, and my kids were just getting to high school. So I said, "Digger, put your ego to rest. Stay another decade at Notre Dame. It's your family's turn to have a life now." Which we did, and I never regretted it. And I always felt good that when I left Notre Dame, basketball was on a par with football.

Now that I'm broadcasting for ESPN, I've really become a basketball fan. I know it sounds funny, but as a coach you've got tunnel vision. You worry about recruiting, you worry about scouting, you worry about your team. I'm a real basketball junkie now. I must watch more than 400 games each year.

I've been able to do other things I wanted to do too. I worked for President Bush's father in the drug office of the White House for a year, and in 1990 LeRoy Neiman started me painting. Last summer I was in the south of France painting for a week. And I've become a big classical music fan. I'll go to the Chicago symphony and just marvel at the hundred musicians on the stage. When the conductor puts his hands up and gives the downbeat and they start playing Mozart, that guy's coaching, baby. He's a coach.

CHAPTER 22

John Thompson: Big Men, Big Changes, and the Big East

Washington, D.C., July 2005

My high school basketball team won two city championships when I was growing up in Washington, D.C., and I was interested in going to Georgetown, but there was no chance of that. The coach, Tommy Nolan, was the sweetest guy in the world, but he sat me down and told me that Georgetown just wasn't ready for an African-American player. That's how society functioned in the early sixties—even good men couldn't do anything about it.

We had a lot of good players in the area then, and they all had to go north or west if they wanted to play in college. Elgin Baylor went to Seattle, Ollie Johnson went to San Francisco, and I went to Providence. I ended up there partly because it was run by the Dominican fathers. My mother went to St. Dominic's Church in Washington, and she thought they would take care of me. I still go to St. Dominic's, by the way.

What bothers me is how everybody accepted what was happening then as a fact of life. It's so misleading to think that Jackie Robinson integrated sports,

because he didn't end the quotas. When I played in the NBA, Bill Russell told me that if I looked around, I'd see that there were three blacks on every team, no more. It hadn't even occurred to me, but I looked and—damn!—there *were* three on every team. We were never competing for one of the 12 spots on a team. Anybody who says that is telling a lie.

We had a lot of good players in the area then, and they all had to go north or west if they wanted to play in college.

You know the story they tell about Texas Western beating Kentucky for the NCAA championship in 1966 with five black starting players? It was supposed to be such a big moment for integration, but that's all just BS. The game was in College Park, Maryland, and I was here at the time. Nobody was talking about it as a big deal. Texas Western wasn't even a big underdog. It was the number three team team in the country. Sure, in the black community we quietly said, "Good," but nobody was running around saying how great it was.

The story that Don Haskins, who coached Texas Western, was this great man and Adolph Rupp was a racist was created after the fact. Haskins wasn't playing those five black kids for a social cause. Haskins didn't say, "I'm going to kick down this wall." I've heard him talk about it, and he was honest about what he did. He said, "I'm going to win this championship, and this is who I've got to play with." He wasn't even thinking about anything else, but they never listened to him. So he's not the one perpetuating the lie. We all are. It's crazy.

Rupp was just a product of his times. Wes Unseld got on me once when we were talking about this, and I said, "Wes, understand what I'm saying. I'm not condoning what Rupp did, but you can't just lay it on him. Our whole society is to blame for what happened then." They're making Adolph seem like the cheese that stood alone, when there were a hell of a lot of teams in this country that wouldn't play African Americans, including Georgetown.

It's not that sports haven't played a big role in our society. They have. College athletics did a lot for integration. But they didn't finally start taking black players at Georgetown because they wanted to be humanitarians. They did it because they wanted to win. And the result was people being exposed to blacks as human beings, not seeing just their color anymore.

I had never thought about being a coach, but the NBA expanded when I was playing for the Celtics, and the Chicago Bulls took the rights to me. Bill Russell was getting older and I had confidence that Red Auerbach would give me a chance to play more, but I didn't know what would happen in Chicago. So I decided to go back to Washington and get involved in something that would let me enjoy myself and have control over my life.

I had a degree in economics and a teaching certificate, so I worked in a poverty program, the United Planning Organization. But then Father Bailey, the parish priest at St. Anthony's, which was the only co-ed Catholic high school in Washington, asked me if I would coach the basketball team. I said I'd come by and take a look. He had the players form a straight line. All I could think was, "Man, all these guys are the same height—below 6'. (laughs) But I said I'd do it if I could coach in the late afternoon after I had finished my job. So that's how I got involved in coaching.

I started liking it when I started winning. I said, "Hey, this is fun." So I started going around Washington and getting some good players to go to St. Anthony's, and after a while we had a very good team. I stayed there six years. Then, in 1972, Georgetown asked me if I would apply for their head coaching job. I told myself, "Georgetown isn't going to hire a black person. There's no way." But a friend from high school, Maurice Lancaster, worked in the admissions office, and he said, "You've got to apply for this job."

I said, "Mo, who are you kidding? I couldn't even go to school there. I'm not going through any charade." And I started thinking about the reputation of Georgetown, the sophistication and all the rest of it. It was west of the park, on the other side of the city from where we were. We lived east of the park, and we always knew the difference. But Mo insisted, and when the director of admissions came to my house and talked to me before the formal interview, I got the sense that maybe they would consider me seriously, and they did.

A lot of the time I was there I felt like an invited guest. I had to adjust to Georgetown, and Georgetown had to adjust to me. Basically, it had a prep-school mentality and there I was bringing in African-American kids to play basketball. But when they saw I had gotten to know the kids and that I was serious about them graduating, they became more supportive and I became more comfortable.

Then we started winning some ballgames, and the attitude was, "Well, they're good boys, aren't they?"

John Thompson celebrates Georgetown's victory over Houston to win the 1984 NCAA championship with Patrick Ewing. Thompson took Georgetown to the NCAA Tournament in 20 of his 27 years at the school and to the Final Four three times.

It's like a story the priest told at mass this morning about a man who loved his donkey. When it died he asked his priest to bury it. The priest said, "No way am I going to bury a donkey in the church." The man said, "I told the minister at the Lutheran church I'd give him $2,000 if he'd bury the donkey." And the priest said, "I didn't know that donkey was Catholic." (laughs)

But Dave Gavitt, who was the athletic director at Providence and the brains behind starting the Big East, said it would take all of us to a whole new dimension. It would put us on television nationally and give us the kind of recognition we never had before.

The best advice I ever got when I first started coaching was from Dean Smith. Television was just coming in in a big way—you were putting so many games on TV, Eddie—and Dean said, "Television will change your program." He said it was amazing how many people were watching these games, and the fact that parents could see their kids play was so important. So one of the first things I did when I got to Georgetown was to tell them to fix the lights. They looked at me like they didn't know what I was talking about. But I said, "We're going to win, and we're going to be on television." That's something I owe Dean Smith.

The next big thing that happened was Georgetown joining the Big East Conference. I was against it from the start because I liked being able to control our schedule, and I didn't like the idea of the officiating being centralized. I thought, "Oh my God, I'm going to lose my creativity." I told Frank Rienzo, our athletic director, "We're going to be in a conference with Syracuse and St. John's? Who's going to run it?" You know, the usual paranoid things coaches go through. But Dave Gavitt, who was the athletic director at Providence and the brains behind starting the Big East, said it would take all of us to a whole new dimension. It would put us on television nationally and give us the kind of recognition we never had before. I said, "Yes, and it's going to put us under a lot more pressure too."

But it turned out to be great because of the people who were running it. Dave, in particular, was just so damn creative. He was the master hustler, and he knew how to handle things. When I was upset about something, he would never confront me in a meeting. He would just sit and listen, and then he would call and say, "I'm going to come down and talk to you." He was the best at getting things done I've ever seen, the absolute best.

One of the things I was upset about was the decision to play the Big East tournament in Madison Square Garden every year. I was paranoid about that because I thought it would give Louie Carnesecca and St. John's the home-court advantage. But then I saw the excitement over the tournament because the fans of all the teams loved to go to New York, and the publicity was tremendous. It just became huge. I can't tell you how important the exposure we got was. It made us more appealing to the NCAA Tournament because we were playing a tougher schedule. And rather than fighting for ourselves to get recognition, the league fought for us, which I was too stupid to understand when they were putting the conference together.

The exposure helped us with recruiting too, because people knew us on a national level. Suddenly we could walk into the house of a kid in New Orleans or California. We got players like Patrick Ewing at Georgetown and Chris Mullin at St. John's. And the other coaches were smart enough to see that even though they didn't want to play against Ewing, his coming into the league would help *them* recruit better players too. After a while, coaches around the country started whining that the Big East was exposed *too* much on television and that it was hurting their recruiting. But they learned from what we were doing too, and they started consolidating and getting TV contracts. The competition motivated them to do better. That's how the game grew.

One thing that was very significant in building the Big East was the personalities of the coaches. We had some real characters and some real jackasses. I'm probably the biggest jackass of them all. (laughs) We fought, we argued, we got angry at each other. We fought about who was going to referee the games, where we were going to play, who was getting more publicity than the other guy. But it was more of a competitive anger than a personal one because we all respected each other.

Just look at the characters we had then: Louie Carnesecca at St. John's, Rollie Massimino at Villanova, Jim Boeheim at Syracuse, P. J. Carlesimo at Seton Hall, and Rick Pitino at Providence. I remember when Rick and Rollie got into the biggest argument at a meeting once. Rollie said Rick was the new guy on the block and that he should sit back and just listen. But Rick wasn't buying it. He was going to be heard. We had guys whose personalities were such that even if their team wasn't good, they were enough of a household name to still be marketable. We were always putting on an act, getting into an argument, having fun about something.

Another important part of it was that we all stayed at our schools for a long time. But here's something important: it never would have happened if it hadn't been for the shoe companies because none of our schools could afford to pay us. We got so much publicity that other schools with bigger budgets came after us. Oklahoma tried to get me, for instance, and other schools tried to get some of the other guys. There was no way our small Catholic schools would have been able to compete. If it hadn't been for the money I was making from Nike, or Jim Boeheim

and Rollie Massimino were making from their shoe contracts, we would have had to leave. So the league helped us get exposure, the exposure got the shoe companies interested in us, and we got to stay where we were. People talked about our dedication, and I thought, "Dedication, my foot." It came down to the fact that we were playing in New York, and we were on television all the time. Nike and Puma and the other shoe companies said, "Hell, we can advertise with these guys."

One thing that was very significant in building the Big East was the personalities of the coaches. We had some real characters and some real jackasses. I'm probably the biggest jackass of them all.

I had a lot of personal feelings when I became the first African-American coach to win an NCAA title. I was very aware of the fact that there was a barrier that said African Americans couldn't coach, and I told myself, "I want to knock this barrier down." After we won, I said, "I don't have to win 10, just the one." If I had one wish it would be to go back and have the luxury of just being a coach, to focus only on basketball and not to have to deal with social issues. I will tell you one thing that made me proud, though. After I stopped coaching, Jesse Jackson said one thing he respected about me was that I stood up for the things I believed in while I was still working—not after I retired. Hearing him say that meant something to me.

I think the world's a better place than it used to be, and I've always thought there were a lot of people both white and black who helped me. Had I not been helped by Dean Smith and Dave Gavitt, I would not have known how to make it through the briar patch. Dean told me some things I never thought a white man would tell a black man. He told me the truth, and I appreciate it. I'll never forget when we were getting ready to play North Carolina in the 1982 NCAA championship game—that's the one Michael Jordan won on a shot with 15 seconds left in the game. It was one of the biggest games of my life, and it was against the guy who helped me more than anybody else. I said, "Now I've got to generate dislike for him? This is going to be the worst thing in the world." But it turned out to be a great game, and I used a lot of the stuff Dean Smith taught me. And you know what? It was *fun*. I enjoyed it even though we lost.

Here's another barrier I was proud of breaking. Can you tell me one coach who played the center position who is in the Hall of Fame? I'm the only one. Big guys don't get jobs as coaches. Stop and think about it. How many big-man coaches can you name? I think we all owe a debt to George Mikan, who was the first one to show the world that big guys weren't just clowns running around out there on the floor. I'm for the big guys. Maybe that's just a bias of mine.

I am still close to some of my players. Some of them I hope I never see again. (laughs) I am close to Patrick Ewing. He'll always be special to me. I remember the first time I saw him was when we went to the old Boston Garden to see Patrick's team play against another player we were scouting. I don't even remember the other player's name. I reached over and touched Billy Stein, my assistant, and said, "See that sophomore on the Cambridge team? Get me him and I'll win the national championship." He was just in the 10th grade, but you could see the talent.

And Patrick was just a beautiful kid. There were so many questions about his academic ability, but when he came to Georgetown he worked hard, and any time a teacher wanted to work with him he did. And he was kind to everyone, from the custodian to the president of the university. When the other players came along, I said they couldn't act like fools because the best player I ever had was a perfect gentleman.

I had a reputation for being protective of my players, and I guess I was. I wanted to create an environment where I could teach what I wanted. A lot of times I said things to the players I wouldn't want other people to hear because they would have been offended by it. But I talked to my players privately, and they understood where I was coming from. Now I hear all the love from the Patrick Ewings and the Alonzo Mournings and the Allen Iversons. I hear them say, "Oh, Coach is so nice." I just say, "Why don't you tell people the truth?" (laughs)

How many big-man coaches can you name? I think we all owe a debt to George Mikan, who was the first one to show the world that big guys weren't just clowns running around out there on the floor.

Here's something that I think is important. Not one of my players has had trouble playing for anyone else. Patrick had a lot of coaches in the NBA, and they all liked him. Alonzo has played for everybody. They say things about Allen, but he plays hard and he plays hurt. So they all adjusted to other people. That's the role of a teacher, I think—not to make a person dependent on you.

In the end, I think the greatest thing you take from coaching is a lasting relationship with your players. I like to tell people that I have a ring associated with every possible championship in basketball, and I've lost every possible championship. It's been a great experience, but nothing surpasses just talking to your players after they've left you, sitting and reminiscing with them, and laughing and relaxing.

Now my son is the head coach at Georgetown. He went to Princeton, and I think he was more influenced by Pete Carril than by me. I'm very pleased with John's progress. I was a little worried when he came here because he would always be hearing his daddy's name. But John came behind the guy who came behind me, so I guess that makes it a little easier. He's always going to hear his daddy's name, though, and he'll always hear my mouth. He may never listen to a thing I say, but he's always going to hear my mouth. Not during the games, though. I go up in the skybox so I can sit there by myself and say whatever I want to.

I work for TNT now and as an adviser to the president of Georgetown. And I've got my radio show, where we talk about sports for a couple hours a day. People hear me telling jokes and laughing and singing, and they say, "Damn, I didn't know you were like that."

I say, "You didn't know me because I didn't *let* you know me." I see so many people who become incarcerated by their reputations, by what others think they are. I'm always going to be what *I* want to be, not what other people think I am.

CHAPTER 23

Dean Smith on Building Tar Heel Greatness

Chapel Hill, North Carolina, June 2005

Phog Allen was probably 65 years old when I got to the University of Kansas in 1951. Can you imagine playing for a coach who learned the game from James Naismith? Allen was really a motivator more than anything else. And what a salesman! He could fire up a team—"Go! Jayhawks! We're going to beat those Tigers!"—like nobody else I've ever seen.

Dick Harp, Allen's assistant, was the *X*'s and *O*'s guy, and he was the first coach I ever saw who used a real pressure defense. I remember we had one game where the other team couldn't even get a shot *off* for the first eight minutes of the game, let alone score. After a while, more and more coaches started picking up on that. I know I did. I emphasized pressure defense with all my teams. I remember one summer when Phil Woolpert, the coach at the University of San Francisco, came in to see Dick to learn about his pressure defense. He said, "I have a guy named Bill Russell coming in, and he's going to be a good shot-blocker." He was right about that, wasn't he?

We won the NCAA title in 1952—I got in for about 30 seconds—and after I graduated, I worked at Kansas as a graduate assistant. Then I went to the Air Force Academy as an assistant coach. Later Dick Harp asked me to come back to be his assistant, and I almost did. What's funny is that long after Dick retired at Kansas I brought him to the University of North Carolina to be my assistant.

I've always been blamed for the introduction of the 30-second clock into college basketball because of my four-corners offense. I guess in a way it was a compliment, but I was pretty steamed at the time.

How I went to North Carolina is a pretty good story. We were at the 1957 NCAA Tournament—that's when Wilt Chamberlain was at Kansas and they lost to North

Carolina in the championship game—and the next day I had breakfast with Frank McGuire, who was the coach at North Carolina. "I know you were cheering for Kansas," he said, "but I might have an opening next year. Would you want to be my assistant?"

I told Frank that Kansas was my school and that I was thinking about eventually going back there. Well, it turned out that he didn't have an opening after all, but the next year one of his assistants left and Frank called again. I accepted. I spent three years coaching under him and that was really great for me. He had such charisma.

I've been close to Bob Knight ever since I was a young coach, and once he called me about Mike Krzyzewski, who was coaching at West Point at the time.

In 1961 Frank left to coach Wilt with the Philadelphia Warriors, and I took over as head coach. I stayed 36 seasons, which seems hard to believe now. Later Frank returned to college to coach at the University of South Carolina. It wasn't considered to be as good a team as North Carolina was, but as soon as he got there he told everybody South Carolina was just as important as North Carolina. He had a good career there too. He's still the only coach to win ACC championships at two schools.

I've always been blamed for the introduction of the 30-second clock into college basketball because of my four-corners offense. I guess in a way it was a compliment, but I was pretty steamed at the time. Somebody asked me about it, and I said you've got to give a team like Bucknell or Princeton a chance to win, which they could only do by holding the ball. Now they have the three-point shot, which gives the have-nots a chance to win.

When the three-point shot came in, I told my best outside shooters they had a green light in certain situations, while other players had a yellow light or a red light. The only time I wanted my outside shooters taking three-point shots was if there were three seconds left and we were behind by three. Pretty soon everybody was out practicing three-point shots to try to get me to give them the green light. (laughs)

I think the number-one reason the Atlantic Coast Conference got so much attention initially was because of our postseason tournament. There was a tremendous amount of opposition to it because the NCAA only took one team from a conference to its tournament. So if you won the regular-season championship, you had to prove yourself all over again in the tournament, and some of the coaches hated it.

But the tournament became very popular—it was hard to get a ticket and it was huge on TV—and it really set our conference apart. Now, of course, they're all doing it, except for the Ivy League, but it's different because just about any team can get in the tournament. Some coaches are hollering, "Let's make it like Indiana basketball where everybody is in it." Well, that's what we have now, isn't it? I remember the first year when *none* of the teams at the Final Four were regular-season champions in their leagues. It was 1989, and the teams were Michigan, Illinois, Duke, and Seton Hall.

I'd say our rivalry with Duke is as intense as any in college basketball, and here's something I guess North Carolina fans might not appreciate: I've been close to Bob Knight ever since I was a young coach, and once he called me about Mike Krzyzewski, who was coaching at West Point at the time. "Mike can go to Iowa State or Duke," Bob said. "Don't you think he should go to Iowa State? It's a pretty tough league." I guess he thought Mike could really make his mark there.

But I said, "No, Duke is so easy to recruit to. It's your call about what to tell him, but I really think he can get better players at Duke than he can at Iowa State." I've often wondered if North Carolina fans can blame me for the games we lost to Mike's teams. (laughs)

Dean Smith, shown here with his greatest player, Michael Jordan, retired from the University of North Carolina as college basketball's winningest coach with 879 victories. Smith's teams appeared in 11 Final Fours and won two national championships.

I helped Roy Williams get his head coaching job at Kansas too. My assistants tended to stay with me a long time—Roy, Bill Guthridge, and Eddie Fogler were with me for years. When the Kansas job opened up, I called Bob Fredericks, who was the athletic director and a close friend of mine, and I said I knew Roy could do the job. But Bob said, "No, we want to get a head coach who's already proven himself."

But Roy went after the job, and they must have liked what they saw. A week later the athletic department's opinion of Roy had been turned completely around. There was fear that Roy wouldn't come to Kansas because he said he would miss Carolina so much. So in the beginning I had to beg them to take Roy, and then after all his years of success at Kansas, they got mad when he came back to North Carolina.

People want to know how we got Michael Jordan to come to North Carolina. We first heard about him when we got a call from his high school coach in Wilmington, North Carolina, who said, "You may want to come down and check out this guy. He didn't even make the team when he was a sophomore, but now he's a junior and he's really come on." So I sent Bill Guthridge down, and he said he thought Michael would get an ACC scholarship and that we should keep following him. Well, the next summer he came to our boys camp, and we knew then we were definitely going to go after him because he was so quick.

In the first practice, we were working on our pressure defense, and there was something about it Michael didn't like. I explained why we wanted it done a certain way, and I told him, "You'll have it down in a couple of weeks." But at the next practice he was doing it just right. I never saw a guy listen and then do what you told him so easily. It just showed how bright he is.

Michael didn't do so well when he quit the Bulls and took up baseball with your White Sox, did he? But I'll bet the hitting coach was impressed at how he listens.

Mike Krzyzewski has made winning a habit at Duke University, where his teams have been to 10 Final Fours and won three national championships. In recent years, Krzyzewski has become one of the leading spokesmen for the importance of values in college basketball.

CHAPTER 24

Mike Krzyzewski Tells of the Spirit of the Game

Durham, North Carolina, June 2005

It's good to sit here talking to you, Eddie. You were there when the train pulled out of the station, weren't you?

That's just another way of saying how old I am. (laughs)

It's amazing to think how much the game has changed over time. When I played for Bob Knight at West Point, the National Invitation Tournament was every bit as popular as the NCAA Tournament. In fact, my junior year we were invited to the NCAA but we went to the NIT instead, and nobody thought that was a strange decision. I'm glad the NIT is still going on, but just look at what the NCAA Tournament has become.

I honestly think it's the most important sporting event in the country, a national treasure, because it unifies us for the month of March the way we're not unified at any other time of the year. It brings teams and people together from small towns and big cities, rural areas and urban ones, the East Coast, the South, the Midwest, everywhere. People fill out their brack-

ets, everybody talks about it—even those who don't follow basketball are following it then—and there's just such a spirit about it. It's the spirit of the underdog, but it's also the values and the traditions of the game. It's pure, and it's followed with such an enthusiasm that I don't see happening anywhere else.

It brings teams and people together from small towns and big cities, rural areas and urban ones, the East Coast, the South, the Midwest, everywhere.

When things are going right, you're in the Sweet 16. And if you win, you're in the Elite Eight—there are names for each of your junctures. And then all of a sudden, you hit the promised land, the Final Four. It's this progression that has changed things from when nobody seemed to care. People didn't really pay attention until the Final Four. But now they're watching every step of the way. You hear them say the "Road to the Final Four" and sing "One Shining Moment," which has become the anthem of college basketball, and it gives you the feeling, "Let's get on the road."

Here's another thing: the kids who play in the tournament come from great universities all over the country, and they will always be members of those communities. That's one of the beautiful things about college sports. There is free agency in the NBA, so if you play for the Bulls or the Lakers there might not be that loyalty or commitment of player to team or team to player. But a player can have a relationship with his college that he'll benefit from for the rest of his life.

I grew up on the north side of Chicago and was a Cubs fan. I've grown to respect the White Sox, though.

That's very diplomatic of you. (laughs)

You hear them say the "Road to the Final Four" and sing "One Shining Moment," which has become the anthem of college basketball, and it gives you the feeling, "Let's get on the road."

When I was growing up, I was looking at Midwest colleges—Wisconsin, Minnesota, and Detroit—and I was leaning toward Creighton because I have a Catholic education and it's a Jesuit school. But then this young coach named Bob Knight came along. You have to understand that my dad never went to college—he only had two years of high school—and was an elevator operator at the Willoughby Tower in Chicago. My mom never even *went* to high school and used to clean offices at the Chicago Athletic Club at night.

For them to think their son might be able to go to the United States Military Academy, well, they just could not imagine it. They thought it was for the rich and privileged. So it was because of them, and espe-

cially the impression that coach Knight made on my dad, that I went to West Point. It was a decision based on the input of two parents who had a combined education of two years in high school.

Was I ready for West Point and coach Knight? No. But nobody is. That's the beauty of going to college. You're the golden boy in your neighborhood and you think you know everything, and all of a sudden you're in an environment where there are other golden boys from other neighborhoods. Your outlook changes. What West Point did for me, and what coach Knight did, was redefine my idea of success. What I learned during my time there was that failure is part of the process and not to stop when you fail. Then, when you succeed, you do it again and again, and all of a sudden good things happen.

It's nice that coach Knight told you that I was good at adapting to his system. If I had heard that when I was younger I probably would have said it's like saying somebody's got a good personality but is not good-looking. (laughs) But I appreciate it. Being his captain and point guard taught me things I've been able to use throughout my life. I think one of the reasons I'm a pretty good basketball coach is that I've learned to adapt.

I'll tell you one more story about coach Knight. When I was a senior at West Point I got word that my dad was really ill. There was a huge snowstorm, and I was trying to get out to go home. A few hours later I got another call telling me my dad had died. He'd had a cerebral hemorrhage, and it was just such a shock. I didn't even know anything was imminent. What coach Knight did those next few days was remarkable. He got me down to the Newark Airport to fly out in the snowstorm, and then he followed me. We had two games left in the season and we were trying to get into the NIT, so we had to win them. But on Monday and Tuesday he was in Chicago, and he stayed for the funeral on Wednesday. He was so good with my mom, and he told me, "You stay here as long as you need to stay."

Now, I was his point guard and he was 25 or 26 years old, and this was an important game for his career. But he was completely committed to helping me and my family. I came back and played both games, and we won and made the Final Four of the NIT. So that's another lesson I learned. Do what's right. Do what you're supposed to do. That's a commitment I've tried to have for each kid that I've coached, and I truly believe I learned it from coach Knight.

I was 28 when I became head coach at West Point. They had won only nine games total in the two previous years so we had to work like crazy, and I loved being back. We won 73 games in five seasons. After the fourth year, I interviewed at Vanderbilt University, but I pulled my name out. I just wasn't ready. The next year I was offered the job at Iowa State, but I wanted to interview at Duke too. I told Lou McCullough, the Iowa State athletic director, that I knew he couldn't keep the job open, so we should part ways. He said he could wait a while, but I didn't want to hurt them, and finally we just cut ties. They ended up hiring Johnny Orr, who did a great job.

Well, I interviewed at Duke and they didn't offer me the job, so my wife Mickey and I went to the airport. She flew to Virginia to visit her family, and I was getting ready to fly back to West Point when an assistant athletic director showed up at the airport and said Duke wanted to talk to me again. They offered me the job, and I called Mickey and told her the news.

She said, "That's great. How much are we going to make?"

And I said, "You know, I didn't ask them." (laughs) I wouldn't advise anybody to negotiate that way today, but at the time it never occurred to me. It was crazy, but it was good.

I'm proud of the honors I've gotten, but really it's the result of being with a good group of players. When an athlete gets an honor, it can be an individual accomplishment within the team structure.

But a coach is solely dependent on his players. I was named Coach of the Decade in the nineties, but if you trace it back I probably had most of the good players of that decade: Bobby Hurley, Christian Laettner, Grant Hill, Jason Williams, Elton Brand. They were outstanding athletes, they played together, and they won. Coaching is part of it, I guess, but you can drive a really good car fast for longer periods of time than you can a jalopy. (laughs)

When an athlete gets an honor, it can be an individual accomplishment within the team structure. But a coach is solely dependent on his players.

Last season I did a commercial where I talked about coaching as a profession, about how it plays a leadership role in society, and some people thought I was just talking about myself. But one of the reasons I did it was to put coaching in its proper perspective. If you're one of the top coaches, I think it's your responsibility to give people a higher view of your profession.

I still remember my best teachers in high school and college because they had an impact on me beyond the subject they were teaching. They had a passion that brought out something in me that made me better, and as coaches that's what we're trying to do—make youngsters better. I wanted to be a coach in high school because of the impact my teachers and coaches had on me. I wanted to have that impact on other people. Then when I went to West Point I put coaching on the back burner because I was going to be a military officer. But I learned that being a leader in the military was actually like being a coach. I was able to play on an all-Army team and do a little coaching, so even while I was an officer I knew this is what I wanted to do.

Duke has been such a wonderful place for me. The Atlantic Coast Conference was born out of small towns, not big cities, and its tradition is deeply entrenched in the hearts and minds of families. And as the ACC has gotten so big, we have to remember how it started and why people are so passionate about basketball here. It has produced national champions, Players of the Year, and some of the most incredible games in the history of the sport. And it will continue to do so if we remember where we came from.

I think that if something gets too big, whether it's sports or business or whatever, it stops recognizing the core values that make up its foundation. It's not the amount of money that determines if something has become too big. It's like when you're growing up and somebody says, "Eddie is getting too big for his britches." What you're saying is he's probably done something good, but he's forgotten where he's from. That's how I look at sports. It's growing, but let's not forget where it came from. That way, it can only grow more.

CHAPTER 25

Roy Williams: I'm Not in Kansas Anymore

Chapel Hill, North Carolina, June 2005

I remember exactly when I decided I wanted to be a basketball coach. It was the summer after the ninth grade in Asheville, North Carolina. Buddy Baldwin, my high school coach, was the first person I'd met outside my family who really made me feel good about myself, and I thought, "You know, I'm not the only guy he's done that for." It made me want to do it too.

Buddy had played for Frank McGuire at North Carolina, and he thought it was a great school. He also had a lot of respect for Dean Smith. And because I was a pretty good student, Buddy thought it would be the best place for me to be. I wanted to see if I could play on that level, but after my freshman year I realized I wasn't good enough. But I kept up my interest in coaching and eventually came back to North Carolina, where I spent 10 years with coach Smith. It seemed as if he was trying to prepare all of us to be head coaches someday, so even though I loved it here, I knew that somewhere out there was a job with my name on it.

During my last four years there it seemed as if I was offered a head coaching position every year, but the jobs never seemed like the right fit, so I was patient. I'll admit I was dumbfounded when I was able to get the Kansas job. It was only because of

One of the great things about the tournament for the fans is a bad thing for the players and the coaches. You have one bad day and you're gone. It makes no difference how good you were or what your record was.

their respect for coach Smith that a guy like me, who was his second assistant at North Carolina, could become the head coach at a school like Kansas.

My cell phone rang. It was Mike Krzyzewski confirming my interview with him the next day. This is very embarrassing, I said.

Don't worry. We're all members of the same brotherhood.

Except when you're playing each other. (laughs)

I've been to the NCAA Tournament 16 of the 17 years I've been a head coach—the only time we didn't make it was my first year, when we were on probation. And of course, being at Kansas for 15 years, I heard all about the 1957 national championship game, which they lost to North Carolina. So when we made our first trip to the Final Four in 1991, who did we have to beat in the semifinal? North Carolina and coach Smith.

When I think about the tournament I go back to 1981, the first year I went as an assistant at North Carolina, and coach Smith talking about how it had grown in terms of media attention in just a few years. Has the tournament gotten too big? I would say no. I don't think something is too big until people start losing interest in it, and I don't see that happening. I believe interest in the NCAA Tournament is unsurpassed.

So, yes, I thought he was going to be a great player, but anybody who says he thought Michael Jordan was going to be *Michael Jordan* is not telling you the truth.

One of the great things about the tournament for the fans is a bad thing for the players and the coaches. You have one bad day and you're gone. It makes no difference how good you were or what your record was. The San Antonio Spurs won the NBA title this year by beating the Detroit Pistons in the finals, but the Spurs' first playoff game was against the Denver Nuggets, and they lost. If it had been the NCAA Tournament, they'd have been finished. There's such a swiftness to how your season can end. There are no do-overs. And I think the coaches, even those of us who have been around a long time like myself, still can't handle the way it's boom! and you're done. I lost two national champion-

ship games before we finally won this year, so I know what it feels like.

But I'll never be one of those coaches who grabs the second-place trophy and throws it to the floor and says, "This is not what we play for." I think in college athletics you do the absolute best you can and you don't second-guess yourself. That's what I tried to do at Kansas when we lost in 1991 to Duke in the championship game and when we lost in 2003 to Syracuse. It's a crushing feeling, but you have to sit back and realize that you enjoyed the journey and you did some really good things to get that far. You can't let the feeling of losing wipe away what you did the entire year.

People often ask me about Michael Jordan. The first day he came to campus for our basketball camp I told one of our other assistants I had just seen the best 6'4" high school player I'd ever seen. We won the national championship his freshman year on his jump shot, and then, the day before practice started the next season, I measured and tested all the players, which was my job for 10 years. Michael had grown two inches, his vertical leap had gone up, and his time in the 40-yard dash had gone down. Here was a young man who was already a fantastic player, and he had exploded athletically and physically even more in that year. So, yes, I thought he was going to be a great player, but anybody who says he thought Michael Jordan was going to be *Michael Jordan* is not telling you the truth.

Part of his success, I think, had to do with the fact his high school team never won a district or a state championship. So when he got to North Carolina and won a national championship his first year, it made him hungrier. I have never seen a guy who could focus so clearly on getting everybody else to raise their level of play. He would challenge guys to a point where it became uncomfortable for some of them. But I believe Michael is the greatest winner the game has seen since Bill Russell. Remember those passes he made to John Paxson and Steve Kerr for shots to win

NBA championships with the Bulls? It didn't matter to him that someone else was taking the last shot. All he wanted was for his team to win. To me, that's the greatest example of a team athlete.

Do you know the story about me beating him at pool? It's true. I beat him three straight games, and he didn't speak to me the rest of the night. Then the next day he didn't speak to me at breakfast, and when we got on the team bus he accused me of telling everybody I'd beaten him. He's the greatest competitor I've ever met, no question.

It's tough not knowing when your players are going to leave or if the kid you've signed out of high school has decided to go straight to the NBA.

I'm convinced that the rivalries in the ACC aren't matched anywhere else in the country, and I think proximity has something to do with it. Duke is eight miles away from us, North Carolina State is 28 miles away, and Wake Forest is 75 miles away. There are people who are great friends but are fans of different schools, and even some families that are split. I think people have picked up on that around the country.

I'll give you an example. We were recruiting a youngster this spring who was considering a very good school in the Northeast. I didn't want to badmouth anyone, but I said, "You're one of the premier players in the country, and you should play on the biggest stage. This other school you're thinking about, when they play their biggest rival, the next day the people who played in the game and the fans of the two teams will know who won. But if you come to North Carolina and you play against Duke, the next morning every college basketball player and fan all over America will know who won." A lot of that is because of television. TV has made everybody in the country know what happens between two schools that are eight miles apart.

There are two changes in the game that worry me. One is the way international players are catching up to American players. Part of this is our own doing because for years we've been sending coaches over to give clinics, and their players have been coming here too. So it's becoming more of a global game. Also, I don't know if we'll ever have the kind of success we used to have in the Olympics because we don't have the passion for them that other countries have.

Last year I was an assistant coach for the U.S. Olympic team, and we had 14 practices whereas China had 88. Puerto Rico beat us in a first-round game in August, and Carlos Arroyo said they had been waiting and practicing for that day for months. They're doing a better job of building their teams and keeping them together.

The other thing I'm concerned about is the changing landscape of players going to, and staying in, school. It's tough not knowing when your players are going to leave or if the kid you've signed out of high school has decided to go straight to the NBA. When we won the national championship this year, we already knew we were going to lose Rashad McCants and Raymond Felton, who were juniors, and Marvin Williams, who was just a freshman. When we got back to Chapel Hill we had a great celebration with fifteen thousand people in the Smith Center. Then I took the whole staff to dinner, and we went home happy. The next night I came home and my wife said Sean May, another junior, had called and said that he wanted to talk to me. I called Sean, and he said he thought it would be best for him to go too.

We also lost three seniors, so 48 hours after becoming NCAA champions, we'd lost our top seven players. If you add J. R. Smith, a high school player in New Orleans who was going to play for us but turned professional instead, that's five guys in the NBA who would have been playing for us. So that put a damper on things in a hurry. It's unfortunate because I think playing in college gives you more time to evaluate your abilities. I would bet every team in the NBA now has several people on their staff just to make sure the young kids coming in are—I don't want to say they're babysitting because that sounds rude—but are keeping tabs on youngsters to make sure they're not doing something silly and making mistakes.

I think back to Kirk Hinrich at Kansas, who wanted to play in the NBA, but also wanted to wait and enjoy college life. So he stayed all four years, and now he's having a great career with the Bulls. I don't think it's bad to enjoy being a kid. Especially because after you take that next step, when you start earning money and paying bills, it's hard to go back to being a kid.

Roy Williams followed a lengthy career at the University of Kansas, where his teams went to back-to-back Final Fours, by moving to his alma mater, North Carolina, in 2003. The Tar Heels won the NCAA title in just his second season.

CHAPTER 26

Hank Raymonds: Remembering Al McGuire

Milwaukee, Wisconsin, February 2005

always wanted to coach, starting in the seventh grade when I coached the sixth-graders in my elementary school in St. Louis. This goes back to the late thirties, when they were just getting rid of the center jump. When I played at St. Louis University I got all the gals who were dating guys on our team together and asked them if they wanted to play. We called them the Billikenettes—St. Louis' mascot is the Billiken—and we played all the women's colleges in the area.

Then one day I got a letter saying no more male coaches would be allowed to coach the women. I was fired from my own team. (laughs) It was gender discrimination, wasn't it? I also coached a Catholic Youth Organization girls team in St. Anthony's Parish in South St. Louis. We were 31-0, and there was one young lady who was pretty good. I ended up marrying her. Jenny's been with me for 54 years now.

After I came back from the Marine Corps I couldn't get a coaching job, so I sold insurance. But then a priest at St. Louis University High, where I'd gone to school, asked me if I wanted to coach there.

I said yes, even though I was making more money in one year selling insurance than I could in five years coaching high school. In the mornings, Jenny would say, "I'm going to work, enjoy your hobby." (laughs)

I knew Al McGuire before either one of us came to Marquette. I'd gotten a job at Christian Brothers, a small university in Memphis, Tennessee, and Al was at

Al and his wife, Pat, were looking around for a house. He found the one he wanted, but he had to go back to North Carolina. So he made out a blank check, signed it, and told me to buy the house for him.

Belmont Abbey in North Carolina, which didn't have a home court. They played all their games on the road. I'd never met Al, but I called him one day and asked if he'd be interested in playing us the following year. I told him we'd give him $700, which was a lot of money in those days, especially for a small school. Al probably kept the money. (laughs) But the next season I came up to Marquette to be an assistant to Eddie Hickey, my old coach at St. Louis, so I wasn't there when Al took Belmont Abbey to Memphis for the game we'd arranged. Christian Brothers beat him by 14 points.

Marquette played Loyola of Chicago that year, and there was time for one shot before halftime. Coach Hickey said to run a certain play, but there was a mixup and a player ended up out of position, standing by the bench. Coach Hickey grabbed him by the chest and started shaking him. "What the hell?" he said. "You're supposed to be out there. What are you doing here?" And he shook him some more.

Well, the president of Marquette was in the stands, and with two Jesuit schools playing each other and his coach causing a scene, he got very upset. So he called coach Hickey in and said, "Either you resign or you're fired." So suddenly Marquette was looking for another coach. It came down to me and Al, and they finally chose Al. The next thing I knew the phone was ringing and it was Al. I'd still never met him.

"Hank," he said, "I know you're probably disappointed, but I want you to stay. You can do anything you want. We'll knock 'em dead. And by the way, where the hell did you get those guys down there in Memphis? They killed us." (laughs)

So I finally got to meet him, and I found out right away he was a little unusual. Al and his wife, Pat, were looking around for a house. He found the one he wanted, but he had to go back to North Carolina. So he made out a blank check, signed it, and told me to buy the house for him. That was a real sign of trust between him and me—Pat is still living in the house, by the way—and we had 14 good years together. And he was true to his word. He let me do anything I wanted.

Do you want to know what he told me when we started working together? The first was, "Don't accept any long-distance phone calls from my brother Jack." The second was, "Introduce me to people with money." (laughs)

Al liked to play an offense that was completely structured. "I want everybody to touch leather," he said, and he didn't want the players to have any options. They were supposed to do the same thing every time. He never liked to make any adjustments, either. It got frustrating for the players sometimes, particularly for Maurice Lucas, who I think was the best player we ever had. One day he said, "Coach, I feel like a robot," and I said, "Maurice, you may think you're a robot, but someday you're going to be a million-dollar robot in the NBA." And he was.

What was funny was that our practices were completely unstructured. We would scrimmage a lot—just play games against each other, really. Al didn't care if people watched. A lot of coaches don't like outsiders watching practice, but it didn't matter to

Our first game was against Massachusetts, and during the game he pointed at the best player and said, "Who the hell is that guy out there?" I said, "If you would pay attention to the damn scouting reports you'd know. That's Julius Erving." We beat them, though.

Al. We were going to play one of Jerry Tarkanian's teams once, and Al invited Jerry in to watch us practice. Jerry left in a cold sweat, saying, "How in the hell could you guys be so unorganized in practice and so organized in a game?"

Al didn't always pay attention to details. In 1970 he got mad when the NCAA wanted to send us out of our region for the tournament, and Al decided to go to the NIT instead. Our first game was against Massachusetts, and during the game he pointed at the

Hank Raymonds (right) was the legendary Al McGuire's chief assistant at Marquette from 1963 until 1977, when the team won the NCAA title. Raymonds then coached the team for six years and became Marquette's athletic director. Photograph courtesy of the Marquette University Department of Special Collections and University Archives.

best player and said, "Who the hell is that guy out there?"

I said, "If you would pay attention to the damn scouting reports you'd know. That's Julius Erving." We beat them, though.

One of Al's great strengths was that when the game was over, it was over. He'd get on the officials pretty good during a game and get frustrated, but he never let anything carry over to the next game. Every day was a new day. And we never second-guessed each other. I never said, "Dammit, why didn't you listen to me?" and he never complained to me.

Al was never big on rules, but he had some life lessons that he wanted the players to pay attention to. They could be pretty crude sometimes, but he'd get his point across. He'd say, "I don't want anybody out after 1:00 in the morning. The only thing left out there are pigs." (laughs) The players understood what he meant.

Here's one of my favorite stories about Al. In 1976, the year before we won the NCAA championship, we played in an international tournament in Brazil. It was an Olympic year, and we wore uniforms that said USA instead of Marquette. Our first game was against Brazil, and one of their players spit on Bill Neary, who was our hatchet man and who was playing a little rough. Bill complained to the official, who gave him a technical. Then Bill came over to our bench and started breaking up everything in sight—the bench, the water cooler, anything he could find. I was pretty hot too, so I told the official, "We're not putting up with this crap. We're going home."

And the official said in broken English, "Remember what happens with soccer players down here sometimes. They get shot."

I said, "We'll finish the game."

We lost the game and had a police escort back to the hotel. We played Puerto Rico the next day, and Al came in and said, "Hank, you coach them. I'll take Pat and Jenny, and we'll sit up in the stands. And if they shoot you, I'll say a prayer for you." Well,

we beat Puerto Rico, and he rushed into the locker room and said, "I'm going to come back and coach. They'll think they can win without me." (laughs)

We played Notre Dame one year and we were up by 14 points at halftime, and he was doing a little dance he was so happy. Then he came up to me and said, "If I was coaching, we'd be up by 20."

What's funny about us winning the NCAA Tournament in 1977 is that neither Al nor I thought we had one of our best teams. We probably shouldn't even have been in the tournament, if you want to know the truth. We lost our last three games at home—even Senior Night, which was pretty embarrassing—and we had to finish the regular season with five games on the road. Everybody knew it was going to be Al's last year, so it was really tense.

We beat Wisconsin at Madison, and then we had to go to Virginia Tech, which was another tough place to play, and we won there. Then we went to New Orleans and beat Tulane in the Superdome, which was being tested to see if it could hold an NCAA Tournament. Then we had to go to Creighton and Michigan, where we won too. What helped us was only two teams from a conference could go to the tournament then. Some of those teams might have played harder if they could have gone. But we were an independent, so we had a chance to make it to the tournament, and the games were more important to us.

The things that happened during the tournament itself were pretty crazy. We were playing Cincinnati in the Midwest Regionals in Omaha, and they had beaten us by one or two points in Cincinnati earlier in the season. That was a really controversial game, but we were beating them in the regionals, when

Bernard Lee ran by their bench and yelled, "We're kicking your ass." A technical was called on Al. He'd gotten technicals that really cost us in the previous two tournaments, and he looked at me and said, "Hank, if we lose now, I'm finished for life." He knew everybody would remember the other technicals if we lost again. We won by one point.

Did you know Al almost didn't make the championship game against North Carolina in Atlanta? We were staying way out in the boondocks—nobody knew where we were—and Al had rented a motorcycle and just taken off. Well, the damn thing broke down, and he didn't get there until 10 minutes before the game. I just laughed at him and said, "Hell, I'm ready, Al."

One amazing thing was that representatives of the shoe companies were in the locker room before the game, hanging around talking to the players. I don't know how they got in there, but here we were trying to win a national championship and the shoe companies were talking about deals with our players.

I wasn't worried about coaching after Al, following a legend and all that stuff. What good is thinking about it? Are you going to be worried the whole time? And Al was always great about it. He broadcast some of our games on TVS, and he was always rooting for us. We played Notre Dame one year and we were up by 14 points at halftime, and he was doing a little dance he was so happy. Then he came up to me and said, "If I was coaching, we'd be up by 20."

It was very hard seeing Al when he got sick. He'd try to go places, but he was so tired he could hardly walk. At the end, the transfusions were keeping him alive, and he could have lived longer if he'd taken more of them. But he said, "No. If I have to do that, forget about it."

The last time I saw him was in a hospice, and we both knew he wasn't going to make it. I brought him a program from his first game at Marquette—the varsity against the freshman—and we talked about that for a while. I thanked him for everything, especially for keeping his word about letting me do anything I wanted. Then he thanked me and said—very matter-of-fact, no outward emotion—"Hank, that's all she wrote. I've had a good life. There's no more Al McGuire."

Jerry Tarkanian, who won the NCAA title at the University of Las Vegas in 1990, retired after 31 years of coaching major-college basketball with the highest winning percentage of all time. A lengthy legal battle between Tarkanian and the NCAA resulted in a $2.5 million settlement in his favor and led to changes in that organization's rules.

CHAPTER 27

Jerry Tarkanian: My Battles On and Off the Court

Las Vegas, Nevada, April 2004

I guess I've always had an unorthodox approach to coaching. I started at California junior colleges in Riverside then Pasadena and won four consecutive state championships. Denny Crum was coaching at Pierce Junior College in the San Fernando Valley, and we were in the same league. We beat him a couple of times, but he had the only team that could give us tough games.

I was a junior college coach when I went and saw my first Final Four. Loyola beat Cincinnati in Freedom Hall in Louisville, and it was the most exciting event I'd ever been to. I thought that if I could ever get a four-year job and get to that position just once in my life I'd be happy. Well, I was fortunate. I got there four times. I just wish it had been more.

When I moved to Long Beach State in 1968, I was able to take some California junior college all-stars with me. It was automatic in those years that every top junior college player in the state wanted to go with me. The other coaches didn't think you could win with them, so they didn't recruit them, which was great for me.

I had five great years at Long Beach. I didn't make any money, but I didn't know any better. UCLA knocked us out of the tournament three years in a row. The last two years it was in the regional finals. If we had won either of those games, we'd have gone to the Final Four.

In my whole career, I've never had anybody steal a game from me worse than Art White did. For months after that his picture was on every billboard and in every bar and restroom in Long Beach.

In 1971 we led for 39 minutes and 37 seconds. We played out of our heads and were ahead by 11 points in the second half. All of a sudden, UCLA's athletic director, J. D. Morgan, came down to the sideline, where he had no right to be, and started yelling at Art White, one of the referees. "You saw that, Art, you saw that," J.D. was yelling. "You've got to call those." And then every call started going against us. It was the only game Ed Ratleff, our best player, fouled out of all year. We were posting him up, and UCLA couldn't stop him. It was a low-scoring game, 57–55, so every call was vital.

I was a nervous wreck all week long. I walked into the arena, and there was Al McGuire, eating a hot dog and drinking a Coke as calm as he could be. He called me over and said, "They want to interview us on television. I told them I'm not going to do it unless they pay us."

They took the lead with 23 seconds to go and won by two points. In my whole career, I've never had anybody steal a game from me worse than Art White did. For months after that his picture was on every billboard and in every bar and restroom in Long Beach. And just to show you how much clout J. D. Morgan had, Art White called both UCLA's Final Four games that year too.

Do you remember when TVS did Long Beach's first nationally telecast game, Eddie? It was 1973. We were ranked number four in the country, and Marquette was number three. I'll never forget it because it was my first game on national television, and it was the only sellout we ever had in the Long Beach Arena. I was a nervous wreck all week long. I walked into the arena, and there was Al McGuire, eating a hot dog and drinking a Coke as calm as he could be. He called me over and said, "They want to interview us on television. I told them I'm not going to do it unless they pay us."

I said, "Al, I'm excited to be interviewed on national television. I don't want to get paid."

"Tark," he said, "if you go on for nothing, you ought to wear a brassiere." (laughs) That was Al. The game went right down to the wire, and we won. The place went crazy. It was the biggest game in Long Beach State's history, and my last home game there.

I came to Las Vegas the next year, and I got here at just the right time. The program was really just starting up in a major-college way, and this town of three hundred thousand people was starved for a good team. I couldn't believe the support we received. We became the hottest ticket in town. In fact, there were stories that it was tougher to get a ticket for Rebel basketball than for Frank Sinatra. Everything seemed to center around the basketball team back then. We had great players, great fans. It was just a wonderful time in my life. I was here for 19 years, and we had a 10-year run where we won 307 games and lost 42. That's an average of 31 wins and four losses over a 10-year period. Pretty good, huh?

Of course, I was like any other coach looking for publicity. I wanted to be on television. You said we had to be willing to go on the road and play tough teams, and I said, "Hell, we'll play anybody anywhere." When you said you couldn't get anybody to play Kentucky, we said we'd play them in Lexington. What I didn't know was that it was Senior Night and they were honoring Rick Robey, who was the big star of their 1978 NCAA championship team. The place was jam-packed, they brought out Happy Chandler to sing "My Old Kentucky Home," and tears were running down people's faces. Then they introduced the Kentucky seniors, which took 10 or 15 minutes, and finally they introduced Rick Robey and his relatives, friends, neighbors, and just about everybody else in the place. It took forever, and I was sitting there thinking, "Boy, this is going to be a slaughterhouse tonight." We led at halftime, but they blew us out in the second half. That was one experience I'll never forget.

Let me tell you about how I started chewing that towel on the sidelines, which became my trademark. I was coaching at Redlands High School in California, and we were playing our championship game. It was February, but it was really hot in the gym and my mouth kept getting dry. I'd run over to a drinking fountain about 20 feet away, take a drink, and run back to the game.

Well, the game went into overtime, and I got tired of running back and forth, so I took a towel and wet it, then brought it back to the bench and put it in my mouth. That's when I won my first championship, so I did it ever since. It was more of a superstition than anything else. Of course, it didn't become a big deal until I was on television, so TVS was probably responsible for that. But you can't believe how many people talk to me about the towel. I'll be in a restaurant and somebody will send a towel over to me.

I went to those four Final Fours, and we won the NCAA Tournament in 1990, but I really think the greatest contribution I made to college basketball— far more than any win—was to make the NCAA change some of their barbaric rules about their enforcement policies and due process. If it weren't for the battles we fought, who knows what would have happened? As far as I'm concerned, they were worse than the gestapo.

Nobody had ever really fought the NCAA before. Usually when you try to fight back they drive you out of coaching, but I was fortunate to be able to hang in there. The longer I battled, the bigger the war became. To me, they were the most vindictive group in America. The greatest satisfaction I ever had was beating them in court. I'm the only guy who's ever done that. They settled with me and paid me $2.5 million because they knew they were totally wrong.

Well, the game went into overtime, and I got tired of running back and forth, so I took a towel and wet it, then brought it back to the bench and put it in my mouth.

I'll tell you one thing that concerns me about the game today. I don't understand how they can pay a college basketball coach so much more than other faculty members. It's totally out of line and can't do anything but create hard feelings toward the athletic program and athletics in general. I don't think you have to pay that kind of money. I really don't.

PART VI

Coming to You Live

When I arrived at the University of Pennsylvania in 1953, I threw my bags in my dorm room and went straight to the school radio station. It was heard only on the four-block campus, but I didn't care. I was a sportscaster. My dream had come true. During the next four years I called hundreds of basketball games, but any thought I had of becoming a professional announcer ended when I sent out more than 100 audition tapes and received only one reply, from a small station in Bradford, Pennsylvania. So I went to law school instead. One thing I learned in college was that if I owned my own company nobody could fire me, and when TVS began I did some of the broadcasting. But then I decided to fire myself and hire people who were good at it.

Nothing I did at TVS makes me prouder than the fact that we were able to hire so many great announcers, including a large number who went on to become some of the top sports broadcasters in the nation. I am only sorry that there wasn't time to interview them all, and I hope this cross section of men who made such great contributions to the development of college basketball will give some indication of the outstanding talent not only at TVS but on the other networks as well.

Dick Vitale, who grew up in the town adjacent to mine in New Jersey, was a successful coach at the University of Detroit when TVS televised some of its games, and later he coached the Detroit Pistons. He called the first college basketball game ever shown on ESPN—Wisconsin at DePaul in 1979—and has broadcast close to one thousand games since then. He has become one of the most distinctive and popular announcers in the business.

Billy Packer broadcast ACC games for many years—he told me only recently that he also sold the advertising—and has covered the NCAA Tournament for NBC and CBS for more than 30 years. It is hard to conceive of the tournament without him. As a player, Packer led Wake Forest University to the Final Four in 1962 and later served as an assistant coach at his alma mater. He only broadcast one game for TVS, but I count him as an alumnus and good friend.

I think of Jim Nantz as the new kid on the block even though he has been the play-by-play announcer for CBS' broadcasts of the Final Four since 1985. He also has covered many other events, from the Olympics to major golf championships to the NFL.

Al Michaels was a young broadcaster for the Cincinnati Reds when I hired him—I had always been a Reds fan and liked to hire their announcers—who has gone on to become one of the most versatile announcers in broadcasting history. Michaels has covered "the Miracle on Ice" at the 1980 Winter Olympics, *Monday Night Football*, the World Series, Super Bowls, and NBA and NHL championships.

Rod Hundley was one of college basketball's most prolific scorers and most colorful characters when he played for West Virginia in the fifties. After his six-year NBA career, he came to work for TVS, and I gave him only one directive: "Be yourself." He always was. Hundley has been the voice of the Utah Jazz for more than two decades and remains a free spirit and a true original. I was proud to see him elected to the Basketball Hall of Fame as a broadcaster.

John Ferguson, who called Louisiana State's football and basketball games for many years, was the first announcer I hired when TVS began its affiliation with the Southeastern Conference in 1965. He stayed with me for 18 years. No one has a better knowledge of how precarious and how hilarious those start-up years often were. Now in his mideighties, Ferguson has called me with the latest sports and broadcasting news and gossip from the South several times a year for the past four decades.

After broadcasting the first college basketball game ever shown by ESPN, Dick Vitale has gone on to call almost one thousand more. Vitale was head coach at the University of Detroit, and later the Detroit Pistons, before becoming one of the most distinctive and popular announcers in broadcasting.

CHAPTER 28

Dick Vitale on Coaching and Calling the Game

Sarasota, Florida, June 2005

How did I become a basketball announcer? Here's what happened. I went from teaching sixth grade in East Rutherford, New Jersey, to coaching the Detroit Pistons in eight years. Is that unbelievable or what? And then all of a sudden—bam!—I got fired. Twelve games into the 1979 season, Bill Davidson, who owned the Pistons, came to my house and said, "I've decided to make a change." He wanted me to be patient and understanding because he didn't think you could build in one year. But I can't be patient. I wanted to build immediately. I was my own biggest enemy, and he had to fire me.

But it was the best thing that could have happened to me. I was so intense and hated to lose so much that I really believe that if I kept coaching I'd have been a dead man at age 50. Today I'm 66 and I act about 13. (laughs) Television gave me balance in life. And I've developed such a passion for it. I look at what I have today and I just pinch myself. Seven books, movies, commercials, appearances with Bill Cosby and David Letterman, and speaking engage-

ments. I used to get $5 to speak and I was happy. Today they pay me $40,000 to $45,000. It's unbelievable. I've been very blessed.

Anyway, I went from teaching sixth grade to assistant coach at Rutgers to head coach at Detroit to athletic director to the Pistons all between 1970 and 1978. I was lucky every step of the way. I was coaching at the high school level while I was teaching. I had some great kids, and we won back-to-back state championships.

If you want to know who your friends are, just try getting fired.

Then I went to Rutgers and it was same thing. We were lucky and had some great players—I recruited Phil Sellers and Mike Dabney, who went to the Final Four in 1976. A couple years later I was hired at Detroit. Dave DeBusschere, the great Knicks star who played his college ball at Detroit, won't admit it, but he got me the interview. We created a lot of excitement, got a lot of people in the building, and started winning.

My last year, 1977, we had a great team and played Michigan in the Sweet 16. They were the No. 1 team in the nation, with Phil Hubbard and Rickey Green, and it was a big deal in Detroit because after we beat them my first year they wouldn't play us anymore during the regular season. We took them down to the wire before they beat us, and to this day I think we cost them a national title. We took so much out of them they were shocked by North Carolina, Charlotte—remember Cornbread Maxwell?—which beat them and went to the Final Four.

> "Dick, you've got three things we can never teach: your enthusiasm and energy, which are unbelievable, and your knowledge. What you don't have is a clue about TV. I'm going to assign a real pro to work with you. Trust me, Dick. Be patient. You've got a career in this."

NBC was broadcasting college basketball then, and we were playing Marquette in Milwaukee. Al McGuire was one of my idols, and who was watching us practice that day but John Wooden. I was just in awe. I got all fired up and had my players taking pictures with him and gave them an emotional speech. We ended up beating Marquette, which went on to win the national title later that season.

A year later I got fired by the Pistons. I was down and depressed. Nobody was returning my calls. If you want to know who your friends are, Eddie, just try getting fired. Then one day the phone rang, and a guy said, "Dick, you don't know me. My name is Scotty Connal. I hired Al McGuire, Billy Packer, and those other guys at NBC, and I'm in charge of this new network called ESPN. I want you to do our first national game, DePaul

and Wisconsin in Chicago." I had never broadcast a basketball game in my life, and I had no idea why he even thought of me. Scotty said, "I heard you talking to your team at that practice session in Milwaukee, and I said to myself, 'This guy's enthusiasm is really something.'"

I said, "I really appreciate it, but I still want to coach. So thank you very much and good-bye."

A week later he called again and said, "Dick, you're not doing anything. You're just sitting at home. How about it?" By then my wife could see how not having anything to do was driving me crazy, so she said, "Go do that game. Get out of here. Have some fun."

I went to Chicago and broadcast the game, and I had no clue what I was supposed to be doing. I had guys talking in my ear and I started answering them, and they said, "Shut up, you're on the air." It was awful. Plus, they were only paying me $350 a game, so you don't have to be a genius to figure out it's not a lot of money. Well, after the game, the phone rang and it was Scotty Connal. He said—I'll never forget this—"Dick, you've got three things we can never teach: your enthusiasm and energy, which are unbelievable, and your knowledge. What you don't have is a clue about TV. I'm going to assign a real pro to work with you. Trust me, Dick. Be patient. You've got a career in this."

I still had no idea what he was talking about, but he assigned me to work with Jim Simpson, who is a pro's pro, and we spent that year together. Then I started applying to colleges again—I really wanted to coach—and Chet Simmons, who was the president of ESPN, called me and said, "Don't do it, Dick. Don't leave. You've got a chance to make a lot of money, have a lot of fame."

I didn't know what he was talking about either, and I never really understood until 1983, when I went to my first Final Four for ESPN in Albuquerque, New Mexico. That's the year Jimmy Valvano cut down the nets. Well, I walked into the arena and everybody wanted to take my picture. They were yelling, "Dicky V! Dicky V!" I was thinking, "What is this?" when

Scotty Connal came over and said, "Didn't I tell you? You connect."

I always loved John Wooden. I remember that as a young coach I wrote him a letter and got one back from him along with his Pyramid of Success. I was like a kid in a candy store running around my sixth-grade class showing it to everybody and saying, "This is from John Wooden!" So of course I ended up working with Digger Phelps, and I must have heard him say about 5 million times, "Hey, Dick, did you hear about the time we beat UCLA when they'd won 88 in a row?"

I tease Digger about how when I was at Detroit, he wouldn't give me the time of day. He'd just walk right by me. Then all of a sudden, I was on ESPN, and we were the best of buddies. I said, "How come you didn't say hello to me when we were coaching?" and he said, "Now we're equals." (laughs) Or I'll be sitting on the set and he'll say, "Take a look at those

And March Madness is a whole month of absolute bedlam. For one month, there's no sporting event that captures the imagination the way it does.

cuff links," and he'll roll up his sleeve to show, "White House, President George Bush." And I'll say, "Well, look at my cuff links. I got them at Kmart." (laughs) We really have a lot of fun working together.

You started all this, Eddie. And you did a great job initially. I think the move to ESPN, which gave America the chance to see colleges from all over the country they'd never had a chance to see before, was so important. Prior to 1979 it was always Kentucky and North Carolina, Indiana and UCLA on the weekend. We set the table all year by letting people see the Davids *and* the Goliaths, and by the time March Madness came along there was such a fever pitch that even people who didn't watch the

games during the season got turned on to it. They saw the passion.

And March Madness is a whole month of absolute bedlam. For one month, there's no sporting event that captures the imagination the way it does. Think of all the unknown teams that make things happen you never could imagine. A Bucknell goes out and beats Kansas. A Vermont beats Syracuse. These teams are not going to win four or five in a row, but for one given night there's the magic of an upset, where a three-star player on a scale of five can play with incredible passion and his team can shock the world. That's the one thing that makes college basketball compelling: it's not four out of seven, where the cream gets to the top. One bad night and the party is over.

People say to me, "You're always singing the praises of coaches." OK, maybe I am. Maybe I do it because I've *been* a coach. I know what the locker room is like. I know what they go through—the pain and the hurt, how difficult it is when things don't go well. And I know good coaching when I see it too.

I've watched Bobby Knight. They can talk about his X's and O's. They can talk about his motivational ability and about his screaming too, because they don't like some of the things he's done. And knowing Bobby, there are things he's done that if he could do them over, he would. But we've all done some wrong things, haven't we? I love so much what he stands for—getting the most out of people, doing things the right way. What's wrong with asking kids to play their hearts out? What's wrong with asking kids to go to class and act like a man? I'll tell you, Indiana is synonymous with Bob Knight, and I'm still having a hard time with the fact that he is not there anymore. That thing should have been resolved. The man should have finished his career at Indiana.

If you'd ever told me that basketball would allow so many people to become millionaires, I never would have believed you. I like the fact it's all happened to me by being positive, doing things the right way, smiling, and being nice to people. Sometimes, people get on you, though. My daughter called me up from work one day and said, "Dad, they've got an NCAA Tournament pool going. Give me some tips." So I gave her some tips, and she called me back later and said, "Dad, I finished last. That shows what you know."

CHAPTER 29

Billy Packer: How the NCAA Tournament Became the Greatest Show on Earth

St. Louis, Missouri, April 2005

My first year broadcasting the tournament for CBS was 1982, which I think may have been the first time we ran the selection show on television. That was one of the things that really helped to build interest, the fact that people could fill out their ballots as the teams were announced. And that was the year Michael Jordan hit his big shot to beat Georgetown in the Superdome in New Orleans. To me, that was where what we now know as March Madness started.

Maybe the big star today is the kid you never heard of yesterday. Maybe that was the only time in his life he's going to have a moment like that, but it was the day you were watching.

With all due respect to the NFL and the Super Bowl, I don't think anything touches the grass roots of American sports the way the NCAA Tournament does. There are more than 300 schools that have the potential to be in the tournament right up through the final weekend of the postseason conference tournaments. There have been some huge upsets in those tournaments, so everybody has a chance—even the teams in last place in their conferences. People say the tournament should be expanded, but I think it's expanded now because everybody has a shot at it through their conference tournaments.

It used to be so different. I had arguments with John Wooden, whom I admire so much, because I was in favor of multiple teams from conferences getting into the tournament and he thought only the champion should go. This goes back to when Southern California was the second- or third-best team in the country and couldn't go because UCLA was No. 1. He's kind of mellowed on that now, I think. Allowing multiple teams from conferences is another thing that really made the tournament take off.

I will say, though, that the UCLA dynasty was extremely important in building interest in the game.

People who weren't around in the era of those incredible teams don't remember how big Goliath really was in those days. I'm not sure you could have gotten NBC to buy college basketball then if it hadn't been for all the interest in UCLA and the way it dominated the sport. We'll never see teams like Kareem Abdul-Jabbar's and Bill Walton's again. Even today you wouldn't want to think about going up against them.

Another important innovation in the tournament was moving teams outside their territory in the regionals. In the old days you only had to play against teams in your area, which might have been from some of the weaker conferences, so some teams had a big advantage. And you might even get to play them on your home floor, which was really unfair.

The NBA psychology says that if you have individual statistics then you've accomplished something. But it's when you make your teammates better, and when you win games and championships, that you become great.

Here's another thing I think has helped build the tournament over the years: college basketball is not built around any individual player. The base that has been built is around a team, around watching a bunch of guys battle. Maybe the big star today is the kid you never heard of yesterday. Maybe that was the only time in his life he's going to have a moment like that, but it was the day you were watching. If you're building a sport, you need your base to keep increasing the fans' appreciation of the game, not an individual player.

The NBA, on the other hand, has gone in a different direction, turning basketball into an entertainment commodity. I think it has turned off people who are interested in the sport for itself. It's not that I don't like the pro game—obviously they are superior athletes—but I think that the people running

professional basketball have lost sight of the fact that it's a sport. It's basically looked upon as a marketing commodity. David Stern is really the CEO of an international marketing group. He's done a great job, but I think there should be a balance, a way to redirect the sport in a healthy way.

They talk about the NBA being a player's league, and that's wrong. Basketball is a team game, and when you lose sight of that, when you have individuals acting and being treated as if they are the sport, then you've got a problem. The NBA psychology says that if you have individual statistics then you've accomplished something. But it's when you make your teammates better, and when you win games and championships, that you become great. That's what John Wooden taught—everything he did was team-oriented even though he had phenomenal players—and that's what's missing from the NBA.

In fairness to the NBA, though, we all fell into this trap a little. A group of great athletes came along to college basketball at the perfect time. You had Larry Bird, who loved to kick your rear end. You had Magic Johnson, who was so entertaining. You had Michael Jordan, who was the ultimate combination of both of them. These three guys transcended the game, sure, but they also brought teamwork to it. They were not selfish in terms of how the game was played. That was an incredible era led by three guys who were special to the history of the sport.

I worked with Al McGuire for many seasons as a broadcaster, and when it came to understanding people and situations, he was the most brilliant person I ever met. Al was really a very simple guy in terms of knowing what he wanted to do. As a coach he knew how to work a crowd and get it all excited. The only one who equaled him at that was Digger Phelps, who could really motivate a team and rile a crowd. Digger could orchestrate a situation as well as anybody who's ever coached, I think.

Dale Brown was good at that at LSU too, and Mike Krzyzewski also knows how to milk a situation. You

Billy Packer has broadcast college basketball for more than 30 years and become synonymous with the NCAA Tournament. As a player at Wake Forest, Packer played in the Final Four and later was an assistant coach at his alma mater.

know that song "One Shining Moment" they play after the NCAA championship game? Well, before winning one of his championships, Mike had a television station make a version of it as if Duke had already won and the players were celebrating. He showed

National recruiting was not really in vogue in the sixties, and schools basically recruited in their own geographical territories. But after the 1957 NCAA championship game between North Carolina and Kansas, ACC basketball was shown on television. For the first time parents got a chance to see their kids play.

it to them back at the hotel so they would see what it would feel like to be up on the big screen in the arena after winning the title. That was completely different from John Wooden, who didn't believe in getting a team up too high for a game. He believed that balance and consistency, playing without peaks and valleys, is more conducive to being a champion.

I'll tell you who I think might have had a more positive effect on how college coaches are recognized by the NCAA than anyone else, and that's Jerry

Tarkanian. He stood up and fought them, and a lot of things about the enforcement process and the right to a fair hearing were changed because he had the guts to do that. Had it not been for Tarkanian, those changes might never have been made.

I know the ACC is the one conference that TVS didn't broadcast, but television was extremely important to its development too. National recruiting was not really in vogue in the sixties, and schools basically recruited in their own geographical territories. But after the 1957 NCAA championship game between North Carolina and Kansas, ACC basketball was shown on television. For the first time parents got a chance to see their kids play. If you lived in West Virginia, you could see your kid play at Duke.

Then they started showing the games outside the conference area. You could see ACC games in Philadelphia, for instance. Well, when kids from the Northeast saw this, a lot of them started going to ACC schools, and by the time the other conferences caught up, through TVS' influence, the ACC schools had already gotten a big foothold. The television exposure also led to the ACC tournament, which helped generate a revenue stream nobody else had.

Did you know there was a guy in Indiana who owned the rights to the term *March Madness*? He claimed the NCAA infringed on it, and I think there was a lawsuit, but finally they settled it. It's become a staple of American society now, hasn't it? You can't imagine life without it.

CHAPTER 30

Jim Nantz on His Shining Moments

St. Louis, Missouri, April 2005

I always wanted to be a broadcaster. When I was growing up, I studied the announcers in the big games more than I watched the players. For instance, I know that Gary Bender called the NCAA championship game in 1982, when Michael Jordan's jumper won for North Carolina over Georgetown, the North Carolina State–Houston game the next year, and Georgetown over Houston in 1984. Then Brent Musburger called the game six years in a row.

I would record the television broadcasts and listen to the announcers, which wasn't easy because there were no VCRs then. I would wrap a mike around the dial used to change the channel and drop it down to the audio output. That way I could record the play-by-play, the opening teases, the music, everything. I would listen to the announcers and dream of being one of them. I still have all those old tapes. TVS was a big deal then, and one of the guys I listened to was Hot Rod Hundley, who was one of the top announcers, never dreaming that one year out of college I'd

be doing games with him. I went to work for the CBS affiliate in Salt Lake City, and along with anchoring the news, I did the Utah Jazz games with Rod.

The fans are so passionate, the bands are playing, the building is filled with so much hope. You're at the Final Four, springtime is in the air, and everybody is convinced that it's their year to win the national championship.

My first Final Four was in 1981. I was a senior at Houston, and Guy Lewis gave me my start in television when I hosted his coach's show. We did the final installment from the Final Four in Philadelphia. That was the year Ronald Reagan was shot, and they had to decide whether to go on with the game or not. I went to my next Final Four in 1985, and now I've been to 20 straight tournaments for CBS.

There aren't many people who can say they were ahead of their time in broadcasting, Eddie, but you're one who can. One guy wrote that you created a monster, but that makes it sound like it's something bad. You created something wonderful. Who could have imagined there would be this kind of interest? CBS is now on the hook through 2013 for $6 billion. That's just astonishing, isn't it?

What I love about college basketball is the purity of it. I know a lot of people hear that and say, there are so many ills in the game, what are you talking about? But I really believe it. The fans are so passionate, the bands are playing, the building is filled with so much hope. You're at the Final Four, springtime is in the air, and everybody is convinced that it's their year to win the national championship.

I don't spend a lot of time with the players during the tournament—the sports information directors give me all the anecdotal stuff—and sometimes I wonder if they even know who I am. But when I see them again in later years, I can't begin to tell you how much they connect me with those halcyon college days.

You have to have some kind of emotional attachment to appreciate it. I'll always remember April 4, 1983, when my alma mater, Houston, lost to North Carolina State. It really crushed me, and it's burned in my mind forever. There could never be any loss in sports that could be more devastating to me. And I dare say all those players who were on the floor, like Hakeem Olajuwon and Clyde Drexler, have replayed that game in their minds more than any other. They went on to win championships in the NBA, but that one really had to hurt. If Shaquille O'Neal loses the seventh game of the NBA Finals, he has 30 million

reasons to be happy when he wakes up the next day. But for these kids, there is such an emotional attachment to the university, to the people in that community, to the kids on campus, to the other players on the team. And to know they'll never go into that locker room again is the biggest hurt of all.

I hope I can express this well because this is the important part. College basketball is a transient sport—by that I mean the players move on after four years—so the losses are more hurtful or devastating than anything else I've seen in team sports. You can't compare it to college football because football doesn't have a playoff system. In basketball, when a team ends its season, it is so final. I'm never going to see Chuck Hayes play in a Kentucky uniform again, that kind of thing. It's crushing, devastating. There's more pain in the loss than anything else I can think of.

I feel it every time I broadcast an NCAA Tournament game and I see a senior walk off the floor at the end. He knows he's not going to win, and maybe his coach is on the sideline waiting to give him a hug. You can't even begin to describe everything that has gone into that kid's life the last four years. It was the first time he's been away from home, and the coach is his guardian in a way, and now suddenly that relationship is over. There will always be a bond, but he'll never be on the floor playing for that man again.

After I had been doing the tournament for a while I saw how the players all carried themselves in a sort of cool manner. But that doesn't mean they haven't all dreamt that someday they'd be down on that floor after winning a title. I don't spend a lot of time with the players during the tournament—the sports information directors give me all the anecdotal stuff—and sometimes I wonder if they even know who I am. But when I see them again in later years, I can't begin to tell you how much they connect me with those halcyon college days. They come up like I'm a long lost brother and say, "Gosh, those days were great. I remember the game you called. You said this and you said that."

Jim Nantz watches the NCAA Tournament in CBS' New York studios with Billy Packer. Nantz has called the play-by-play for the Final Four since 1985.

I got to know Chris Webber quite well in his days at the University of Michigan and he said, "I can remember the feeling of every game, every locker-room speech." The players all have a wistfulness in the way they talk about playing as though they wish they could tap into it again. They might have financial security now, but they don't have the purity they had in college.

He started singing "One Shining Moment" and I let him go on, and then I said, "All right, thank you. Let's go back up to the studio." I knew they would be running the song *that* night.

And even some of the players who do go to the NBA never have moments like they did in college. You take a guy like Tony Delk, who played on Kentucky's national championship team in 1996. He made seven three-pointers in the title game and was named Most Outstanding Player of the tournament. He's in the NBA now, but when is the last time you saw him play a game on television? But when he hit those seven three-pointers, everybody saw it.

Let me tell you a story about that song we play at the end of the championship game. It's called "One Shining Moment," and we ran it for a number of years. I always liked it. But in 1993, when we were in the Superdome in New Orleans, where North Carolina won the championship, I started hearing some rumblings that CBS was getting a little tired of it.

Well, Billy Packer and I were on the floor after the game waiting to interview Dean Smith, and the whole team was behind us. They cut away for a commercial, and while we waited for them to come back to us, I heard one of the players, Pat Sullivan, singing the song. I turned to him and said, "Hey, Pat, would you do me a favor? When we come back, I'm going to stick a mike in your face. Would you sing, 'One Shining Moment?'"

He said, "Are you serious?"

I said I was, and then they came back to us. We interviewed Dean Smith and Donald Williams, who was named the Most Outstanding Player. Then I said, "Hold on, here's Pat Sullivan. Pat, do you have something to say?"

He started singing "One Shining Moment" and I let him go on, and then I said, "All right, thank you. Let's go back up to the studio." I knew they would be running the song *that* night. (laughs)

And just to show you how much it caught on, a couple of years later we were in the Hoosier Dome in Indianapolis when Arizona beat Kentucky in overtime, and all of a sudden "One Shining Moment" started blasting out. Everybody in the dome paused, froze, and looked up at the screen. Then I looked over at the Arizona kids and they were all arm in arm, looking up at the screen, watching it together. It was such a rich moment. I think it's my favorite memory of the NCAA Tournament. I get goose bumps right now just thinking about it.

CHAPTER 31

Al Michaels: The Education of a Sportscaster

San Antonio, Texas, June 2005

When I first started broadcasting for TVS, Eddie, I could never figure you out. In the late sixties you were paying me $250 per game and putting me up in Holiday Inns. But every flight I took was first class. I never understood it. Why would you fly me first class and put me up in a dump? I guess I figured I was really getting about $1,700 per game because that was the price of a first-class plane ticket.

I know this is open to argument, but I have always felt that UCLA's 88-game winning streak and John Wooden's run of titles belongs near the very top, or even at the top, of any list of sports accomplishments.

You had me broadcast a doubleheader down in Charlotte, North Carolina. As soon as I got there you said I'd be doing two games and a show between games too, which meant I'd be on two and a half times as long as for one game. But you said you were only going to pay me $375. I said, "Wait a second, you should be paying me a premium." But you said no, the second game came at a discount. That's how you had enough money to buy the White Sox—by hiring announcers at a discount. It wasn't until a few years later, after I left TVS, that I was able to make any money. (laughs)

I succeeded Dick Enberg doing UCLA games in Los Angeles in 1973, for what turned out to be John Wooden's last two seasons. Bill Walton was there then, and Jamaal Wilkes, and it was a wonderful experience. After Notre Dame broke UCLA's 88-game winning streak, which Dick broadcast on NBC, they had a rematch at Pauley Pavilion the next week. I called that game with Tommy Hawkins. UCLA just killed them—no contest—and I interviewed you at halftime. What a setup. Imagine taking a young announcer and compromising his journalistic integrity like that. It almost ended my career. (laughs)

Right, and tomorrow you'll be promoting Desperate Housewives *at the NBA finals. (laughs)*

I know this is open to argument, but I have always felt that UCLA's 88-game winning streak and John Wooden's run of titles belongs near the very top, or even at the top, of any list of sports accomplishments. Now we have revisionist historians who want to diminish what John did by saying that it was different then, that you could do something like that then. There are some who never want to give John his due. That's crap as far as I'm concerned. What John did is unparalleled in sports. We never saw it before, and we will not see it again.

One thing that worries me a little about what's happening today is the complete dumbing down of sports.

I'm one of those who thinks that John Wooden has not only been a phenomenal man in terms of what he's done as a coach, but as a human being as well. I think the influence he has had on so many people is extraordinary. I'm awed not only by what he has done as a coach, but the way he has looked at life and the way he has influenced young people. Thank God this man has lived into his midnineties, and I hope we get a lot more years out of him.

It's amazing how much college basketball has grown, isn't it? It used to be just a regional thing. But now there are so many teams getting into the tournament—all these schools we didn't know existed back then that have come out of nowhere.

What's great, I think, are all these office pools where you have secretaries and executives, people who don't even know there are five guys on the court, putting a few bucks down. I don't think it's gambling as much as social interaction. When you put $20 into an office pool, that's not gambling. But the fact that so many people care shows you what a spectacle the game has become. That's why people love sports, I think, because of the spectacle, the entertainment value.

One thing that worries me a little about what's happening today is the complete dumbing down of sports. You hear these sports talk shows where the host can't speak the language, and the fans who call in are loud and obnoxious. It's just plain stupid.

The difference between now and when I started is that with the advent of cable and publications like *USA Today*, a plethora of information is available, almost too much sometimes. They break the game down 24 hours a day, day after day, and they run out of things to say. You can vaporize the game by breaking it down that much. So I've taken to stepping back a little, telling myself that a lot of people will tune in knowing very little about what they're going to see. You never want to insult the real fan, but you don't want to lose the casual fan, either. And you have to approach it from a personal standpoint because ESPN is on two hours before the game, and they're going to be on two hours after the game.

I'm a lucky guy. As a kid growing up, I always loved baseball, and I got to do a World Series for the first time when I was very young. Then I went on to do eight of them. And I was always fascinated by the Olympics, and I wound up doing five of them, including, fortunately, maybe the greatest sporting event of the 20th century—the "Miracle on Ice" at Lake Placid. I've done the NBA Finals, the Stanley Cup Finals, the Kentucky Derby, and the Indianapolis 500, and I've loved all of it. I still think you owe me for those college basketball doubleheaders, though. (laughs)

CHAPTER 32

Rod Hundley: Spinning the Ball and Spinning Tales

New York City, New York, March 2004

My friends call me Rod, but my professional name is Hot Rod Hundley. I even call myself that when I'm doing a commercial: "Hi, I'm Hot Rod Hundley."

I got the nickname when I was a freshman in college because I played a fancy style of basketball like Pete Maravich did a decade later. I dribbled the ball behind my back and did a lot of other fancy stuff, so the sportswriters started calling me Hot Rod and it stuck. That started in 1954, so they've been calling me Hot Rod for more than 50 years.

When I was a kid in Charleston, West Virginia, I went to the YMCA, where all the good players hung out, and I had to sneak in because I couldn't afford the two or three bucks it cost. We'd play games where the winners stayed on the court and the losers went to the end of the line. They had handball courts in the gym, so while I was waiting I'd go over and throw the ball at the wall. I'd throw it behind my back, catch it, spin it, dribble it through my legs, roll it down my back, all those things. I carried it over to junior high and high school, and then I went to West

Virginia, where I became notorious for playing that way.

Fred Schaus was my coach at West Virginia—he later coached me for three years with the Lakers—and he always told me, "We'd better be 20 points ahead when you start doing those things. As long as we're 20 ahead, I don't care if you drop-kick the ball out of the building." (laughs) I never forgot that. But I never jeopardized a win, and I had a good college career. We won 65 games during my three years, and I averaged almost 25 points per game. And because we played a big schedule, I got to play at Madison Square Garden and made the All-America team. Life was good.

I loved being compared to Maravich when he came along, but there was really no contest. I broadcast his games with the New Orleans Jazz, and he was the best ball-handler and the best showman ever. I remember talking about him to Isiah Thomas, who was an incredible ball-handler people sometimes compared to Pete, and he said, "Are you kidding me? Pete made the ball disappear." He said nobody touched Pete.

Rod Hundley was one of college basket-ball's top scorers and most flamboyant personalities when he played at West Virginia University. After playing in the NBA, Hundley began a lengthy broadcast-ing career that led to his induction into the Basketball Hall of Fame. Photograph of Hundley as a player courtesy of Eddie Einhorn.

Pete was 6'5", and in those days, most guys that tall weren't that smooth. But he was as graceful as he could be when he handled the ball. He played for his father at Louisiana State, which had to be tough. I don't think anybody should play for their father because everybody is going to think the coach is prejudiced in favor of his son. But every year at LSU, Pete's scoring average went up—43.8, 44.2, 44.5. That's just amazing to me. There was no stopping the guy. You'd throw a zone at him or a man-to-man defense, or you'd triple cover him—it didn't matter. Whatever you did, he'd *average* 44 points. And do you know how many times he passed the ball off when he could have made the shot? He was a great passer and a great middle man on the fast break.

I loved being compared to Maravich when he came along, but there was really no contest. I broadcast his games with the New Orleans Jazz, and he was the best ball-handler and the best showman ever.

The sad part of Pete's career was that he never played on a good team—at LSU or as a professional. And he had mood swings. His mother committed suicide when he was with the Jazz in New Orleans, and it really shattered him. He was just lost. His shooting percentage went down.

But he fought back, and in the end he started living a Christian life. He quit drinking, became a vegetarian, drank goat milk, and started doing motivational speaking to kids. In fact, he died after speaking to some kids at a church in Pasadena. He went out and played with them and collapsed at age 40.

I guess the most exciting game I ever covered was the one TVS did in 1974 that ended UCLA's 88-game winning streak at Notre Dame. It was after another loss to Notre Dame, in 1971, that UCLA *started* the streak, and Dick Enberg and I broadcast that game too. The amazing thing about the streak is that UCLA didn't play a kids' schedule. They played the top teams in the country, and for three years they just mowed people down.

The scene at Notre Dame before the streak ended was just incredible. Dick and I were out on the floor before the broadcast, and UCLA was warming up. Then Notre Dame came out of the locker room and the band started playing, "Cheer, Cheer for Old Notre Dame." Bill Walton walked out of the line where he was shooting layups and came over, balled his fist, and looked us right in the eye. "This is what it's all about," he said. "Let's get this game *going!*"

I can still see Dwight Clay making the shot from the right-hand corner with a few seconds left to win the game and make the crowd go crazy. I don't know if you could hear us over the air because we couldn't hear ourselves. Then UCLA got the ball to Walton, and he had to hurry a shot and he missed it. The game ended, and the fans stormed onto the court like bees going after honey. They were all over each other.

After the game I had to get back to Chicago in a hurry if I was going to get home to Phoenix that night, and John Wooden let me on the team bus, which was a very nice thing for him to do. Here were all these players dressed in coats and ties, and they all had tears in their eyes because their winning streak was over. But Wooden talked to them very quietly, like a father talking to his kids, and I thought he said all the right things. He said, "I'm very proud of you. I want you to know that. We've got to go home now and get ready for our next game." It was amazing to me how he could take a situation like that in stride.

I always liked broadcasting Notre Dame's games. I used to interview Digger Phelps, and we'd kid each other. He'd be wearing these expensive clothes, and I'd say things like, "Nice suit, Digger. Did you get two pair of pants with it?" And he'd say, "That's a beautiful tie. How come you couldn't find one to match your outfit?" This would be going out over the air, and we'd be laughing at each other.

I wore some crazy outfits those days, Eddie, and you didn't discourage me. I wore anything with red in it, or green and gold. I had leather pants and leisure suits and blue-and-yellow patent leather shoes with white on top. Basically, I wore anything that would call attention to me. I was living in Phoenix at the time, where I had a deal with a big-and-tall men's store, and after one game, Dick Enberg, who always wore a blue blazer and gray slacks, signed off by saying, "We'd like to thank the big-and-tall men's store in Phoenix for Rod Hundley's wardrobe, and Teens and Tots for providing Eddie Einhorn's daughter's clothes, and personally I'd like to thank the Salvation Army for mine." I was sitting there crying because I was laughing so hard.

Here is one of my most embarrassing moments as a broadcaster. We were doing the NCAA Eastern Regionals in Charlotte, North Carolina, and Penn lost to Providence in the first game. I went over to interview Chuck Daly, who was coaching Penn and who I'd known for years, and I said, "Hi, Rod Hundley here with coach—" and I drew a blank. I said, "I can't remember your name," and I started laughing. And Chuck said, "I hope the athletic director has forgotten my name." Chuck still kids me about it. Every time I see him, he says, "I'm Chuck Daly," and I say, "Yes, you are."

I always wanted to be a broadcaster after I quit playing. I worked with Chick Hearn on the Lakers broadcasts in Los Angeles—he was a master and I learned a lot from him—but I left because I knew if I stayed I'd be Chick's analyst forever. And not talking much, either. (laughs) I got the job with the Jazz, and one day the Lakers were in town. Chick came over and said, "Hey, I've got a lot of friends in Salt Lake City, and they tell me you've been stealing some of my lines." And I said, "Not some of them, *all* of them." He loved it.

I never made the Hall of Fame as a player, but last year they put me in the broadcasters division of the Basketball Hall of Fame in Springfield, Massachusetts. My three daughters got to be a part of the ceremonies, and they were so proud of me. I was so happy I had tears in my eyes. I thought, "This is the ultimate."

CHAPTER 33

John Ferguson on the Legend of Pete Maravich

Baton Rouge, Louisiana, December 2003

I was born in northern Louisiana, and after going to school at Louisiana Tech I went to work for a large radio station in Shreveport. After World War II, which I spent flying military aircraft in India, China, and Burma, I thought it would be a good idea to get an advanced degree. I went to Louisiana State, where they were looking for somebody to announce football on the radio. I got the job, broadcast games for three years while I was going to grad school, and then did games all over the Southwestern Conference until I came back to LSU, where I worked from 1961 through 1985. That was the heyday of college football on the radio, and I felt fortunate to be there.

Basketball was around at that time too, but it was not the popular sport football was. LSU played basketball in the Cow Barn here on campus, which doubled as a rodeo arena. It had a capacity of about nine or ten thousand people, and a lot of times the crowds weren't very large. I remember the first time TVS broadcast one of our games, and the cameras were on the north side of the building. You had everybody move to the south end of the court to make it look like a sellout.

Except for Vanderbilt and Kentucky, which were always good places to play, the gyms in the conference were all pretty old and dilapidated back then. Alabama, Mississippi, and Mississippi State all played

During my first year broadcasting basketball I think I was paid $15 per game, and then I got a big raise to $25.

in what were nothing more than Quonset huts, really. They had their fun, though. I'll never forget going to the Mississippi State gym in Starkville, Mississippi, of all places, and all of a sudden a 13-piece dance orchestra started playing at halftime. It was really good music too, and all I could think was, why did people make fun of Starkville?

Now, of course, everybody has marvelous new arenas. I remember Joe Dean, who announced a lot of games with me, saying that you were responsible for that, Eddie. All of a sudden, people woke up and said, "Hey, we're on regional, or even national, television. We've got a chance to make some money with this sport and gain some recognition." So the next thing you know, LSU, Ole Miss, Mississippi State, Georgia, and Florida all built brand-new arenas. And Kentucky moved into Rupp Arena. They all make big money from television now, of course. You created a monster for them by making them build quality facilities. And it's happened all over the country now too.

During my first year broadcasting basketball I think I was paid $15 per game, and then I got a big raise to $25. And I did my own engineering, arranged for the telephone lines, and did all the setting up. Just to show you how basketball rated back then, when LSU went to the Final Four in 1953, I had to do a real selling job to our station manager just to get him to let me go. I remember going into the main arena in Kansas City, and there were 25 other guys there broadcasting the game at the same time because nobody had the exclusive rights. It became a battle to see who could talk loud enough so viewers wouldn't hear somebody else in the background like an echo. Again, I did all the announcing and engineering myself and made $25 a game.

Bob Pettit, a great All-American, and Joe Dean, who was an All-Conference guard, were on that LSU team. Later I ended up broadcasting with both of them. Bob was incredibly popular, and he is still revered as one of LSU's great players. He was one of the most graceful players the game has ever known. He had a reverse layup along the baseline that was a thing of beauty. Everywhere we went together people wanted to take pictures with him and get his autograph. And Joe became one of the most popular announcers in the South. When a player made a long shot, he'd say, "String music" in his gravely voice, and it became his trademark. Even today people will see him on the street and say, "String music." Later he became the LSU athletic director.

One of the things you had going for you was that when you offered regional college basketball broadcasts to stations in the South, they needed programming. And you were giving them shows with local flavor at very little cost because you sold the commercial time yourself. I don't think any of those stations thought it would become as big as it did. But you also came along at a good time because the game was really blossoming. I remember Joe Dean telling me that you had a lot to do with improving the quality of college basketball. You'd bring Kentucky into schools and Kentucky would win by 40 points. It was embarrassing to be on TV and lose like that. So schools would say, "Wait a minute, we need more players here." They wanted to be on TV for the exposure, but they didn't want to get beaten like that.

The crowd really got on him, so every time he made a long shot or one of his fancy plays, he ran past the part of the crowd that was making the most noise and gave them the finger.

The one player who had the most to do with showing what college basketball could be on television was Pete Maravich. In my opinion, Pete is the greatest player this game has ever seen with the ball in his hand. He was easily the equal of Michael Jordan, although defensively he didn't concentrate all that much. He would spin the ball on his finger or dribble it between his legs or double-clutch and stay in the air forever. When he was a freshman here at LSU, people would fill up the Cow Barn to watch the freshmen play and then leave when the varsity game began.

One of the most interesting games I ever broadcast was in 1970, when we were in Alabama. Pete was playing hurt, but he was just incredible. He scored 47 points in the second half and ended up with 69 points, which was the NCAA record at the time. The crowd really got on him, so every time he made a long shot or one of his fancy plays, he ran past the part of the crowd that was making the most noise and gave them the finger.

What he didn't know was that a lot of players on the Alabama football team were sitting in that part of the arena. So after the game there was a huge fight on the floor involving at least 600 or 700 people. It was really getting out of hand until the campus and state police managed to get things under control. The SEC officials asked us not to show the fight on television, and we didn't. We just sat there and talked about other things and alluded to the fact that there was a problem on the court without showing it.

Another game that same season was when Kentucky came to the Cow Barn to play LSU. That was one of the games you broadcast, and I think it may have been the first time Pete had been seen on national television. I remember Joe Dean asked you how many stations you had signed up for the game, and you said more than 200. You blanketed the country.

Joe Dean and I were on the sidelines before the game, and Joe interviewed Press Maravich, Pete's father, who was the LSU coach. Joe asked him what they were going to do in the game. Press said, "Joe, our offense is Pete, and we're going to give him the ball and follow what he does. If he's on, it will be a hell of a game."

Then I interviewed Adolph Rupp and asked him, "Coach, what do you people at Kentucky plan to do with this big offensive power?" And Rupp said, "John, there is no player in the game like Pete Maravich. We know he puts on a show, and we want to see the show too. We're going to let him do what he wants. We're just going to stop the other four players if we can."

Pete was incredible in that game. He was making shots from everywhere. At times it appeared as if his jumper was going 100 feet in the air, all the way up to the rafters. And nine times out of ten, it would come down and hit the bottom of the net. He

ended up with 64 points. LSU's fast break was great that day too, but Kentucky was better. They just had more depth. Dan Issel had 51 points, and Kentucky won 121–105. I remember that game as if it were yesterday. I thought we were on the cutting edge of a momentous event in college basketball because people were watching it nationwide. To me, it was an NBA game times 10, just a fabulous show.

We broadcast some other wild games too. We were in Alabama once, and one of their players started yelling at someone on the other team. C. M. Newton, the Alabama coach, stopped the game. He called the player over and said, "What are you doing? We don't talk to members of the other team during the game."

And the player said, "But Coach, I have to."

"Why do you have to?"

"Because the guy is spitting in my face." (laughs)

Then there was the time LSU was playing at Kentucky at the old Memorial Coliseum, and a lot of fouls were being called against LSU. So Dale Brown, who was coaching LSU, went out to midcourt, took off his coat, and put it right on the floor. He said, "If you're going to beat me like this, then just take the coat off my back and beat me that way too."

TVS once sent me to Madison, Wisconsin, for a tournament where Marquette was playing. Connie Alexander was the other broadcaster, and Al McGuire called us over and said, "This is what's going to happen." He started painting scenarios of how he would do certain things in certain situations. For instance, he said if a guy committed an unexpected foul, Al would pose for us in one way. And if a player made a shot to tie the game or break a tie, this is what his reaction would be and the director should be ready for a close-up. So we had a camera on him every moment. What a showman Al was. I mean, who would think of something like that—planning out in advance how you were going to react and telling the television broadcasters?

It's hard to overstate the influence some of those old-time coaches had. One time we were broadcasting at Mississippi State, and they had fallen behind in the game. The crowd just went berserk. The officials couldn't control them, and it was really getting a little scary. Well, Babe McCarthy, the Mississippi State coach, got up, walked over to the public-address podium, picked up the microphone, and said, "We're trying to play this game, and we can't play it if you're too unruly. *Keep quiet!*" You could hear a pin drop for the rest of the night.

"We're trying to play this game, and we can't play it if you're too unruly. *Keep quiet!*"

Not everybody liked the coaches as a group, though. I remember talking with Boyd McWhorter, the SEC commissioner, who never really cared much for basketball. He thought it was vastly oversold. He said, "John, if you turned the world over to basketball coaches for 24 hours, the universe would be in hopeless chaos." (laughs) I'm not sure that's true, but it might be partially.

TVS had us covering games all over the South, and sometimes it could get pretty interesting getting from one place to the other. Once we did a game in Kentucky then had to drive to the Cincinnati airport approximately 65 miles away. It was a snowy afternoon, and I had an hour and a half to catch my plane, so I figured I had to pick 'em up and put 'em down. About halfway there I got stopped by the Kentucky Highway Patrol, which was hiding in one of the revetments along the highway. Luckily, the officer recognized me and said, "John, why are you traveling so fast?" I explained the situation, and he said, "Follow me." He took me all the way to Kentucky with his lights flashing. When we got to the airport, he said, "Don't worry about your car. I'll send you the receipt." And he took my rental car, turned it in, signed the papers, and sent me the receipt in the mail.

Another time I wasn't so lucky. You had sent us to Oxford, Mississippi, for a Friday night game, and we had to drive to Nashville for a Vanderbilt game the next afternoon. Joe Dean was driving, and we drove up through the rolling hills of north Mississippi and into Tennessee. With all due respect to Joe, he's a heavy-footed driver, and we were going 90, 100 miles per hour late at night. But we were awake and having a good time when suddenly we came over a hill and down at the bottom was a creek and a bridge—and 10 police cars waiting for us. They recognized us and took us to a small town. By then, it was about 1:00 in the morning. Joe said, "What do we owe you? Let us pay you, and we'll get on out of here."

But they wouldn't talk to us, wouldn't say a thing. I was so tired that it didn't really bother me, but you don't do that to Joe. He got angry and his face turned red, but they wouldn't pay any attention to him. They kept us there all night long and never charged us with a thing. They just wanted to keep us from driving so fast at night. At 5:30 in the morning they let us go, and it was all we could do to get to Nashville, take a bath, and go to the arena. That was an interesting night.

Another time, I was following Joe through Georgia—we had two hours to get to the Atlanta airport—and we were going at least 95 miles per hour. We came around a curve, and there were two police cars. Joe didn't slow down, and we went on for 15 or 20 miles before they pulled us over. They charged us $75, which I don't think was legal, but we were happy to pay it. They said, "We're going to let you guys go because we know you have to make a plane." And Joe said, "Don't follow us." They didn't, and we made the plane.

I believe the biggest change in basketball since we started doing telecasts is the introduction of the black player. When I started broadcasting, there was one black player in the conference, at Vanderbilt. And now so many of the players are black. I think television had

I think people found out in a hurry that when a white man and a black man played in the same basketball game it was not necessarily a bad thing.

a lot to do with the quote-unquote "acceptance" of the black athlete into the game and into life in this part of the country as a whole. I think people found out in a hurry that when a white man and a black man played in the same basketball game it was not necessarily a bad thing. So I think the basketball games you put on television on a regular basis had a lot to do with that, and I think you should take some credit for that.

Let me tell you one more story. We did a Vanderbilt game in Nashville one night and met a guy who was the watchman for the stage door at the Grand Ole Opry. He invited us over one night, and we walked into a room where we could stand and see the stage. Ernest Tubb was singing " I Don't Want Your Greenback Dollar." Dottie West, Porter Wagoner, the Scruggs Brothers, the Statler Brothers, and I've forgotten who else were there too.

I looked down from the side of the stage, and there were people with blue coveralls and high-topped brogan shoes chewing tobacco, with a spittoon on the floor, tapping their feet in unison. I thought that was one of the biggest shows I'd ever seen. Those were great days, Eddie.

PART VII

The Networks—TVS and Beyond

Television programming cannot exist without the hundreds of people whose faces the viewers never see and whose voices they never hear. These are the network executives, station managers, producers, directors, camera operators, ad salespeople, and so many others behind the scenes.

When TVS, which started on a regional basis in 1965, went national three years later, we were called an independent or "occasional" network in comparison to NBC, CBS, and ABC. But we all competed for the same sponsors and the same viewers, and it took a special group of talented and dedicated people to get us on the air every week. One of the great joys in working on this book was catching up with some of them after so many years.

Alan Lubell was my first employee and a supersmart salesman who ran the TVS office when I was traveling. Chris Zoulamis was indispensable in handling station relations and talent assignments. Howard Zuckerman was the lead producer and director on a large number of TVS games and coordinated the production of many more. Phil Olsman and John Crowe were producers who were always available to travel around the country as we added more and more conferences to our network.

Unlike the major networks, TVS had no full-time affiliates, so much of our success was dependent on relationships with the managers of individual stations around the country. No one represents this group of executives better than Irving Waugh of WSM in Nashville, Tennessee, a great sports fan who somehow managed to carry almost every game we offered.

Eventually, TVS had to hand college basketball off to the larger networks, as first NBC and then CBS signed contracts with the NCAA. Fortunately for the game, and for their networks, the men who took over were some of the most talented and dedicated in the business.

Chet Simmons was the president of NBC Sports when his network assumed responsibility for production and station clearances from TVS in 1976, and he later became the first CEO of a new network called ESPN. Neal Pilson was at CBS Sports after that network acquired the rights to the NCAA Tournament in 1982, and later he became its sports president. Sean McManus is now president of CBS News and Sports as it nears its 25th year broadcasting the tournament.

CHAPTER 34

Alan Lubell on Lining Up Stations, and Advertisers, One at a Time

New York City, New York, November 2003

My title was executive vice president in charge of sales for TVS, but you were on the road most of the time, Eddie, so basically I was the TVS office. We met in 1966 when I was working at the Dancer Fitzgerald Sample advertising agency. Before that, I had spent four years at NBC, so I had a basic understanding of buying and selling television ads.

I went around to the agencies to try to sell the MAC or the SEC, and the buyers asked me if I could get them Knicks tickets.

When TVS started, we really only had one advertiser, Shell Oil, and it wasn't buying nationally. To make our operation work, we had to come up with national advertisers, like beer and tobacco companies, so that's where I went to work. The problem in those early years was that we hadn't gone nationwide yet. You had signed up some conferences—the Big 8, the Southeastern Conference, the Southwestern

Conference, and the Mid-American Conference—but they only covered about 25 percent of the country. So we kept talking about ways to add additional conferences or import games from other areas.

While I was trying to sell advertisers on college games, the Knicks were the glamour team in New York. I went around to the agencies to try to sell the MAC or the SEC, and the buyers asked me if I could get them Knicks tickets. (laughs) So even though the college game wasn't big in New York then, I could see that basketball itself was getting a lot of attention. One of the first big sales I made was to Pabst, which was shut out of other sports properties by Anheuser-Busch. I convinced Pabst that college basketball was going to be the next big sport, and they became a two-minute sponsor of all our games. That was a big deal then because two minutes meant companies were buying four 30-second spots.

In addition to Shell and Pabst, some of our other two-minute sponsors were Schick, Warner-Lambert, and tire companies like Firestone and Goodyear.

And in the Midwest, I found American Motors, which didn't have the big bucks to advertise on the NFL. By then college basketball was on the national landscape, so I was able to go to the ad agencies and get a cordial reception. They still asked me for Knicks tickets, though. (laughs)

The first couple of years we sold nationally, we overdelivered on some of our ratings, which is the best thing you can do when you're coming out of the gate.

Then in January 1968, we did the Houston-UCLA game, and that put college basketball on everybody's radar screen. For that game I signed up some of my old Dancer Fitzgerald Sample clients—like R. J. Reynolds and General Mills—and after that I was able to market the concept of a national college basketball package. It was so much easier to market on a national basis than it was to market regionally. After the Houston-UCLA game we were able to renew the Shell deal and bring in R. J. Reynolds on a regular basis. Back then the tobacco companies were usually 20 percent of every sports television package. That was before they were banned from the airwaves, of course.

I thought if we had a true national college basketball package we could go to the same advertisers who were buying NFL games and other national television sports properties. And it wasn't long before we were able to sign up 85 to 90 percent of the country. You were expecting a ton of advertisers that first year, but I kept telling you they wanted to see how we did first. They wouldn't buy on the come, but off past performance.

We almost went bankrupt waiting for that to happen. (laughs)

We were actually selling the same concept as the NFL. They showed the Packers in Green Bay and the Giants in New York, but they sold the ads nationally. We did the same thing with the SEC in the South, the Big 8 in the Midwest, and other conferences around the country. So I was competing with the guys selling commercials for the NFL. We were all calling the same buyers. But even when our ratings weren't strong in some areas, the advertisers stayed with us because we had good numbers elsewhere and it averaged out. And because we were the only ones broadcasting college games nationally, our ratings were good. We would get a seven or an eight rating, whereas today if you get a one or a two it's a big deal. You have a choice of so many games today that it's a different universe.

The first couple of years we sold nationally, we overdelivered on some of our ratings, which is the best thing you can do when you're coming out of the gate. So we made believers out of the ad agencies and were able to get new clients for our package. Then when I walked into the big agencies like J. Walter Thompson and BBDO, I got a cordial reception because we were in 85 percent of the country on 120 stations. They still didn't really understand what you and I were seeing, though, that college basketball was about to explode as a spectator sport. We saw all the new arenas being built around the country, and we tried to convince the buyers that the excitement taking place at Pauley Pavilion in Los Angeles and in the SEC arenas in the South eventually would make for a revival of the game in New York. We told them there was a lot of enthusiasm on the college campuses and a lot of mini Madison Square Gardens being built.

One thing that helped was that we were preempting NBC stations all across the country for our games. The local stations wanted the games of teams in their areas more than they wanted whatever the network was giving them. It made my job easy when I'd go into an agency and they'd say, "Who is your station in New York?" And I'd say, "WNBC." And they'd say, "Who is your station in Chicago?" And I'd say "WMAQ," and so on. That gave us all the credibility we needed. In the end we became a programming threat to the networks because we controlled a lot of their stations, approximately two-thirds of the country sometimes. We basically took all of Saturday afternoon away from them—we went from two hours to four hours by the late seventies—on stations across the country.

UCLA was the standard-bearer for college basketball. The whole country got used to seeing John Wooden year after year, sitting on a seat on the bench, holding his folded program, calmly talking to his players.

Toward the end we were accumulating so much scheduling power that the coaches were coming to us and saying that we had to stop putting Notre Dame and Marquette on television every week—it was getting to be the Al McGuire–Digger Phelps show—because it was hurting their recruiting. So you said if they'd play big intersectional games, we'd put them on too. A lot of teams were afraid to do that because back then they had to win their conference to make the NCAA Tournament, so you said, "Well, maybe you should get that changed." Eventually they did. Now there are a lot of big intersectional games during the season, which is great for the game.

One of the biggest breaks we ever got was around 1970 when the Sports Network, which later became the Hughes Sports Network, sued the phone company, saying their transmission rates were unreasonable. We couldn't afford to join the lawsuit, but they won, and the irony is that it cut *our* rates in half too. That saved us $200,000 or $250,000, which enabled us to turn the corner. And the Sports Network had contracts with the Big Ten and the Pac-10, which we later took away.

By then the game was really taking off. In the late sixties, the game had not only Lew Alcindor and Elvin Hayes, but also Pete Maravich and Spencer Haywood. And UCLA was winning all those championships, which gave college basketball the brand name it needed. You see it now in golf, where Tiger Woods is the brand name everyone measures their performances against. UCLA was the standard-bearer for college basketball. The whole country got used to seeing John Wooden year after year, sitting on a seat on the bench, holding his folded program, calmly talking to his players. It came to be a regular winter event.

If UCLA won, it was expected. If someone upset them, it was a huge story. Some of the biggest games TVS ever broadcast were upsets of UCLA. When Notre Dame broke UCLA's 88-game winning streak in 1974, it was on all the network shows and was one of the highlights of the year in all of sports—not just college basketball. And those highlights were from a game we had shown on little TVS. That was a big moment for us. It put us on the map. The other thing that was great for us was that the audience for college basketball was young—the magic 18–49 audience that every advertiser is looking for. Those good demographics helped us establish credibility in a hurry.

Now, of course, the NCAA Tournament is one of the biggest sporting events of the year, and I have to admit that I was surprised at how quickly it exploded into such a huge moneymaker and became a three-week event. I knew the foundation was there because I'd seen the excitement, but I didn't understand that the Final Four would become so big. Even when the season is just starting, they're talking about the Road to the Final Four. It's amazing to me.

CHAPTER 35

Chris Zoulamis on Putting the Pieces Together

Boston, Massachusetts, August 2005

After TVS moved from the building on Fifth Avenue, Eddie, where you used the phones in the lobby until you could afford an office, our office was across the street from the Warwick Hotel. I think we were on the 38th floor, and it was the first time we weren't all in one room. You and Alan Lubell and I had our own offices, and we even were able to hire a secretary. I wish I could remember her name, but what I do remember is that she was an actress who was in one of the daytime soap operas on television.

Then around 1965 we moved to 1330 Avenue of the Americas, right across the street from CBS headquarters known as Black Rock. What I remember about our new place is that for the first time we had a teletype and could send messages directly to the stations. That was a big improvement in how we worked.

I was in charge of booking the talent and the production facilities and clearing the stations. I've still got some of the records from those days. It's amazing to me to look at the figures and realize how much less expensive everything was back then. In 1976,

for instance, TVS put on 66 games, and our total expenses were $491,375. That's $7,445 per game for everything—production costs, equipment costs, talent costs, travel, the works. That's pretty good when it comes to holding the line, isn't it?

We used to shoot from the hip and make our decisions right away.

We certainly used a lot of great announcers in those days, guys who went on to have long careers: Marv Albert, Dick Stockton, Marty Brennaman, Merle Harmon, Jay Randolph, John Ferguson, Monte Moore, Bucky Waters, Frank Glieber, Joe Dean, Tom Hawkins, and Ross Porter. We used all of them in one season. They're all here on one piece of paper. What we used to pay them is written down too, but I guess I'd better not tell much of that. Some got a little more than others, and they might get mad at us. (laughs) Nobody got rich, I'll tell you that. Look at John Ferguson, for instance. He started at $250 per game, and 11 years later he was up to $300.

Seriously, though, they didn't care. They weren't looking around to see if somebody was making more than they were or telling us to call their agents. They all *wanted* to be there. It was a break from their normal routine and a treat for them to do our games. And we never had a complaint from any of the stations, either, which is a great tribute to their professionalism when you stop to think about it. The directors didn't make much money, either. Our highest-paid director was Howard Zuckerman, who did our national games, and he made $486 per game.

One place where TVS did pretty well was in the first few rounds of the NCAA Tournament. When NBC had the rights to the tournament, it only carried the Final Four, so we'd go to the markets where the teams were from and get the local stations to compete against each other. A lot of times these weren't the big markets, but the people in them wanted to see the games, which made it a big deal for the stations, and they'd bid like crazy. We used the leverage we had with the tournament games to get them to clear time for us the following season too.

I was sorry when it all came to an end. In 1976 TVS made a deal with NBC, giving them the responsibility for sales and station clearances. After that we were just caretakers, really. I could see how hard it was for you to get new ideas on the air. There were the memos, the accountants, the salesmen, and the fact that they wanted the money in the bank before we even went on the air. It was as if they needed to keep their jobs, and the way they did that was to make your job tougher. That was how they justified themselves, I guess.

It was so different from when you ran it alone. We used to shoot from the hip and make our decisions right away. Those were very vibrant times for me. It was a joy to come to work, knowing we were going to get things done. We were a family. Toward the end, I felt like I was back at a big company, and I didn't like that. I work for myself now, and it's like when I used to work for you, Eddie. Those were such great days.

CHAPTER 36

Howard Zuckerman and Phil Olsman: The TVS Circus Comes to Town

Los Angeles, California, August 2003

HOWARD ZUCKERMAN: I was working for a station in Detroit when you rented our mobile unit and hired me and a crew to do a game in western Michigan. A few years later I became one of your producers, going around the country handling games for you. We would talk on the phone every week and figure out where to go that weekend.

I'll tell you, Eddie, some of the working conditions were pretty crazy. I remember one game we had in Kansas City, where we didn't have a production truck for some reason, so all the equipment was brought into the field house and set up under the bleachers. The game was going on, and all of a sudden Coca-Cola started dripping down on us. We were sitting under the stands, and the fans were pouring Coke on us. (laughs)

But we did some pretty innovative things too. At halftime of one game at Notre Dame, Digger Phelps let us into the locker room, and we broadcast his speech to the team live. They were losing, and he was giving it to the players pretty good, and there he was

wearing our microphone. I think it was the first time anybody had done something like that.

PHIL OLSMAN: I became involved with TVS in 1968, when I was a student at Southern Illinois when Walt Frazier was there and we won the National Invitation Tournament. Howard came down to produce the game and was looking for crew, so he called the athletic department and said, "Can you give us some bodies?" That's literally what he said: "some bodies." (laughs)

I felt like the Music Man, a one-man band dragging everything we needed into town.

So I went to work for him operating the camera. Do you remember what happened that day, Howard? The SIU mascot is the saluki, which is a kind of greyhound, and you wanted to show everybody what one looked like, so the announcer, Gene Kirby, brought one out on the floor. Unfortunately, the dog hadn't gone to the bathroom recently, and Gene got a little wet. I wish we had some of that stuff on tape, but there wasn't any in those days.

From that day until I graduated, I operated the camera for various games around the Midwest. Then I went to work for Howard full time in Indianapolis, producing and directing three or four games each week in different sports, but always basketball on Saturdays. I was by far the youngest person working for TVS, and I didn't look quite like the others. I had a beard, and my hair was down to my shoulders. You called me Tevye. But that didn't seem to matter to you. You were much more interested in putting together a team. Every year we would have a meeting where the producers and the announcers would show up, and for three months people who often didn't know each other came together and became a team.

But that's when we knew we were making an impact, because the kids wanted the banners for their dorm rooms.

We made schools important when TVS came to town. When our 40-foot truck pulled in, it was as if the circus had arrived. And the broadcasts were really freewheeling back then. We would get on a plane, show up in a college town, and there would be your announcer, your microphone, your TVS banner, your reel of commercials, and it was, "All right, go!" I felt like the Music Man, a one-man band dragging everything we needed into town.

ZUCKERMAN: And here's your tan blazer with the TVS logo, don't forget that.

OLSMAN: One of the amazing things about those broadcasts was that there was no central control point where Eddie could see them. He was totally dependent on the people out in the field. We would have our Monday phone calls, and all you really cared about was did we get on the air on time, did we get off on time, did the commercials run, and did the banner get hung.

ZUCKERMAN: We had to protect those banners because the students started stealing them. I can remember calling Eddie in New York and having to tell him another TVS banner was gone, another $38. But that's when we knew we were making an impact, because the kids wanted the banners for their dorm rooms.

OLSMAN: Sometimes you'd go to one of those towns and there would be a guy from the local station who directed the news or something. He'd always introduce himself, say, "Hey, how are you doing?" and just hang around. I couldn't figure it out. Why would somebody drive in just to say, "Hi?" Then I realized he was hoping I'd die before the game went on the air so he could direct it. That would be his big break. (laughs)

Getting on the air could be pretty hairy sometimes. I remember driving across the entire state of Washington, from Seattle to Pullman, because the weather was bad and the planes weren't flying. The announcers were Ross Porter and Tommy Hawkins, and they took a Greyhound bus and got in at noon for a 1:00 game. They hadn't showered, they hadn't slept, and they looked like death. But they did the game and, wouldn't you know, it was over quickly, and we had a lot of time to fill.

Ross and Tommy were doing their wrap-up, and I'm sure they were thinking they could finally get some sleep, and we had to tell them, "Twenty more minutes." You should have seen the look on their faces. They'd already summarized the game and done all their interviews—the only person left to talk to would have been the guy sweeping out the arena— but they had to keep going.

Tommy is this big, good-looking guy who played for Notre Dame and the Lakers. One day we did a game in Eugene, Oregon, and went out to a bar afterward, where Tommy was the only black guy in the place. He started talking to some of the girls, wanting to dance with them and so on, and I wasn't sure how the local guys were taking it. I was thinking, "You know, Tommy,

TELEVISION NETWORK

if you could tone it down just a little bit we might get out of here alive." (laughs)

Did I ever tell you about the time Stu Nahan caught on fire before a game? He was a local sports guy in Los Angeles, and Eddie sent him to Seattle to do the play-by-play at the University of Washington. I picked him up at the hotel, but he insisted on driving to the arena. He was all dressed up to do the game and smoking a pipe. I made some kind of smart-ass comment while he was driving, and he laughed and blew out the embers from the pipe, which lit up his shirt. All of a sudden he was wearing sackcloth and ashes. There were black streaks and holes all over his shirt and smoking embers all over the car.

We got to the arena, and I found a kid and gave him $100 to run out and buy Stu a shirt. But he didn't get back until after the tip-off, so Stu did the first quarter with things piled up in front of him on the table so that no one could see his shirt. Then the quarter ended, and Stu stood up in full view of everybody in the arena, took off his shirt, and put on the new one so he could do the standup at halftime.

ZUCKERMAN: The one thing we always tried to do when you were at the games, Eddie, was to keep you out of the truck. When you were there, you'd be saying, "Let's change this, I don't like that," so we made sure to keep you out on the floor whenever possible. That way you couldn't say what you didn't like. We always kept a camera on you too, so we would know you were still out there and we didn't have to worry about you.

Do you remember what happened with the national anthem at the Houston-UCLA game in the Astrodome? Dick Enberg had finished his opening, and they had put up the first words to "The Star-Spangled Banner" on the big screens. Everybody stood up to start sing-ing, but we were still playing a tape explaining Lew Alcindor's eye injury, so you called upstairs and said, "Don't start the anthem until I tell you to." You kept fifty thousand people standing for two minutes waiting for you to give the cue for the national anthem.

I really think TVS started a lot of what college basketball has become. Once we had those games on Saturday afternoons, they were the talk all the following week of anybody who cared about the sport. And the newspapers would start talking about what had happened in the games, so all of a sudden there was a lot of interest.

OLSMAN: We also started attracting the younger viewer—what they now call the key demographic—because a lot of other sports programming was aimed at older people. When Eddie started putting college basketball on TV on a regular basis, he got 18-year-olds sitting at home watching their own colleges on TV who never used to watch much on weekends.

ZUCKERMAN: We also pioneered a lot of the technology. When NBC started doing games, they would call me and ask what kind of headset we used for the announcers and where we got them. They had no clue. And we had some great telecasts. I'll put them up against anything that's on the air now, considering what we had to work with. Or rather what we didn't have—a lot of the technical stuff they have today and a crew of maybe 10 people instead of 30 or 40.

OLSMAN: I'll tell you, Eddie, for a young guy like me to have that opportunity to go out and do those things for you and Howard was great. I just loved it. My girlfriend used to say we could be lying on the beach in Hawaii in the middle of February, and if Howard called and needed me to go to a game in Kansas, I'd be on the plane. She was right too. (laughs)

CHAPTER 37

John Crowe on the Birth of the TV Timeout

Houston, Texas, January 2004

We met when I was working for the CBS station in Baton Rouge, Louisiana, Eddie—this was in the midsixties—and TVS needed someone to edit the commercial reels for its Southeastern Conference game telecasts. I agreed to do it for one simple reason: I thought TVS was the wave of the future, and I wanted to direct some of its basketball games.

The advertising agencies would send me the film of their commercials and instructions about which ones to put where, and I would record them on a roll of videotape. Then I would ship the tapes to the sites of the games on a Greyhound bus. I found that it was more efficient than the post office. What I'd have given for FedEx back then. You let me direct a few games that first year, and one was LSU against Kentucky in Baton Rouge. Just to show you how different the interest in college basketball was then, the gym wasn't full, and we asked the public-address announcer to tell everybody to move across from where the cameras were. You said, "You're all going to be on television," and they moved in a hurry. That gets it done every time. (laughs)

Adolph Rupp was really upset—not enough to give up a chance to be on television, though.

Anyway, LSU upset Kentucky for maybe the first time in Baton Rouge, and Adolph Rupp was really upset—not enough to give up a chance to be on television, though. John Ferguson was interviewing Frank Truitt, the LSU coach, after the game and Rupp walked over and stood beside John. And right while John was talking to Frank, Rupp said in a loud voice, "John, if you need me, I'm right here." (laughs)

After that I started traveling all over the country for TVS. The South, the West, the Midwest—wherever you needed me. In those days we had only three cameras. One was used for wide-angle shots that let viewers see the plays develop. Another one down on the floor was for close-ups. And the third was on a tripod and wheels so we could roll it around the court to use when the players were shooting foul shots and so on. We put the wide-angle camera up in the stands and took a shot of the scoreboard after every basket. When the schools saw what we were doing, they started selling advertising for the scoreboard, which caused some problems because we had sold advertising too, and there were some conflicts. We had no instant replay, of course, and very rudimentary graphics.

The announcers were Merle Harmon and Gary Thompson, really solid guys, but as soon as the game started, I never heard from them again. The grandstand noise was so deafening that I couldn't hear the play-by-play.

The first game I ever did in the Big 8 was in the men's gym in Lincoln, Nebraska—a lot of the arenas were called the men's gym, come to think of it—and a station in Topeka, Kansas, convinced us that it could provide all the equipment we needed. What they didn't say was that they didn't have a production truck, so they rented a truck from Ryder and piled in all the equipment.

They pulled up at the game and started unloading everything, and I said, "What are you doing? Aren't we going to do the production out of this truck?" And they said, "There's not enough room. We have to do it inside the gym." So they piled everything underneath the grandstand—camera monitors, video equipment, audio equipment, everything. The announcers were Merle Harmon and Gary Thompson, really solid guys, but as soon as the game started, I never heard from them again. The grandstand noise was so deafening that I couldn't hear the play-by-play. I could only pick up Merle's commercial cues by watching him.

Another problem was that Merle was sitting four rows back in the stands, and we didn't know that the fans always stood up until Nebraska scored its first basket. So for the first 35 or 40 seconds, he had to make it up. Somehow we got through the game, and, in fact, we continued to use that station in Topeka whenever we went back because they knew what they were doing. We convinced them to let us work inside the truck, though. Not that that was always so great. It gets cold during basketball season in the Big 8, and there was no heat in the truck, so we'd sit there in 8 degree weather on a Saturday afternoon and the snow would be blowing and we would be freezing. We'd wrap ourselves in blankets and try to stay warm.

One big problem we had was with timeouts. We called four per half, and we devised a system where we'd let the coaches know within about a minute of when they were going to come. We'd call them with 16, 12, 8, and 4 minutes left in each half, but if a coach called one at, say, 17 minutes, I would bypass the one at 16. Or if the flow of the game was such that we couldn't call one at exactly 12 minutes, I'd wait until there were 11 left.

The real problems came when we got down to the four-minute mark because timeouts became critical then. I'll never forget when we broadcast Oklahoma against Kansas State in the men's gym in Norman, Oklahoma. We were down to 30 seconds left in the half, and I still needed one commercial. I was screaming at Bill Hancock, who was the sports information director for the Big 8, to get me a timeout. He said, "I can't stop play now. Kansas State has the momentum." I said, "Bill, I have got to get this commercial in or they're going to kill me."

Finally, with three seconds left, I called the timeout myself. The Kansas State coach just went berserk—screaming and hollering and jumping up and down. We went into the truck at halftime, and there came a knock, knock, knock on the door. It was Chuck Neinas, the commissioner of the Big 8, who happened to be at the game.

"Did you call that timeout?" he asked.

I said, "I sure did. I'm sorry, but I had to do it."

He said, "I'll talk to you next week," and left. That's the way it was back then.

Of course, the coaches learned to save their time-outs. When they knew we were about to call one, they'd use ours instead. I can't tell you how many times I've heard an analyst say a coach should call a timeout but he's waiting for the next TV timeout, and it's going to cost him.

Another thing we introduced was a commercial after the starting lineups were introduced. The coaches hated it because they wanted to tip off right away. The home coaches particularly wanted to start play immediately because the crowd was on their feet cheering for the team.

One coach who really orchestrated the introductions was Johnny Orr at Iowa State. They had a brand-new arena, the Hilton Coliseum, that seated fourteen thousand people, and they were trying to fill it on a regular basis. Johnny was a promotion-minded guy, and when we went Iowa State for a game against Missouri, they told me about an opening they had cooked up. All the lights would go out, they would turn on a spotlight as the team ran out onto the court, and the band would strike up *The Tonight Show* theme. Then the announcer would say, "Heeere's Johnny!" and Orr would run out onto the court, go over to the people in the front row of the stands, and start shaking hands. I thought this would look good on television, but I had to convince them

not to turn out all the lights because the picture would be black.

The only problem was nobody told Norm Stewart, the Missouri coach, what they were going to do, and when he saw it he went berserk. "You're hyping the crowd!" he yelled. "You're hyping Iowa State! You're making my team stand here all this time." Oh, was he mad. He came to me after the game and chewed me out up one side and down the other.

Then the announcer would say, "Heeere's Johnny!" and Orr would run out onto the court, go over to the people in the front row of the stands, and start shaking hands.

Here's another great story about coaches. We were at Oklahoma for a game against Nebraska, and instead of blowing a horn at the end each half, they fired a gun. It was a really close game, and we were getting close to the end when Joe Cipriano, the Nebraska coach, started running up and down on the sideline. Joe, who was a very excitable guy, ran over to the timer's table with about 30 seconds left, grabbed the gun, and shot it. Bang!

John MacLeod, the Oklahoma coach, came running up and said, "Who shot that gun?" And Joe just smiled and said, "Yeah, who shot it?"

CHAPTER 38

Irving Waugh: The Role of the Station Manager

Nashville, Tennessee, December 2003

When I was living in New York, I was interested in the theater, but I didn't have any talent, so I drifted into radio. I ended up as a correspondent for NBC in the Pacific during World War II, and then went to Nashville where we put the first television station on the air in 1950. I loved sports, and I tried to get control of everything NBC didn't already have, which meant dealing with independent sport networks like TVS.

I think the first game you offered me, Eddie, was Vanderbilt versus Kentucky, but it was very difficult to get the signal from Louisville to Nashville. There were no satellites back then, and the transmission offered by the phone companies was spotty. Cities the size of Los Angeles, San Francisco, Dallas, and Denver didn't even *have* network television. It was a very different world.

In 1965 our station received a call from Bernie Moore, the commissioner of the Southeastern Conference, who said he had proposals from three promoters to show SEC basketball games. One of them was the Hughes Sports Network, which was

well established then, another was a promoter from Louisville, Kentucky, and the third was a guy from Paterson, New Jersey, named Eddie Einhorn.

Bernie said "Irving, what should I do?"

"If the dollars are even, go with Hughes. They're established; they know what they're doing," I said.

He said, "Everything isn't even. I can get more money from these other two guys."

So I told him, "I've had a few dealings with Einhorn. He's inexperienced, but he has lived up to everything he said he would do. So if you are trying to decide between Louisville and Paterson, New Jersey, go with Eddie." (laughs)

So you got the SEC package, and before long you had signed up some of the top stations in cities like Atlanta, Miami, New Orleans, and Jackson, Mississippi. I was surprised that you were able to sell it to them because I knew the managers of some of those stations, and they didn't care much about sports. Obviously, they must have had sales managers or somebody else who did.

A couple of years later you called and said, "Would you like to show a game between UCLA and Loyola of Chicago?" At first I thought, "Who would be interested in that in Nashville?" But then I thought, "Wait a minute—Lew Alcindor. Hell, *I'd* like to see *him* play." I brought in our local sales manager and some other people because we had never shown a game that wasn't from our area and explained it to them. They all had blank looks on their faces, and I realized that none of them had ever heard of Alcindor. So we ended up televising that game just because I wanted to see him play. (laughs) Then the game was delayed by a big snowstorm, and TVS showed it on Sunday instead of Saturday.

I first heard about the Houston-UCLA game before you were involved with it. About a year before it was played, I received a call from one of the other independent networks—Hughes or Sports Network, I can't remember which—asking if I was interested. Lew Alcindor versus Elvin Hayes? Of course I was interested, and we cleared the time.

But the network couldn't get enough station clearances to show the game live on Saturday night, so the deal fell through. That's when you came along, and what I remember is how you waited until the press began to build as both teams went through the season undefeated. A lot of the stations that had wanted to delay the broadcast until late Saturday night or Sunday morning had to fall in line, or you'd go to their competitors. By the end, you'd put together a hell of a lineup, and it turned out to be a tremendous event.

NBC gave us some guff when we told them we were going to wipe out their programming for that game, but we just said, "This is a service to our audience, so we're clearing the time." NBC never did seem to get the picture when it came to college basketball. It had absolutely no interest. I had meetings with the brass where I would push for them to become involved, but they didn't see it. They thought pro basketball had a future, but college basketball was only good for the market where the universities were located. Of course, none of us could have foreseen the growth of the game, could we? It's just amazing to me.

Looking back on it, Eddie, you and I had an unusual relationship. I don't believe we ever had anything in writing. We'd talk on the phone, and that was it. I remember once when the CBS station in our market was thinking about bidding against you for the rights to the SEC package, and you said it was going to cost you another $20,000 to keep from losing the rights. I wasn't very happy about that, but I said, "OK, we'll pay the extra $20,000, if necessary."

NBC gave us some guff when we told them we were going to wipe out their programming for that game, but we just said, "This is a service to our audience, so we're clearing the time."

We went through the rest of the season, and I called and said, "How much do I owe you?"

You said, "Irving, I made out all right. You don't owe me anything." It turned out that the other station never made a bid, and you didn't have to pay more for the rights. That really surprised me because you could have said anything up to the $20,000 we had agreed on.

I remembered that years later when a reporter in Chicago called me and said, "I understand you know this scumbag Eddie Einhorn." That was when you and Jerry Reinsdorf were negotiating for a new stadium for the White Sox and talking about moving the team to St. Petersburg.

We weren't very popular in Chicago then. Jerry and I had round-the-clock body guards.

I told her, "Let me tell you something about Eddie. He's an honest guy." I don't think that's what she wanted to hear. (laughs)

CHAPTER 39

Chet Simmons Traces the Rise of Sports on Television

Stamford, Connecticut, March 2004

I owe my career to Ed Scherick. Ed is the guy who gave Roone Arledge his first sports job even though he had no background in sports. Roone was the producer of Shari Lewis and Lamb Chop—remember her, the lady with the hand puppet?—on a local channel in New York. But Ed saw something in him—God knows what—that other people hadn't seen.

I had been a premed student at George Washington University, but I failed miserably and was asked to leave. I guess I didn't like cutting up frogs. (laughs) But I got another chance at the University of Alabama and then did a year's graduate work in radio and television at Boston University. I was lucky to go to work for Ed at Dancer Fitzgerald Sample, an advertising agency in New York. Ed saw my love for sports and put me on the Falstaff beer account. Falstaff was probably the largest sports advertiser for beer then, the way Anheuser-Busch is today, and it did the baseball game of the week with Pee Wee Reese and Dizzy Dean.

Then in the midfifties Ed started his own company, Sports Programs Inc., and got the rights to televise Big Ten college basketball. I went with him and did a multitude of things—typing, bookkeeping, filing, and some stage managing. That was really the beginning of what I consider the modern era of televised sports in America. Sports were very much an afterthought at the networks then. There was the NFL, some baseball, a few college bowl games, The Masters, and the U.S. Open. That wasn't much compared to the explosion that was to come.

But Ed was a very creative guy, and he began to romance Tom Moore, who was the president of ABC, which didn't even have its own sports department then, if you can believe that. Ed convinced Tom to let us produce their sports shows. We got the rights to college football, and then came up with the idea for *Wide World of Sports*, which really helped to establish ABC as a sports presence.

One day Ed didn't show up for work at Sports Programs Inc., so I called Tom Moore's office and asked if he was there. The secretary said, "Oh, let me get you his extension."

I thought, "His extension?" and then another secretary picked up the phone and said, "Ed Scherick's office."

"What do you want?" Ed asked when he came on the line.

"What do you mean what do I want?" I said. "It's 3:00 in the afternoon, and we haven't seen you or heard from you. And now you've got an extension at ABC?"

"Yes. I sold the company over the weekend. I'm working here now. We'll talk later. Good-bye." And he hung up. Later Ed went to Hollywood, where he produced a lot of top movies like *The Taking of Pelham One Two Three* and *The Stepford Wives*. He's remembered today as a movie producer and very rarely thought of as the guy who gave such a big push to sports on television.

So I got my job while standing at a urinal in Tokyo.

So now Sports Programs Inc. was owned by ABC. Roone Arledge ran the programming, and I ran the business side. In 1964 I went to NBC as sports director and later its first president of sports. I stayed 13 years. Things had been getting a little tense at ABC because Roone wanted more control, and I felt it might be best for me to leave. I went to the Tokyo Olympics for ABC, although NBC had the rights to the Games, and I was standing at a urinal with Carl Lindeman, one of NBC's top executives. He said he was looking for an experienced sports hand. I told him I was looking around, and he said we'd talk when we got back to New York. So I got my job while standing at a urinal in Tokyo. (laughs)

I'll tell you when we first heard about you, Eddie. It was when all the attention was focused on the Houston-UCLA game. That made us all aware of college basketball and TVS, and the fact that you were keeping us from doing the weekend programming we wanted because so many of our stations were running your basketball games. The conversations were along the lines of, "Who is this little punk taking up all our time?" and "What do we do about him?" (laughs)

We weren't stupid, though, and we began looking around to see how we could get involved with college basketball ourselves. The next year we bought the rights to the NCAA Tournament for a little more than $500,000. Then a few years later, after you sold your company, we picked up some of what had been TVS' programming too. I can't for the life of me remember why we didn't just buy the rights from you. Maybe if we had, and kept you around, we wouldn't have lost the rights to NCAA basketball to CBS. Oh, what a sad story that is.

It happened because just as it was time to renew the contract, NBC got a new president, Fred Silverman, who had very little interest in or knowledge of sports. I always thought the problem was he had two daughters and no sons to ask him to go out and throw a ball around. He just didn't understand how important sports were. All he cared about was whether it was going to lose money now, not what it would be worth in the future. He was so myopic.

There are so many stories I could tell you about Fred. Remember the 1979 World Series when it was so cold in New York that Bowie Kuhn wore long underwear and refused to put on a topcoat? NBC had the rights to baseball then, and one day I got a call from Fred saying, "I just got this invitation from Bowie Kuhn to sit in his box during Game 1 at Yankee Stadium. What do I do?"

I'm thinking, "What do you *do*? My God." I said, "Fred, you're the president of the company. He's the commissioner. You want to keep the rights to the World Series. Go sit with him at the game and schmooze him." He said, "OK, OK," and he went to the game. I came over about the eighth inning and sat behind him so we could walk out together. And do you know what he said when we left? He said, "If you ever do that to me again, I'll fire you."

Then there was the time when we were going to broadcast the 1980 Moscow Olympics—this was before

Chet Simmons was president of NBC Sports when it began broadcasting college basketball in 1976 and became the first CEO of a new sports network called ESPN. Later he became commissioner of the U.S. Football League. Photograph courtesy of Bettmann/CORBIS.

the U.S. boycotted them—and the Moscow organizing committee invited us to come over to look around. We got there late at night, but we were so excited that

> ## "We piled in some cars and drove up a bit of a slope, and there it was—Red Square, all lit up. We were looking at it through a kind of ghostly mist, and God, it was magnificent. Silverman got out of the car and said, "What the hell did you bring me here for in the middle of the night?"

nobody wanted to sleep, and we said, "Let's go out and see Red Square." We piled in some cars and drove up a bit of a slope, and there it was—Red Square, all lit up. We were looking at it through a kind of ghostly mist, and God, it was magnificent. Silverman got out of the car and said, "What the hell did you bring me here for in the middle of the night?" (laughs)

But losing the NCAA Tournament was the worst. It sickens me to this day. We had a really good relationship with Walter Byers, the executive director of the NCAA. Every time the contract was up Walter gave me a number, we met it, and we got a new contract. In 1980 we had an option for a two-year extension, and when Walter called over the weekend he suggested a four-year deal. I thought great, we would wrap it up for a long time. I knew all the network executives would go for it, and the sales guys were particularly supportive. Walter said he needed an answer by Monday morning.

So I called Silverman at home and said, "Fred, we have a terrific opportunity to renew NCAA basketball for four years." He gave it about eight seconds' thought and said, "No, only two years," and he hung up the phone. I called the top financial guy at the network and said, "What do we do? We can lock this sucker up for four years, and if we do that, we'll have it forever. If I go back to Walter with just a two-year extension, he'll never give us another shot." He tried calling Fred, but the answer was still no.

So I had to call Walter, and when I told him two years, there was silence on his end. Finally he said, "What did you say?" I told him and, bang, the phone went down. We had the tournament for two more years and never saw it again.

Around that time we began to hear a lot about something called ESPN, a network that an entrepreneur named Bill Rasmussen was starting up in Connecticut. Nobody knew the guy, but he had made a deal with the NCAA for a lot of minor sports that was being pooh-poohed in the industry. I got a call from a headhunter, asking me if I'd like to talk to ESPN. When he told me Getty Oil was putting up some of the money I decided to take a shot at it. Fred Silverman was still at NBC and we were not compatible, so I took the job as president of ESPN.

That was the summer of 1979, just a few months before ESPN went on the air, and when I got to Connecticut I found nothing. No equipment, hardly any people who knew what they were doing. Literally nothing. Just realizing what we would have to do to get on the air made it the most frightening time of my life. Luckily I got Scotty Connal and some other folks from NBC to come with me, and somehow we made it.

I remember that after our first night of programming I gathered everybody around me, and we all gave a big cheer: "Hooray, we made it through the night!" Then I said, "You guys did a wonderful job, but remember you have to do it again tomorrow and the day after that and the day after and the day after and the day after that."

A 24-hour sports network seemed like such a long shot at the time, but one thing I remember saying about ESPN was that if it could acquire the rights to the major sports, there would be nothing that could stop it. I was right about that, wasn't I?

CHAPTER 40

Neal Pilson on NBC's Big Mistake— and CBS' Big Break

San Antonio, Texas, April 2004

I was 6'6" when I became president of CBS Sports, and when I left 14 years later, I was much shorter. (laughs) That network took a lot out of me.

Let me tell you how we got the rights for the NCAA Tournament away from NBC in 1982. CBS wanted to build some major sports properties, and it looked like a real growth opportunity. One of the things we did was offer to give the tournament many more hours of coverage than NBC did, and that was very attractive to the NCAA. We also offered to put the selection show on national television, so overall I think we made a very persuasive case.

I never knew until recently what was going on at NBC that caused them to lose the deal, but I remember very clearly Walter Byers and Wayne Duke walking into our suite, looking us in the eye, and saying, "You've got it. You've won the rights. We look forward to working with CBS." It was an enormous shock to NBC, I know, because it had been a very big event for them.

Back then, the early rounds of the tournament were carried by ESPN, but about two or three years later I was in the shower—that's where I do some of my best thinking (laughs)—and I thought, "Why don't we take the entire tournament? Why don't we take all the games, regionalize the first and second rounds, and put them all on CBS?" We worked out a financial plan and went back to the tournament committee, and they were excited about it. The advertisers were excited too, and our affiliates were *thrilled*. Many of them were more excited about covering the colleges in their states or regions than they were about the NBA, which did not have significant affiliate allegiance.

Eventually CBS made a decision to give up the NBA and to stay with college basketball because we felt it was a more important property. And that is true to the present day. I talked to the president of CBS recently, and he assured me that their commitment to the tournament is 110 percent. It's a glue for the affiliates, it's a great product for the sports division, and it's a franchise for the parent company, Viacom. I can't tell you how important that last part is. Sports have gotten so big now, and the major events are so expensive, that they've gone way beyond the financial ability of the sports divisions to pay for them. You have to go to the parent company—General Electric, FOX, Viacom, Disney—to support them.

I've described the NCAA Tournament as America's Olympics. For three weekends in March, the entire country focuses on it in much the same way it focuses on the Olympics.

I'm involved in selling the Olympics now, and we direct our pitches to the parent companies. We tell them about the value of the Olympics to the corporation, rather than just the sports division. There are maybe 10 events on the sports calender of this magnitude—and the NCAA basketball tournament is certainly one of them—events that are successful because they deliver for the parent company.

I've described the NCAA Tournament as America's Olympics. For three weekends in March, the entire country focuses on it in much the same way it focuses on the Olympics. There are teams from almost every state or region of the country, and it gets an incredible amount of media attention. I think it is on an equal basis with the Super Bowl and the World Series, which is a statement you couldn't have made five or ten years ago.

To me the tournament is a perfect sports event. I think of it as a movie with a beginning, a middle, and an end. If you watch the first weekend, you see the stories developing among the teams and the players, and then you follow them through to the end. There's a logic to it, a clarity, and there's no mystery about how it works. You win and you move on. You lose and you go home. Every game is an elimination game.

The other important thing is that these are just kids. Ultimately, there is a difference between the amateur athlete and the professional athlete. A lot of people predicted that with many potential stars either leaving early or not going to college at all the tournament would suffer. But I always took the position that while the players are certainly a critical element, they're not the only element. The rivalries and the coaches and the fans are all a part of it.

Frankly, I think television is responsible for a lot of this because so many more schools get exposure now. Kids know about schools that may be far away from where they live because they see them on TV. This equalizes the quality of competition around the country and has led to the fact that almost anyone can win the NCAA Tournament, or at least get in it. One great team can't load up on all the great athletes, and when you get to the top 16, the difference in quality is really quite small. Most of the games can go either way—all it takes is one missed foul shot or one out-of-bounds call—and I think the public recognizes that. Then every year several hundred thousand fans graduate and create their own homes and buy their own television sets. So then you have new fans.

I love the way it has grown and prospered, Eddie. I think sitting here with you watching two Final Four games made us both feel very proud of the sport. I know you're proud of what you've done, and I'm proud of the contribution I made at CBS.

CHAPTER 41

Sean McManus on Keeping Up with the Growth of the Tournament

New York City, New York, June 2005

I was working at NBC in 1982 when it lost the NCAA Tournament, and looking back, I can see what a big moment it was for college basketball when CBS took over. Whenever a big event changes hands, the new carrier often puts a lot more energy, effort, and creativity into it. And when you pay a lot more money than the other guys did, there's almost an obligation to reinvent the product, and that's what CBS did.

Neal Pilson gets the credit for how it all worked out because it was his decision to do the entire tournament live. That's what really put the event on the map, what more than anything else catapulted it into the television spectacle it is today. Neal and his team showed a lot of foresight in what they did. Look at the way the selection show has become must-see appointment television. It's one of the few sports programs that has no athletic competition in it whatsoever but is eagerly anticipated every year by sports fans. People can't wait to see who has made the field, who hasn't, who is seeded No. 1, No. 2, and so on.

When I got to CBS in 1996, we didn't have the NFL, which made the NCAA Tournament and The Masters our two biggest properties. And because we were doing the tournament from the opening tip on the first Thursday through the championship game three weeks later, it became a part of the culture of CBS Sports. I don't want to say it's our most important event, but it gets as much attention as anything

I'll tell you, those first four days of the tournament are like being in the boiler room of a big ship. People are screaming at each other—"You've got to go to this game!" "No, *this* game!" It's the most exhilarating and probably the most challenging production job in all of television.

else we do because of the complexities. The first weekend we do 16 games on Thursday from four different sites, and 16 games on Friday from four other sites, so other than the Olympics, it is by far the most complex production done by any sports network. And in some ways it's more complex than the Olympics because you don't know which game is going to be worthy of national attention when you go on the air.

And here's the thing about underdogs and Cinderellas. They're great, but only to a certain extent. What you really need to build an audience are teams with great national followings and tradition, like Duke, North Carolina, and Kentucky.

I'll tell you, those first four days of the tournament are like being in the boiler room of a big ship. People are screaming at each other—"You've got to go to this game!" "No, *this* game!" It's the most exhilarating and probably the most challenging production job in all of television. A game that is programmed to 5 percent of the country may end up being the one everybody sees because it turns out to be the biggest upset or the best game in that particular time period. So it's an amazingly complex and challenging event to work on.

I like to think that in the eight years I've been here we've done a better and better job of presenting the tournament, particularly when it comes to switching back and forth between games. It's not always easy, though. We know that every time we switch from one game to another, we're going to annoy a large group of people. Duke can be beating up on Vermont and you might want to go to a tie game between Syracuse and Michigan, but there are a lot of people who will really annoyed. They'll say, "I want to watch Duke. I don't care if they're winning by 100 points." So we

make decisions based on what we think will please the largest amount of fans.

I learned all about this the first day of the first tournament I was ever involved in. Kentucky was playing somebody, I forget who, and they were up by about 40 points in the second half. With four minutes remaining, we switched from that game to what turned out to be the biggest upset of the opening round. It was just a thrilling game. Well, the switchboard in all of our stations in Kentucky just blew out. We got more complaints than you can possibly imagine. So our philosophy now is that we never take a Kentucky game away from a Kentucky audience. You just don't want to take the chance of frustrating a loyal fan who wants to watch his team no matter what the score is. Maybe we'll occasionally go away for 30 seconds if it's literally a buzzer beater, but we'll get the audience right back. In Kentucky, you're going to see 100 percent of the Kentucky game, no matter what the score is.

Here's another example. A lot of times a game will be winding down—there will be 45 seconds left, say—and we'll switch there live, and as soon as we get there, a coach will call a timeout. Then somebody will say, "How could CBS go to a game when the coach is going to call a timeout?" as if we had some special knowledge of what he was going to do.

And here's the thing about underdogs and Cinderellas. They're great, but only to a certain extent. What you really need to build an audience are teams with great national followings and tradition, like Duke, North Carolina, and Kentucky.

So you don't want a Vermont beating a North Carolina?

Not while I'm president of the sports division. (laughs)

One of the most satisfying things to me now is that people start talking about the tournament in early January. They start wondering if Illinois, say, can go undefeated. Or they say that if such and such a team is going to make the tournament it had better win four or five more games on the road. The tournament has become the focus of the entire regular season, which

Another thing that has happened is the tournament has gotten bigger in terms of the amount of attention it gets in the national media—television and newspapers and radio. I think a lot of that is because of office pools.

Sean McManus is president of CBS News and Sports as it nears its 25th year broadcasting the NCAA Tournament. The Final Four is one of the network's most important properties, and CBS has created an entire division just to sell the marketing rights.

is terrific for us. It's a solid three and a half months of promotion for the tournament and our broadcasts.

The biggest development in recent years is a deal we have with the NCAA that is unique in all of sports. The tournament is the only major sports property where one network has bought all of the rights: television, radio, sponsorship rights, licensing rights, archive rights, and the Internet. It was owning all these rights that made us think the $6 billion we paid for an 11-year deal was justified.

It was not an easy decision to make. When the NCAA came to us with the idea of bundling all the rights together, we thought long and hard about it. Finally we decided that it would dramatically increase the amount of revenue that could be generated, and so far we've been right. The marketing aspect alone has generated tens of millions of dollars in new revenue, which in turn has generated more revenue for ad sales

on the telecasts. We actually created an entire division at CBS just to sell the marketing rights. It's an expensive deal, and it's going to be challenging to make it work financially, but so far we're achieving the numbers we had hoped for. In today's world it is becoming more and more difficult to get people to watch network television. Events like the NCAA Tournament are guaranteed to bring a large and demographically attractive audience. So it's a very important product for us to have, and one we didn't want to lose.

Another thing that has happened is the tournament has gotten bigger in terms of the amount of attention it gets in the national media—television and newspapers and radio. I think a lot of that is because of office pools. I'll give you an example. My sister-in-law is a very casual sports fan who doesn't follow baseball or football. All she'll watch is the Super Bowl and perhaps a little bit of the Olympics. But every Selection Sunday for the past five years she has called me and said, "I've got to fill out my brackets. Tell me who you like in this region and that region." And she follows every single game, not so much because she loves college basketball, but because she loves the tournament.

I think people get addicted to it because of the brackets too. It's a national phenomenon unlike any other sport, and I wouldn't really call it gambling. It's just so engaging because you can lose for two and a half weeks and then move way up in the final round. It's a lot of fun for a lot of people.

Walter Byers (left) and Wayne Duke (middle) opened the first NCAA office in Kansas City, Missouri, in 1952. Later, they were joined by Art Bergstrom (right). Photograph courtesy of Wayne Duke.

PART VIII

The Stewards of the Game

Over the years I worked closely with a number of NCAA executives and conference commissioners. Their growing realization of how important television would be in exposing college basketball to a wider audience was indispensable in getting TVS on the air, and in paving the way for the explosive growth that was to come.

Wayne Duke was a chief assistant to Walter Byers, who was the first full-time executive director of the NCAA when it opened its offices in Kansas City, Missouri, in 1952. He taught me everything I needed to know about NCAA rules and policies, and he was a big supporter of TVS' efforts in its early years. Later Duke became commissioner of the Big 8 and the Big Ten. He was a member of the NCAA basketball committee for more than two decades.

Tom Jernstedt is the senior vice president of the NCAA and has overseen the NCAA Tournament since 1972. He is on the board of the U.S.

Olympic Committee and recently completed a term as president of USA Basketball.

Jim Host is the founder of the highly influential Host Communications and the man who pioneered the NCAA Tournament's lucrative promotion and marketing operations. Today he is the commerce secretary for the state of Kentucky.

Chuck Neinas followed Wayne Duke as assistant executive director of the NCAA and later became commissioner of the Big 8 and director of the College Football Association.

Dick Schultz was a successful basketball coach and later became the athletic director at the University of Iowa. He then succeeded Byers as executive director of the NCAA. He held that post for seven years before becoming executive director of the U.S. Olympic Committee.

Dave Gavitt was the founding father of the Big East Conference in 1979, which makes him as responsible for the growth of March Madness as anyone else. The Big East led to a revival of big-time college basketball in New York, which brought the game the attention it had been sorely lacking. As the coach at Providence College, Gavitt had eight 20-win seasons and made a trip to the Final Four in 1973. He was chairman of the NCAA Tournament Committee during some of its most important growth years.

Larry Albus was the athletic director at St. Louis University when he became the youngest member of the NCAA Tournament Committee. He organized a number of midwestern colleges into the Metro Conference. Later he became the head of sports marketing for Anheuser-Busch, and he now heads his own sports marketing firm.

CHAPTER 42

Wayne Duke on the Indispensable Man

Barrington, Illinois, September 2004

Walter Byers was 29 years old and I was 23 when we opened the NCAA's first offices in Kansas City in 1952. They were located in a palatial three-room suite at 11th and Baltimore that was literally over a saloon. The rooms weren't air-conditioned so when it got really hot in the summer we would go down the back stairwell to the bar, where not only was it air-conditioned, but you could get an ice cube or two in a glass, perhaps with a little libation poured over it. (laughs) The only other person in the office at that time was Marjorie Fiever, who was Walter's right-hand person for many years.

It's hard to believe now, but until that time the NCAA had been run out of the Big Ten offices in Chicago. Walter had been an executive assistant who spent a lot of time working on NCAA matters, and it was clear that the NCAA was going to have to go out on its own and take on greater responsibility. For one thing, so many veterans had returned from the service that intercollegiate athletics were burgeoning, and the NCAA needed some semblance of order. Another fac-

tor was the infractions taking place at that time—the biggest one was a gambling scandal in the Kentucky basketball program—which served as an alarm bell that the NCAA was going to have to deal with enforcement.

Walter built the NCAA on four pillars: the enforcement program, television, football bowl games, and the basketball tournament.

Walter built the NCAA on four pillars: the enforcement program, television, football bowl games, and the basketball tournament. I honestly think he had a vision that transcended that of any of the rest of us. And he had a particular vision about the basketball tournament that none of us could match. He got a lot of help in the beginning from Dutch Lonborg, who was the athletic director at Kansas. Dutch and Walter would sit down and talk a lot about ideas that led to the evolution of the tournament.

The first year we ran the basketball tournament was 1953, and I did just about all the administrative work—the finances, the promotion, the press book. At one point I stayed up 48 hours straight. I'm not sure how I did it. (laughs)

From then on he sort of had a chip on his shoulder, and I think he took great satisfaction in being someone who was labeled too small physically but turned out to be one of the biggest men in college athletics.

The key thing Walter did was to develop the automatic conference-qualifying principle. He locked up the champions of the 16 major conferences and added nine at-large teams. That was the guiding principle from which the tournament grew. Walter used the conferences to form the nucleus of the NCAA structure. He would bring them together and they would talk about enforcement, about the tournament, about everything the NCAA was doing. That's how he built such a strong administrative foundation.

I'll tell you how important the conference structure was. I was at a meeting where we voted to have the Ohio Valley Conference retain its automatic qualification status. Arliss Rhoden, who was the president of the conference, sought me out afterward and said, "That made our conference. Being an automatic qualifier is like academic accreditation. It means we belong." I've never forgotten that. What we did far transcended the simple running of the tournament. It affected the entire game.

The one thing Walter loved more than anything else was negotiating the television contract. He negotiated great deals for both football and basketball, and it was as if television was really his business. What you have to understand about Walter is he had been an all-city center in high school, but when he went to Rice, the coach said, "Young man, you're too small to play big-time college football." From then on he sort of had a chip on his shoulder, and I think he took great satisfaction in being someone who was labeled too small physically but turned out to be one of the biggest men in college athletics. In my opinion the tournament was the biggest catalyst in terms of the development and growth of college basketball, and a lot of it was due to Walter's adroit management of how it was presented on television.

Toward the end a lot of people turned on Walter. Some of them were just greedy and were all out for themselves when what he was doing was helping all of college basketball through television programming. But I don't make any bones about it—I'm deeply indebted to the guy. Walter used to say, "Duke, if it weren't for me you'd be back in Dubuque, Iowa." And maybe I would. My dad had a sixth-grade education, and I washed pots and pans and worked in the sports information office at Iowa State. But I've been the commissioner of the Big Ten, I've run the Final Four and the College World Series, and I've been involved with the football *Game of the Week*. And now I've just been inducted into the Rose Bowl Hall of Fame.

That makes a little old Iowa guy feel pretty good, and it's all due to Walter.

CHAPTER 43

Tom Jernstedt: Basketball's Journey Around the World

Indianapolis, Indiana, May 2005

Over the years I have tried to assess what has caused the tournament to explode so dramatically. One reason, I think, is that the game is played with just a rubber ball, and it can be played anywhere—on the pavement or the sandlots, in a city or in a barnyard. That's why it's played all over America—all over the world, really. And I think the fact that it's so easy to play, and that it doesn't cost much, has a lot to do with it.

The magic of the tournament, I think, comes from the fact that we have more than 300 Division I institutions that play basketball, and they're all over the country. People don't have to go very far to find a school to become attached to. They may be alums or they may not be, but they become familiar with the schools that are near them geographically. So every little hamlet, no matter where it is, can identify with a basketball program that, on a given day, can beat the big teams that everyone in the country is familiar with.

That gives you these David-and-Goliath situations where Vermont and Bucknell can beat Kansas and Syracuse, which most people think could never happen because of the difference in the stature of the programs. The sport also benefits from the fact that teams only have five players on the floor at one time, so teams that have one or two outstanding players might be able to beat the more prominent teams.

But just when I think I have it all figured out, the tournament keeps surprising me. When a lot of players started leaving college for the NBA a few years ago, I thought it might hurt the game, but just the opposite has happened. You can't stockpile talent for a period of time anymore, and that has brought the top schools down and the bottom ones up. There are more teams in the middle now, which has increased the level of competition, and I don't think the overall quality of play has suffered.

What's so interesting about this is that teams that rise up and knock off the big guys every now and then come from the schools that are more successful in keeping their players for the full four years. This works to their advantage because they don't have to go through the transition every year or two of losing a star to the pros. They can play together more and be more cohesive, which I love to see because one of my frustrations has been seeing basketball become too much of a *me* game instead of a *team* game. I think it was Dave Gavitt who coined a phrase I have heard many times, that the difference between college basketball and the professional game is that in college it's about the name on the front of the jersey, not the back. That sums it up for me.

The difference between college basketball and the professional game is that in college it's about the name on the front of the jersey, not the back. That sums it up for me.

Here's another very important element. I've had the opportunity to travel the world and watch the game become truly global. A lot of that has to do with the fact that for many years other countries have been bringing over some of our finest college and professional coaches to learn from them, and they have been very good students. They've developed the game in a way we never contemplated. For a U.S. team with NBA players making millions of dollars per year to finish in sixth place in a world championship was something I didn't think I'd see in my lifetime. Or to lose in the Olympics to Puerto Rico and Argentina because those countries played the team game so well. I never would have thought a thing like that could happen.

One of the problems the NCAA has had to deal with is commercialization. We had that back in TVS' days televising the game too, of course. The minute you sell advertising to get a game on the air, you become commercialized. It's just a question of how you handle it. Jim Host was so persuasive when he helped convince Walter Byers that it's possible to be tasteful commercially—that commercialization doesn't have to become crass. I think we've been building on that ever since.

Tom Jernstedt (left), with Larry Brown (center) and Stu Jackson (right), is senior vice president of the NCAA and has overseen the tournament for more than 30 years. He recently completed a term as president of USA Basketball.

CHAPTER 44

Jim Host: Four Million Basketballs and a Pizza

Lexington, Kentucky, September 2004

I got interested in broadcasting back home in Ashland, which is in northeastern Kentucky. I'd lie in bed every night listening to Rosey Rowswell broadcast the Pirates games, Waite Hoyt do the Reds, and Harry Caray do the Cardinals. I just loved radio play-by-play. When I was nine or ten years old I'd walk down the street describing the trees, the sidewalk, everything I saw as if I were on the radio.

My company started broadcasting University of Kentucky games in about the same way you set up your early radio broadcasts, Eddie. There were no exclusive radio rights in Kentucky then, so five of us would do them at the same time. All we had to do was pay a small rights fee.

Remember when you and I rented an old Nash Rambler station wagon, one of the small ones, and we could barely get all our equipment in it? My radio gear and your television gear were sticking out through the middle of the backseat all the way up to the front. I was driving and you were riding shotgun. We put the equipment in, and we were off to another game, laugh-ing all the way. We split the cost of a hotel room too. Neither one of us had any money then, or any idea how to get any. All we had was an idea.

I'll tell you how I finally got the exclusive University of Kentucky radio rights. I was 32 years old, and I had run for lieutenant governor in 1971 and lost. I had $170 in my pocket, owed $76,000 to the campaign, and didn't have a job. But I had a marketing and broadcasting background, so I started my business on the floor above a barbershop.

My first contract was with the Lexington Tourist and Convention Bureau, and it had a relationship with the university, which sold the exclusive rights for the first time in 1974. It was primarily for football, but if you got the football right then you had to take the basketball rights too, so I made a proposal and got them both. Well, that very year both Louisville and Kentucky went to the Final Four in San Diego.

The night of the championship game I was standing on the floor with Tom Jernstedt, who was Walter

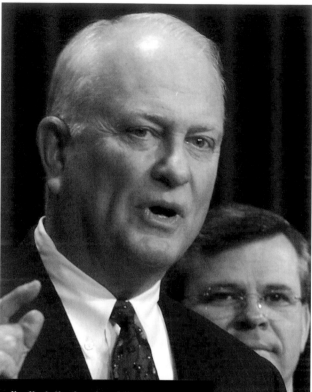

Jim Host, the founder of Host Communications, was the first to realize the revenue potential of marketing and promoting the NCAA Tournament. Shown here with Kentucky governor Ernie Fletcher, Host is now the state's commerce secretary.

There was a guy with long sideburns, cowboy boots, one eye that went in a different direction from the other one, and the worst toupee in the United States. He was also the single smartest guy I've ever met.

Byers' assistant at the NCAA. I said, "How much is Mutual (the network that broadcast the tournament nationally) paying you for the radio rights to the tournament?"

"I'm embarrassed to tell you," Tom said. "You're paying more for just Kentucky than we're getting for the national rights to the tournament." The NCAA was getting $21,000, and it had to assign several people to the production. I said I'd give them $30,000 and do all the work myself. Well, you'd have thought I'd offered him the formula for buttermilk. (laughs)

The next Monday Walter Byers called and said, "Host! Be in my office tomorrow morning at 9:00!" And, boom, he hung up. So I went out to Kansas City, and I walked into his office. There was a guy with long sideburns, cowboy boots, one eye that went in a different direction from the other one, and the worst toupee in the United States. (laughs) He was also the single smartest guy I've ever met. I've met presidents, governors, you name it, but Walter is the only person in my life I've been in awe of because of how intelligent he was.

I would sit in negotiating sessions with Walter and he wouldn't have a single piece of paper with him. But he knew more about your business than you did. He knew how much you were selling time for, how much money you were making, and how much he wanted you to pay him. But he was loyal to the people he worked with, and he wanted everyone to benefit. I remember as if it were yesterday Walter saying, "You should make 15 percent, and I should make less."

Anyway, Walter sat down, looked at me, leaned forward, and said, "I've checked you out. I'm going to give you a one-year trial. The deal is you give me $30,000."

I said I didn't have $30,000, that I was planning to make it selling commercial time for the tournament.

"You give me a letter of credit, and you've got a one-year deal," he said. "If there's any profit, we'll split it 50/50, and then we'll come back and see how you did." And then he said, "But I want one thing from you.

I want you to commit your life to college basketball. I don't want you messing with the NBA, the NFL, or anything else. If you're willing to commit yourself to us, then I'm willing to work with you."

I started with seven stations and cleared up to two hundred by the next year, but with expenses and the cost of building the radio network, I was losing money. I was doing the engineering at a Kentucky game one night when Walter came up and tapped me on the shoulder. I took my headset off, and he said, "I know you lost money this year."

I said I did, and he said, "Well, I'm making it. Our deal is now 50/50 for three years." And that's how I got started.

It wasn't always easy, I'll tell you that. Sometimes I would not have any money in the bank on Thursday and a payroll due on Friday. I would lie in bed at night not having a clue about how I was going to pay the bills, but something always came up, somebody I could cut a deal with or give a 50 percent discount to if he'd give me cash right away. And somehow we always made it. The key to it, I think, was that I never feared failure. I knew something would come to me. And it always did.

As smart as Walter Byers was, there was one thing I just could not sell him on, and that was selling exclusive sponsorship rights to NCAA events. It's common now in all sports and worth a lot of money, but the first time I mentioned it to him, he said, "Over my goddamn dead body." This was in the late seventies and early eighties, and there had never been a single license sold for NCAA T-shirts or hats or anything else. Walter couldn't understand the idea of selling the rights to a single manufacturer. He didn't see why an advertiser would want to put his trademark on things having to do with the tournament.

But I'd learned about the concept of exclusive rights when I was working for Procter & Gamble in the early sixties—we used it to get a competitive advantage in supermarkets—and I kept at him. I kept sending him things about how much revenue

it would bring in and telling him that the idea was to build the NCAA brand. The more you position the brand, the more television revenue you can bring in. Well, it must have worked because in 1984 Walter called me and said, "I'm ready to talk. Come see me." So I got on the next plane and flew out to see him, and he said, "What's the deal?"

There was a big gap between the Super Bowl in January and the Kentucky Derby and the Indianapolis 500 in May, and I thought maybe the Final Four could be the next big marketing event.

I proposed a deal where I'd pay all the expenses and we'd split the bottom line. He said, "No, that's not fair. We'll do a deal at 65 percent for us and 35 percent for you." I said all right and we shook hands. The whole thing took 10 minutes. What changed his mind? I think he finally saw that promoting the NCAA brand would give him an advantage in negotiating with the networks. Walter would never admit he was wrong, but he was enough of a visionary to see what was coming. It just took a while.

The first thing I did was get in touch with Bill Ryan, with whom I'd worked years earlier at Procter & Gamble and who was now at Gillette Company. We looked at a calendar together and I said, "The All-Star Game and the World Series are great advertising vehicles, but you don't have anything in the spring." There was a big gap between the Super Bowl in January and the Kentucky Derby and the Indianapolis 500 in May, and I thought maybe the Final Four could be the next big marketing event.

So I told Bill I would charge him $500,000—don't ask me where I came up with that figure—to put a freestanding insert in the Sunday newspapers that offered a trip to the Final Four and contained coupons redeemable for razor blades. Gillette made a deal with some drug chains and supermarkets for aisle displays that resembled the newspaper inserts, and 141 million coupons were redeemed. It was the

We literally wrote a book on how to do this because nothing like it ever had been done before.

most successful promotion Gillette had ever done. I took those results to Pizza Hut and Pepsi Co. and charged them $500,000 too. Some advertisers bought it because of the advantage it gave them in the marketplace, but others liked the image of being associated with college athletics. They liked being the only people in their field connected with that market. And they liked having tickets to the Final Four too. (laughs)

The biggest single success we had was with Pizza Hut in 1986. David Novak was the president of sales then—he's the CEO now—and we convinced him to do a basketball giveaway. These were mini basketballs with Final Four and NCAA logos on them, and they bought 4 million of them, which was more basketballs than ever had been manufactured at one time in the history of the world. I think they cost $2.25 to make, and if you ordered a pizza for $10, you got to buy a basketball for three bucks. Well, they sold all 4 million in 10 days and finally had to pull their ads from television. Walter Byers watched all that, and he called me up and said, "I get it." He finally understood.

That promotion was what really launched the brand. We kept increasing our prices, and so did the NCAA. The last five years I was with the NCAA, we paid them $97 million. By the time I sold my company in 1997, corporate sponsorship was on its way to becoming a $3 billion business.

During that time I also had deals with individual colleges and conferences all around the country, and I was doing other things for the NCAA too. At the Final Four in 1977 I was sitting at the press table in the Omni Hotel in Atlanta, helping with our radio broadcast, when Wayne Duke started bitching about the tournament program. It had a picture in it that was upside down, a whiskey ad that was an embarrassment, and it looked terrible. And besides that, the NCAA lost $14,000 on it because the Omni had the program rights. I listened to Wayne complain for a while, and then I said, "Do you guys want me to do the program?" And that's how I got in the program business.

Our first year I got lucky because Kentucky was back in the Final Four. I knew how to sell in my own state, of course, and I sold more programs than ever had been sold before and made $48,000. A few months later I went to the NCAA summer meeting and presented a big book outlining everything we had done to produce the program to the tournament committee, and they all said, "Great job."

Then Willis Casey, a tough old guy who had been the athletic director at North Carolina State for years, held up a little black-and-white program I didn't recognize. He said, "Do you see this? That's what we had at the first round of the tournament this year in College Park, Maryland. Don't you agree it looks horrible?" I said it did, and he said, "Do you like doing the Final Four program?"

I said, "Yes, sir," and he said, "Well, if you want to continue doing it, you've got to do the first and second rounds, and the regional tournaments too."

That was before computers—in the dark ages of printing, really—and I was thinking, "How in the hell am I going to get eight first-round programs done and to the sites on time when I don't know which teams are in the tournament?" The Final Four program itself was a nightmare because of the logistics and how little time we had to put it together. But I said I'd try, and I went home and set up a mechanism that is still in place. We had a network of stringers all over the country, and we collected data on maybe 100 teams that had a chance to be in the tournament. On Sunday night when the teams were announced, we'd drop the rosters and pictures into the formats and were ready to go. We literally wrote a book on how to do this because nothing like it ever had been done before.

For years we did a much better job than the Super Bowl program, which was out of date because it had all four teams that had played in the AFL and NFL championship games two weeks earlier. They didn't have their stuff together the way we did. The NFL and NBA asked us to do their programs, but Walter said no, our deal was exclusive to the NCAA. That was all right with me because I was a college guy. I never wanted to do anything else.

I was the exclusive marketing agent for the NCAA for 32 years. Radio, television, coaches' shows, publishing—I had the rights to them all. In all that time the tournament kept building into the top event of its kind in the world, yet at the same time it kept the clean, pristine look that every organization would like to have. I kept potential competitors away by not letting anybody outside the NCAA know who I was or what I was doing. I didn't give any interviews. I wouldn't let anybody use my picture. I never put out a press release announcing we had signed a new contract. And my offices were in Lexington, Kentucky, so that I wouldn't be on the radar screen nationally.

Every year *The Sporting News* would run a list of the 100 most influential people in college athletics, and I was never on it. I told my wife, "As long as it stays that way, I'm successful." And I think the NCAA liked having me around because I was part of the culture. I was a college guy they were comfortable with. I would go around to the various schools and try to be available for whatever extra things they needed. I always paid them on time too. (laughs)

Later we built the first website for the NCAA. Nobody in the organization wanted to mess with it,

but when two bright young guys, Rick Ford and Tim Campbell, called me and said they could get audio from every game onto the Internet to broadcast all over the world, I said, "Damn, that sounds good to me." I realized that alumni would be able to hear their teams' games wherever they were. Rick and Tim needed the NCAA rights to get started, but they didn't have any money, so they gave us 5 percent of the company. That company ended up becoming Broadcast.com, which was later sold to Yahoo!, and that 5 percent became worth $60 million.

He'd give me a piece of ESPN if I'd be his official sales agent. I listened to him and said, "This is not going to work. Who's going to watch all those sports on television? And who's got cable?" So he sold to Getty Oil instead.

Not everything I did was brilliant, though. Walter Byers called me one day and asked if I knew a guy named Bill Rasmussen. I said no, and he said, "Well, he's started up something called ESPN. I want you to meet with him." So Bill came down to Lexington and said he wanted to make a deal with me. He'd give me a piece of ESPN if I'd be his official sales agent. I listened to him and said, "This is not going to work. Who's going to watch all those sports on television? And who's got cable?" So he sold to Getty Oil instead. (laughs)

I knew that CBS, which owned the broadcast rights to the tournament, would wake up one day, and they did. They asked why they should be out there hustling when I had so many of the people they wanted to do business with locked up. They said they were paying more money than I was, and they deserved some of those rights. I knew it was a losing cause—I didn't have the deep pockets CBS had—so finally

I sold out to a subsidiary of Gray Communications, which is the largest owner of CBS stations in the country. When we merged, the company I had started by myself had 600 employees.

Looking back, I think there are a number of reasons why college basketball has become so huge. There is no question in my mind that TVS' national broadcasts led the way. You saw something that nobody else saw, Eddie. If you hadn't put it all together, there wouldn't have been a game of the week on NBC or CBS, and without that regular-season package, there wouldn't have been as much interest in the tournament.

But maybe the biggest thing of all is the growth of the alumni market. After World War II, 1 percent of the nation's population had graduated from college. Today it's 21 percent. The number of college alumni in this country has doubled in the last seven years and will double again in the next five years. As the amount of college graduates continues to grow, the affinity for their schools continues to grow too. I know I'll always be a Kentucky fan wherever I am.

CHAPTER 45

Chuck Neinas on the Expansion of the NCAA Tournament

Clayton, Missouri, April 2005

The first time I met you, Eddie, was around the time I joined the NCAA—that was in 1961, when we had eight employees—and I was administering the basketball tournament. You had left your briefcase in a taxicab, and you were beside yourself. You said, "I've just lost my office." Your office was in your briefcase. (laughs)

Here's how I got started in sports. I went to the University of Wisconsin, and in my senior year the sports information director, Art Lentz, left to go to work for the Olympics. He asked me to broadcast the Wisconsin basketball games, and I stayed on for four more years to organize the football and basketball radio network. We had 52 stations for football and approximately 20 for basketball. So I had a radio and television background that helped me understand how important broadcasting was going to be to the growth of college sports. Later I was involved with a game of the week on radio on WBBM in Chicago, and there's one story I've got to tell you.

Jack Drees was the broadcaster, and at halftime they would throw the show back to the studio for updated scores and so on. But for some reason Jack would conduct dummy halftime interviews anyway, without telling the guests that nobody would hear them. Once he was interviewing a sportswriter from Los Angeles at the halftime of a football game, and they talked about Jess Hill retiring as USC athletic director. The writer started giving Hill all these accolades, and Jack said, "Well, I understand the reason he's leaving is that he's an SOB." (laughs)

Another time, he interviewed Waldo Fisher, the athletic director at Northwestern University, and they were talking about how much Northwestern was struggling in football. Fisher started to give some explanation, and Jack said, "Well, the prevailing opinion is they've got a lousy athletic director." (laughs) It got so we would all run down to where Jack was to listen to what he was saying on his interviews.

In 1961 the University of Cincinnati played Ohio State for the first time, and when they met again the next year, the Final Four was in Louisville, Kentucky.

We had a great shortage of rooms, so we put out a bulletin to the hotels in the area, asking if they had any empty space to please contact tournament headquarters. Well, the afternoon of the first game, we got a call from somebody at one of the hotels who said, "We just had a guy jump out of a 12th-floor window. As soon as we clean up his room, you can have it."

With both schools being so close together, the demand for tickets was unbelievable. We had a great shortage of rooms, so we put out a bulletin to the hotels in the area, asking if they had any empty space to please contact tournament headquarters. Well, the afternoon of the first game, we got a call from somebody at one of the hotels who said, "We just had a guy jump out of a 12th-floor window. As soon as we clean up his room, you can have it." (laughs)

Things were so hit-and-miss in those days. I remember one Finals where we had agreed that no television cameras would be stationed at the end of the court. The cameras had red lights, and the tournament committee thought it would be distracting when a player was shooting a free throw. Isn't that silly? They've already got fans hollering and maybe throwing things at them: shoot the ball, put it in the hoop.

Well, ABC put a camera at the end of the court anyway to tape the game for *Wide World of Sports*, and Bernie Shively, who was the athletic director for Kentucky and the chairman of the basketball committee, asked them to move. The cameraman said no, he had instructions from the director to leave it there. Well, Bernie was about 6'5" and 250 pounds,

and a former Big Ten wrestling champion who had been a lineman for Red Grange. He just picked up the camera and started carrying it off the court. The cameraman said, "Where are you going?" and Bernie said, "I'm taking it outside. You should have put it where we told you."

Bernie and I were in the middle of another situation involving the tournament too. Chicago Stadium was supposed to be the site of the 1966 Final Four, and Bernie and I went there to make arrangements. In those days the ticket sellers at the stadium were in a very powerful union, but we told them Northwestern University would be handling the tickets. So one of them said, "You know, Mr. Shively, if you don't allow us to handle the tickets, there may not be any lights when it's time for the game."

Bernie got up and said, "Chuck, we're leaving. We can't deal with these people." And in a very short time he arranged for the tournament to be played in Cole Field House in Maryland. That's the year Texas Western beat Kentucky, one of the most famous Final Fours ever because Texas Western had an all-black starting lineup.

I'll tell you something interesting that came out of that game. In the semifinals, Texas Western beat Utah handily, while Kentucky beat Duke in a game that went right down to the wire. So Texas Western was well rested in the second half, while Kentucky was just exhausted from getting past Duke, and Kentucky had to play the championship game the next day. At the next meeting, the committee voted to have a day off between the semifinals and the finals. They went to a Thursday-Saturday format.

I think everybody agrees that one of the big things that increased the popularity of college basketball was expanding the tournament. I believe that the commissioners of the various conferences played a big role in that. This was the midseventies, when I was the commissioner of the Big 8, and we kept trying to get the NCAA to loosen up and allow more than one team from a conference in the tournament.

As assistant executive director of the NCAA, Chuck Neinas helped run the basketball tournament. Later he became commissioner of the Big 8 and director of the College Football Association.

all season, both to UCLA. We had Purdue, Missouri, and Tennessee too, which were good teams with large fan bases. The tournament was not a financial success, but it was very competitive, and the NCAA looked at all the attention it was getting and said, "Uh-oh, this could be too good. We'd better allow a second team in." So our tournament didn't last very long, but it accomplished our objective.

I'll tell you a funny story about that Indiana-USC game. Bobby Knight didn't want to play in the tournament. He wanted to go to the National Invitation Tournament. But most of the NIT money was kept in New York, and we thought that because our colleges were making the money, we should be rewarded appropriately. That's one of the reasons we started our own tournament. Anyway, Bobby got two technicals and was ejected from the game. But instead of leaving, he went to the top row of the auditorium. One of his assistants kept running up there, getting Knight's instructions, and then running back down. After that, the rules committee said if you are ejected from a game you have to stay in the locker room or leave the building. You can't come back into the arena.

Here's one more story about you. I was at a meeting at CBS, and everybody was wearing a suit and tie except for you. You had on a colored, short-sleeved sports shirt. Well, the phone rang, you talked for a while, and then you hung up and said, "That was Jerry Reinsdorf. I think we just bought the White Sox."

I said, "Are you nuts?" and you said, no, it had really happened.

So I was there at the beginning, when you lost your office, and I was there at the end when you bought the White Sox. (laughs)

But they refused, so we started our own tournament, the Collegiate Commissioners Tournament, which took the major conferences' second-place teams. People called it a losers tournament, but in our 1975 championship game we had Indiana, which was one year away from going undefeated, and Southern California, which had lost only two games

CHAPTER 46

Dick Schultz: College Basketball Becomes a Billionaire

St. Louis, Missouri, September 2005

Walter Byers had run the NCAA for 35 years when I replaced him in 1987, and he had always been a very private person. I was given one challenge by our executive committee: open the NCAA up, make it more user-friendly. So for the first three or four years I was on the road almost constantly, visiting universities, trying to build a camaraderie.

One of the things I did, and this met with a lot of resistance at first, was give the athletes a voice in what was going on at the NCAA. I started a Student-Athlete Advisory Committee, and now they can speak on the convention floor and have a vote. I thought that if we were making rules that affected their lives, we needed to get them involved.

What really made the tournament was going to 64 teams in 1985. That's when it became a coast-to-coast event for the first time, and we realized that we had a monster on our hands. I don't think any of us knew it would grow to be this big. I did have some sense of what it would be like because I was the chairman of the NCAA basketball committee when we expanded.

When that happened, every college in the country that had 18 wins thought their team should be in the tournament, so for 30 days before the selection, my phone was constantly ringing with reporters asking, what about this team, what about that team? I was the athletic director at the University of Virginia then, and I couldn't get any work done. So the next year we set up a conference call with more than 100 writers. That made life a lot easier.

It wasn't long, of course, before the tournament became the financial lifeblood of the NCAA and very important to the schools financially. I know I had a lot of fun negotiating that first billion-dollar contract in 1990. In all seriousness, though, one important thing we had to do was figure out a formula to share the wealth. There was a time when a Final Four game would be coming to an end, a player was at the free-throw line, and the announcer would say, "This is a $60,000 free throw."

I thought we had to get rid of that. So in that billion-dollar contract, we came up with a new formula, where a conference got paid based on the number of appearances it had made in the tournament. The money was distributed back to the schools on the basis of how many sports they sponsored, how many scholarships they provided, and a number of other things. It didn't all go to the schools that went to the Final Four.

"Do we want the Final Four to be NASCAR or The Masters?"

Here's another question we asked ourselves: "Do we want the Final Four to be NASCAR or The Masters?" In other words, did we want an association with a few major sponsors that we would control, or did we want to allow everybody to cut their own deals? We decided to use The Masters model because we had the opportunity to make lots of money through signage and other things if we had control. And I think it has added a lot of class to the tournament. We had to take a hard line with a lot of the arenas. They'd

say, "We can't cover up that sign. We've got a contract." And we said, "If you want to host the tournament, you're going to have to cover them all up."

When I look at what March Madness has become, I don't think there's any other tournament in America that commands this much interest over a three-week period. One of the things that makes it so popular is that you have amateurs playing their hearts out, and it's sudden death. It's not the best of seven games. One bad night and it's all over. And frankly, I don't see any end to the popularity. I remember when we took the game to the Superdome in New Orleans, Louisiana, where there were seventy thousand seats. We marked the highest seats "distant view." I went up there with a pair of field glasses and thought, "This is a tough place to see a game from."

But when people saw where they were sitting, we had maybe a dozen returns, and there were 500 people standing in line to get them. People just want to be a part of it, don't they? So maybe it doesn't seem as if the tournament can get any more popular, but it will. It will continue to grow and grow.

Dick Schultz, with U.S. Olympic Committee President Bill Hybl, succeeded the legendary Walter Byers as executive director of the NCAA. Schultz later became executive director of the USOC.

CHAPTER 47

Dave Gavitt on the Big Idea
That Was the Big East

Providence, Rhode Island, September 2004

We founded the Big East Conference in 1979 out of necessity. I was the basketball coach and athletic director at Providence, and we were part of a huge conglomerate known as the East Coast Athletic Conference, which consisted of hundreds of schools of all sizes—from Syracuse University to Colby College in Maine. No disrespect to some fine universities, but that meant we had to play teams like Vermont and Maine and New Hampshire, which were just not on our level. We'd had some great players like Lenny Wilkens and Johnny Egan and Jimmy Walker, and we'd been to the NCAA Tournament. We even went to the Final Four in 1973, and we wanted to compete at the highest level.

I thought about dropping out of the ECAC and becoming an independent, but then I realized that we should think about putting together our own conference of the basketball powers in the East. The rest of the country was organized in conferences, and I thought it would be hard to make our mark as independents. My idea was to form a conference

of schools that would cover all the big markets and basketball hotbeds in the East. I wanted St. John's so we'd have a presence in New York, Georgetown in Washington, Connecticut and either Boston College or Holy Cross in New England, as well as Providence. We needed teams in Philadelphia and New Jersey

I thought about dropping out of the ECAC and becoming an independent, but then I realized that we should think about putting together our own conference of the basketball powers in the East.

too, so I approached Temple and Rutgers, but they said no, so we took Seton Hall and, a year later, Villanova. Pittsburgh joined that next year too.

Some people didn't want Connecticut, but I kept pushing for it because I thought it would tie New York together with New England, like the Yankees and the Red Sox. I just thought they needed some time to build up there, and of course, they've been national champions in men's *and* women's basketball. What's happened in that little town of Storrs, Connecticut, is mind-boggling to me.

Anyway, I laid out my plans to the other athletic directors, and it wasn't an easy sell. I remember Lou Carnesecca at St. John's said, "We're winning 20 games a season now. What do we need to be in a stronger conference for?"

"We've got to think bigger. Everybody has got to be willing to give up a little to build the game in our area. The pot will be much bigger if we're successful together."

I said, "Lou, you've got to get used to losing a little. The good high school players in the East are going to the ACC and Notre Dame because their games keep coming in here on television. We've got to think bigger. Everybody has got to be willing to give up a little to build the game in our area. The pot will be much bigger if we're successful together."

We had meetings once a month throughout the winter, where we'd fly into LaGuardia Airport and meet at the Marriott to figure out how to build the conference on a sound foundation. We didn't want to hurt the teams that would not be leaving the ECAC, so we agreed to stay until the end of the ECAC television package three years later. We knew that if we did pull out, TVS would have been at our doorstep the next day trying to sign us.

We sure would have.

We tried to do all this quietly—nobody knew about our meetings at LaGuardia—but finally the word got out and we had a problem. We still needed two more New England schools, but there were four of them in

the ECAC—Holy Cross, Boston College, Connecticut, and Rhode Island—and none of them wanted to be left behind. So they said unless all of them could come in with us, none of them would. That just would have led to more and more schools and created the ECAC all over again. I knew there was no way the bigger schools like Syracuse, St. John's, and Georgetown would have stood for it. So we had to call their bluff. We really wanted Boston College, so we called them up and gave them six hours to make up their minds or we'd ask somebody else. Finally they went with us, and I don't think they've been sorry.

I'll tell you a story about the relationships we had in the early days. Providence had a big TVS game against Penn one day—Chuck Daly was the coach, and we'd known each other for years—and Marv Albert and Bucky Waters were the broadcasters. The night before the game, my wife and I invited Chuck and his wife, and Bucky and Marv, out to a fancy Italian restaurant. We were having this nice dinner when I realized Bucky had gotten very quiet, so I said, "Do you feel all right?" And Bucky said, "I can't believe what I'm seeing."

I said, "What do you mean? What can't you believe?"

He pointed at Chuck and me and said, "You two guys are about to battle it out on television tomorrow for basketball supremacy in the East. You're both highly ranked, it's a huge game for both teams, and here you are having dinner together? In the ACC, the coaches wouldn't even say hello before a game, much less have dinner with each other."

I said, "We haven't been at this long enough to hate each other." (laughs)

The driving force behind the Big East, of course, was television. We had learned so much from you, Eddie, going back to when TVS had the rights to the ECAC *Game of the Week*. We badly wanted to be on that broadcast because we needed the exposure to help us recruit, but you didn't want us on against St. Joseph's or St. John's. You wanted us to play teams from around the country that TVS could show nationally.

Well, we'd play anybody to get on television back then. You sent us to Louisville and Oregon, and one year you asked us to play UCLA in Los Angeles. It turned out to be Bill Walton's junior year. It was a close game for a while, but they ended up killing us. We were working hard to develop Providence as something different, and you helped us do that.

The fact that we had a good team and that our television signal reached Boston, Worcester, and

During our first 12 years or so, the Big East grew faster than I could have imagined. It was a gamble, but college basketball was really catching on.

Cape Cod gave us some huge television ratings even though we were in a small market. So I was learning about television then, about negotiating and getting as many appearances as we could, and about developing relationships with network people like you. That was the beginning of what came later.

During our first 12 years or so, the Big East grew faster than I could have imagined. It was a gamble, but college basketball was really catching on. We were in so many large markets and our conference championship, which we always played in Madison Square Garden, became a huge event. By 1984 you couldn't get a ticket for the tournament.

We had our problems, though, especially when we tried to piggyback onto the idea of *Monday Night Football*. We were naïve and full of ourselves, and we drew up plans for a Monday night Big East basketball series and sent them to the networks. We got zero response. Literally nothing. But one of our schools had done a small deal with a company in Memphis that was a barter outfit—you had to sell your own ads and pay the production costs. We talked to them, and they said, "We can sell the games and clear the

stations, but we don't know anything about production. You'll have to do it yourselves."

So very quickly we had to learn about producing basketball on television. Mike Tranghese, who was my sports information director at Providence and later succeeded me as the Big East commissioner, found someone to take care of the production truck and the satellite time and so on. We hired Len Berman to do the play-by-play, and I did the color commentary because I had been the coach of the 1980 Olympic team—that's the one that didn't go to Moscow because of the U.S. boycott—and was a little bit of a name by then. It wasn't hard to clear stations in our areas because we already had local packages, and pretty soon we were on our way. Everybody thought we were getting a lot of money, when really we were getting zilch. But that wasn't the point. We were establishing ourselves on television.

We started with a Saturday package, but the next thing we knew we were on WOR in New York on nine consecutive Monday nights and getting a good response. There were threats of a lawsuit by a guy who said we were a successor conference to the ECAC and bound by a renegotiation clause, but we fought him and eventually he went away. At the same time, we had our own lineup of stations on other nights. We would have Syracuse play Providence on a Tuesday, for instance, and it would air in Washington and New York, as well as the home cities of the teams. Our goal was to show eight games in every market during the season, plus the Saturday games— eight Providence games, eight Syracuse games, eight Villanova games, and so on. We wanted to saturate the market, and pretty soon we were on television far more often than any other conference.

Then, right when we were getting started, we got very lucky. ESPN arrived on the scene. They were right around the corner in Bristol, Connecticut, and because we knew more about television than some of the other conferences, we were a good partner for them. You could say we grew up together. They ultimately bought our Monday Night *Game of the Week*, and now it's all over the country—starting in the East and moving across the country all evening long. And by then ESPN was paying us good money too.

Looking back, I would say three things were important in building the Big East and our television package. One was the decision to play our postseason tournament in Madison Square Garden every year. Being in New York drove the selling and the publicity. It's fine to have a tournament in Lexington, Kentucky, or Greensboro, North Carolina, but there's nothing like New York City to get the media attention, is there?

Whoever would have thought that a 5'10" guard from Peterboro, New Hampshire, population 1,800, would have seen so much just from basketball?

The second thing that really helped was the Carrier Dome at Syracuse University. It was the first domed campus facility and was a phenomenon. In its first four or five years it was drawing thirty-three thousand or thirty-four thousand people, which made the telecasts really exciting.

And last, we had great coaches who stayed at their schools through the eighties, which helped establish us. We had John Thompson at Georgetown, Lou Carnesecca at St. John's, Jim Boeheim at Syracuse, Jim Calhoun at Connecticut, and Rollie Massimino at Villanova. That helped us a lot, especially with recruiting. All of a sudden, Syracuse was getting Steve Thompson from Los Angeles, Connecticut was bringing in Ray Allen from South Carolina, and Georgetown was recruiting kids from New Orleans. This had never happened before. We got Patrick Ewing, Chris Mullin, and Pearl Washington. It was just unbelievable.

We weren't all big schools, you know. I remember when I took Providence to the Final Four in St. Louis, and the schools were UCLA with thirty-five thousand students, Memphis State with thirty thousand, and Indiana with thirty thousand. A writer came up to me handed me a program, and said, "This is a misprint, isn't it? Your enrollment should be thirty-six thousand, shouldn't it?"

I said, "The Dominican fathers who run the school would like that, but no, it's 3,600." And he said, "I'll be damned." (laughs)

The final piece of the puzzle came when we started having tremendous success. In 1982, our third year as a league, Georgetown went to the NCAA championship game and lost to North Carolina by one point on Michael Jordan's shot. Two years later Georgetown won the national championship. The next year, we sent three teams to the Final Four: Villanova, which beat Georgetown in maybe the greatest upset in the history of the championship game, and St. John's. That's the only time it's ever been done by one conference.

I've done so many things in basketball. I've been on the NCAA Tournament Committee, I've been president of the NCAA Foundation, I've been president of USA Basketball, CEO of the Boston Celtics, chairman of the Basketball Hall of Fame in Springfield, Massachusetts, and a lot more. Whoever would have thought that a 5'10" guard from Peterboro, New Hampshire, population 1,800, would have seen so much just from basketball?

But the game has changed a lot, and I have to admit that there are things about it that worry me. I think that despite its good health, the college game is under attack in several areas. One is the trickle-down effect of the pros. It's like acid rain coming down from above—the money and the style of play, the bump-in-the-chest "me" attitude instead of playing for the team. You can't blame the kids for wanting to leave school early—Al McGuire used to say to look in their refrigerators—but you'd like to see them have enough time to mature as human beings and to learn how to play the game. They'd be better professionals if they did.

And then before college you have people shoving shoes at 14-year-old kids and putting money in their pockets. They're not coaches, they're not educators, they're in it for themselves, and they're getting kids to say, "I got some money, man. Go get yours." And we're sitting in the middle. So it's trickle down from above, bubble up from below.

One thing we have to stop is the pro intrusion on our games. We need to send our own message. I don't want to be watching Louisville play Georgetown and see a promo for an NBA game. You don't see promos for college games on NBA broadcasts. I'm also worried about the fact that coaches move around so

much. In the colleges, the coach is the most important guy in the game. Roy Williams, Rick Pitino, Mike Krzyzewski, and Gary Williams are the recurring images you see. They represent what's good about the game.

What we have to do is accentuate the strengths of the game. Get people to understand that it's played in all 50 states, not just in 30 pockets of the country like the NBA, and that it touches everybody in the same way, from Vermont to Hawaii to Alaska. It's something everybody is passionate about—they paint their faces and the bands blast away. It's John Philip Sousa and apple pie, whereas the NBA is MTV. College basketball is different. It's unique, really, and it has to stay that way.

CHAPTER 48

Larry Albus on Why Conference Tournaments Matter

St. Louis, Missouri, April 2005

I was the athletic director at St. Louis University when we met in 1965, Eddie. Because we didn't play football, I thought we needed a conference that would be focused mainly on basketball. We were in the Missouri Valley Conference then, but it was becoming fragmented into small markets. We were going to places like West Texas State and New Mexico State, and I said, "This isn't where we want to be."

So we formed the Metro Conference, which included St. Louis, Tulane, Memphis, Louisville, Cincinnati, and Georgia Tech before Georgia went into the ACC. Then we picked up Florida State and Virginia Tech. Instead of looking at schools, we looked at television markets: New Orleans, Atlanta, St. Louis, Cincinnati, and so on.

Dave Gavitt and I were both on the NCAA Tournament Committee then, and he said he wanted to set up a conference based on markets in the East. I said, "Dave, you can do it better than we can because you've *really* got the markets—New York, Washington, Philadelphia, the whole East Coast really. So he founded the Big East, which everybody thought was a huge gamble at the time, but has been a huge success. Dave and I worked together bundling our schedules and putting on a Monday night television package.

I remember when people said there was no way the Big Ten or the Pac-10 would ever have a postseason tournament, but now of course they do.

Then we discovered a loophole in the NCAA rules that said you could immediately qualify for the national tournament if you determined your champion in a postseason conference tournament.

Well, we couldn't change our schedules for the season right away, but we could have a tournament. It brought in more money too. At that time, the ACC set the standard for postseason tournaments, which have opened up the possibility of getting into the NCAA Tournament for everybody. I remember when people said there was no way the Big Ten or the Pac-10 would ever have a postseason tournament, but now of course they do.

It was through Eddie that I met J. D. Morgan, and we got to be good friends. Later, when his tenure on the tournament committee was up, I was his

I don't recall us ever saying we wanted to add teams so we could get more publicity or more money. We added teams so we could accommodate the demand to be in the tournament. But because there was more interest, more teams, and more games, we wound up generating more money.

replacement. That was in 1969, when there were 24 teams in the tournament. I remember when they started discussing having 32 teams in the tournament and allowing in more than one team from a conference. J.D. thought that was the end of the tournament, that we were diluting it. But by then the tournament was gaining more acceptance and more conferences were forming, which proved how much interest there was in college basketball. And everybody wanted to get in the tournament any way they could.

So the focus of the committee was how to accommodate this growing interest. That's what drove the expansion of the bracket—the demand from teams around the country. I don't recall us ever saying we

Later we began talking about expanding beyond 64 teams so that everyone would have a chance. But I believed that when you had conference tournaments everybody *did* have a chance

wanted to add teams so we could get more publicity or more money. We added teams so we could accommodate the demand to be in the tournament. But because there was more interest, more teams, and more games, we wound up generating more money.

Later we began talking about expanding beyond 64 teams so that everyone would have a chance. But I believed that when you had conference tournaments everybody *did* have a chance. Even if you're in seventh place in your conference, if you win your tournament you're in. One of the things people were worried about was whether expanding the tournament field would kill the National Invitation Tournament, which had been bigger than the NCAA for many years. But it didn't work out that way. Both tournaments have prospered.

It's funny to think how different things were back then. When we got the NCAA Tournament for St. Louis, we didn't have a logo, and I didn't see how we could sell merchandise without one. So we created one. And for years we tried to get one of the networks to cover the announcement of who would be playing in the tournament, but nobody cared. Until the late seventies, we just sent out a news release. Now, of course, it's a big television show.

The other thing that has really changed is the arenas. When we held the NCAA Tournament in

St. Louis in 1973, the arena seated seventeen thousand and was the largest indoor facility that had ever been used. Nine years later, we went to the Superdome and sold the place out. We printed something like "obstructed view" on the tickets, warning people the seats were a long way away. Now people come to the tournament for the weekend even if they don't have tickets. They just want to hang around. Or they have a lottery for the last remaining tickets. That's how much it has grown.

On December 19, 2003, Michigan State played Kentucky at Ford Field—the site of the 2006 Super Bowl—before 78,129 spectators. It was the largest crowd ever to see a basketball game and immediately was dubbed the Basketbowl.

PART IX

The Future

Television, my TV analyst pal Beano Cook likes to say, is the best thing that ever happened to college sports and the worst thing that ever happened to college sports.

While there is no doubt that television has been the catalyst for the growth of all college sports, I believe basketball has benefited the most because of its unlimited inventory and growing audience. There are more than 300 major colleges in every corner of the country playing basketball, and nearly all of their games are televised nationally or locally. And as the Internet spreads, it won't be long before every school broadcasts every one of its games in one form or another.

But there is a dark side to so much exposure. Bigness means money, and that leads to fierce competition among schools and conferences to win. This, in turn, leads to recruiting excesses, commercialism, alumni pressure, rules violations, and the compromise of academic standards. The debate over the place of sports in an academic setting seems unlikely to end anytime soon. What cannot be argued is the fact that college basketball—and March Madness—will continue to grow. I thought it would be fitting to close this book by speaking with three people who are eminently qualified to tell us what that future might hold.

In her 31 years at the University of Tennessee, a time when participation in women's sports has grown exponentially, Pat Summitt has won more NCAA games than any other coach, male or female. No one has played a greater role in the growth of women's basketball and the expansion and recognition of the NCAA women's tournament, which her teams have won six times. Her teams' exciting games against the University of Connecticut in recent years have had the same effect on women's basketball that the series between UCLA and Notre Dame did several decades ago. In 2000 Summitt was inducted into the Basketball Hall of Fame.

Myles Brand, a former philosophy professor at the University of Illinois at Chicago and later president of the University of Oregon then Indiana University, became president of the NCAA at a time when university presidents have shown their resolve to place greater emphasis on the academic aspects of collegiate sports.

My old friend David Stern has been commissioner of the NBA since 1984, during which time professional basketball has expanded both nationally and around the world. Stern's vision and ability to solve his game's problems have made him one of the most effective commissioners any sport has ever had, and I found his views on the relationship between college and professional basketball to be compelling.

CHAPTER 49

Pat Summitt on Letting Women into the Game

Knoxville, Tennessee, August 2005

Before we talk about the future of women's basketball, maybe we should talk about the past. If you think the men's game has come a long way, just consider where women started from.

When I started coaching at Tennessee in 1974, I was only 22 years old and right out of college, with no coaching experience. One of the first things I did was push very hard for the state high school association to switch from the six-player game. Girls' high school basketball used to have three players on offense and three players on defense. The guards stayed on one side of the center line, and the forwards were on the other side because women weren't supposed to be physically capable of running the full court. It was such a putdown of girls' basketball.

Saying this should be eliminated, that girls should play the same game as boys like they were doing in other states, was a very controversial position at that time, and I took some pretty hard licks from the media. I was even subpoenaed by a young lady in Oak Ridge, Tennessee, and I went to court and spoke on behalf of the five-player game. I said I wanted to see the girls in our state have the same opportunity to earn college scholarships as girls around the country. I'm not one to stick my neck out and bring negative publicity to our program, but that time I felt I had to. Finally they changed the rule, and I'm glad I stood up and said what had to be done to help the game.

The state of the women's game in college back then was maybe one step above intramural basketball. I guess you'd call it extramural.

The state of the women's game in college back then was maybe one step above intramural basketball. I guess you'd call it extramural. When I came here, we were pretty much playing only local teams. A big trip for us was to go down to Mississippi for a few games or to go to Rock Hill, South Carolina,

We were just so much of an afterthought. Then something came along that, more than anything else, changed everything: Title IX.

where they held a national tournament. There would be 16 teams, and on the first day you would play two games to try to advance to the championship round. Can you imagine that? Two games the same *day*? And our budget was so limited that we couldn't even afford a bus, so we'd travel in a van. We had to buy our own shoes, and we paid for our uniforms by selling donuts. I call those the punch-and-cookies days of women's basketball.

As for the NCAA, it didn't even have a women's basketball tournament until 1982. Before that we were in an organiza-tion called the Association of Intercollegiate Athletics for Women. We were just so much of an afterthought. Then something came along that, more than any-thing else, changed everything: Title IX. As soon as the federal government said that there had to be equal opportunity for boys and girls to play sports in high school and college, there was an immediate awareness of the

No one is more associated with the explosive growth of women's college basketball than Pat Summitt of the University of Tennessee, who became the winningest college coach of all time in 2005 and whose teams have won a record six NCAA Tournaments. She was inducted into the Basketball Hall of Fame in 2000.

discrepancies in funding. People began to see that girls just didn't have the same opportunities as boys, and they realized that wasn't right.

I was fortunate enough to be able to coach alongside Bob Knight at the 1984 Olympics, when he coached the U.S. men's team and I coached the women. And being able to watch Denny Crum, Dean Smith, and John Wooden was so helpful.

At that point, a lot of universities—and I'm proud to say Tennessee was one of them—chose to step up to the plate and support women's sports. That wasn't necessarily the popular thing to do, but it was the right thing to do. It gave us the opportunity to start to compete nationally, and soon we had long-standing matchups with Texas, Stanford, and Old Dominion, which were also supporting women's sports.

I'm not going to sit here and tell you it happened overnight. In my time at Tennessee, for instance, I've coached in three different arenas, which shows how we've progressed over the years. Most coaches would have to change jobs to be in three different arenas, but I've done it on one campus. The first place we played was Alumni Gym, next to the football stadium. The capacity was three thousand, and I'll never forget how many people were there when I won my first game. There were 53. Later we moved to the Stokely Athletics Center, where the men's team played—it seated seven thousand. Now we're in the Thompson-Boling Arena, which seats more than twenty-four thousand and is the largest on-campus arena in the country. So that shows you how big the changes have been.

Maybe this sounds funny, but I never thought much about the future. When I first took the job here, I wasn't paying any attention to the big picture. I was just focused on working one day at a time to try to bring a team together. It was really important to build a good staff, which I was able to do despite the fact we had no budget for assistant coaches. They were just grad students who volunteered in their off-hours, but a lot of them went on to fine careers in basketball: Sylvia Hatchell became the coach at North Carolina, Judy Wilkins Rose went to UNC–Charlotte, where she's now one of the few women athletic directors at a Division I school, and Sharon Fanning is the coach at Mississippi State. They've all done well, and I'm very proud of them.

I'll tell you a story about my first few years at Tennessee. Ray Mears was the coach of the men's team, and he had a policy that no one from the outside was allowed to watch the team practice. And that included me. I didn't say anything. I've never been the type of person who would bully my way into a place where I wasn't wanted. But it's interesting that I wasn't allowed to watch the men practice, isn't it? What I did instead was visit with coach Mears' assistant, Stu Aberdeen, who was great to me. We talked about basketball constantly, and I learned a great deal from him. I've learned a lot from other men coaches over the years too.

I was fortunate enough to be able to coach alongside Bob Knight at the 1984 Olympics, when he coached the U.S. men's team and I coached the women. And being able to watch Denny Crum, Dean Smith, and John Wooden was so helpful. I don't know of anyone who wouldn't try to learn something from John Wooden. I also learned a lot from Don Meyer, who was at David Lipscomb University in Nashville, Tennessee, for many years and is now at Northern College in South Dakota. He's one of the great teachers in the game in my estimation. I learned from some of the women pioneers too, like Billie Moore, who won national championships at UCLA and Cal

State–Fullerton, and Sue Gunter, the great LSU coach who just died.

And now you've surpassed them all in victories— men and women. After you broke Dean Smith's record last season, Bob Knight told me there's no way he's going to catch you.

When I don't have the intensity and the passion and the drive, then I'm out of here because I would never cheat the young people who choose to come here and be a part of this.

What was interesting to me as we began to build to the point where we were rivaling the men's program was that I never felt any resentment. I didn't rock the boat, and the men's head coaches were all very respectful. It was important to me that I gain their respect, and I think I did. Don DeVoe, who was here in the eighties, was a great man, and I think he really respected us. I watched him practice and he watched us, and I could talk basketball with him. And that's gone on down the line with the other men's coaches here.

I've always liked the men's game. My oldest brother, Tommy, played in junior college and was recruited by Tennessee, so my family grew up with basketball. I look at the men's game now, and I just can't believe the athleticism, the speed, the size, and the way they play above the rim. It's incredible how much the game has changed. But I still think the purest form of basketball is based on fundamentals and skills. It's the teamwork involved in getting a good open shot and then being able to make it. It's great to see women with the ability to play up around the glass, and it brings a lot of excitement to the game. We had our first practice of the season today, and one of our top recruits, Candace Parker, who is from Naperville, Illinois, was on the floor dunking the ball. She's a great athlete and it was fun to see, but at the same time the fundamentals have been a big part of the women's game for years and I don't think we'll get away from that.

The most important thing that happened in building our program was that when we started winning, people began to take notice. Dr. Ed Boling, who was the president of the university, became a big fan of ours, which certainly helped. But as far as what has happened to women's basketball nationally, I wish I could say I could have seen how it would develop into what it is today, but I can't. I didn't have the vision. The pattern is a lot like what took place in the men's game, isn't it? The athletic directors weren't ready for it. Television wasn't ready for it. The media wasn't ready for it. There are a lot of similarities. The men were on TV long before the women, so we have constantly been playing catch-up. But now I think we both provide a great stage for college basketball, and we both enjoy the benefits of March Madness. Our tournament isn't called March Madness, though, is it? Maybe it should be.

One thing I don't think anybody doubts is that women's basketball is just as competitive as the men's game.

One thing I don't think anybody doubts is that women's basketball is just as competitive as the men's game. I know I'm just like any other coach when it comes to wanting to win. I've kicked my players out of the locker room when I didn't think they were trying hard enough. That's one of the most definitive statements you can make, isn't it? Telling them they're not worthy of going into the locker room. (laughs)

Before we played Virginia in the regional finals in 1990, our marketing people got a little ahead of themselves and printed up T-shirts that said, "Tennessee in the Final Four." We lost the game in overtime, and our athletic director, Joan Cronan, was really upset about it. She said, "Now we've got to eat all these T-shirts." I said, "Don't worry, Joan. We'll save money on practice shirts next season because we're going to practice in them every day."

(laughs) The next year we beat Virginia for the national title, so it turned out to be great motivation for us.

One thing I'm proud of is that every player I've coached who has completed her eligibility has graduated. I grew up in a home where books came before basketball, and I never missed a day of school in 12 years. I tell people I'm sure I must have passed around the mumps, the measles, and chicken pox. (laughs) But my parents were adamant about us going to school every day. So I tell our students that if they don't go to class, they don't play. I wouldn't let them play if they didn't come to practice, would I? It's the same thing. I tell my players I want them to get to class early to

One thing that did touch me afterward was when they named the court in the arena after me. Now they call it The Summitt.

get a seat in the first three rows. I've seen studies that show your retention is much better if you do that, and your professors get to know you. I think it's important that you show that level of respect.

They made a big deal last year when I broke Dean Smith's all-time victory mark. It happened during the NCAA Tournament, and honestly I was more concerned about winning the game. I talked to coach Smith and said, "It's really not that big a deal." He said, "Not until it happens. *Then* it's a big deal." In the weeks leading up to it, I just tried to keep everything focused on the team and the task at hand. And to the players' credit, they did a good job.

One thing that did touch me afterward was when they named the court in the arena after me. Now they call it The Summitt. When it happened, I thought, "Nothing like that could ever happen to honor a woman and a women's team." So to me it

was a huge statement by the university and the board of trustees. It was a tremendous honor, sure, but it was also a tremendous statement.

I'll tell you a funny story about it. My maiden name is Head, and somebody said, "How do you like that, Pat Summitt breaks the record and wakes up the next day and her husband's name is on the court." (laughs)

It's amazing to see how far the women's game has come and to think where it might go. I guess in a way we have it a little better in college than the men do because women's professional basketball doesn't pay the kind of money the NBA does, so the players have no reason to leave school early. It may happen someday, but not when you're talking about making $30,000 a year and not $30 million.

For a coach, I think it's the same with both men and women. It's not about the records, it's about the people. It's about the faces and the relationships. I have fond memories of the teams that came together and cut down the nets after winning championships, but really, they're all family to me. I always say, "Once a Lady Vol, always a Lady Vol." I hope they'll come to understand that it's important while they're here, but it's more important when they leave. What's interesting is that sometimes the players you had the most conflict with are the first ones at your door.

One very nice thing that happened here in Knoxville in the last few years was the opening of the Women's Basketball Hall of Fame. It's a great source of pride for our game and for the people in this area. I can't take credit for it—the city, the county, and the corporate community all came together to make it happen—but I think it shows that we have people in this area who are not only knowledgeable about women's basketball, but are respectful of it too. This knowledge and interest shows how far our game has come, and I think it's only going to get better in the future.

CHAPTER 50

Myles Brand: The University Presidents Take Control

Indianapolis, Indiana, May 2005

I became president of the NCAA as an outgrowth of the Knight Commission report on college athletics that was released in 1991. The problems in college athletics were getting worse and worse—there were a number of scandals—and we were also concerned about the movement of the athletic department away from the rest of the university.

I want to bring college sports back into higher education. We're not a professional league. I have no problem with professional sports—I enjoy them—but they're different from college sports.

The main point of the Knight Commission report was that college athletics could not be brought under control until the university presidents grabbed hold of them. The athletic departments were run by athletic directors, but it's the presidents and chancellors who have the bigger picture, who see the forest for the trees. They understand how sports ought to be a part of the athletes' education. So in the nineties we saw a lot of reform efforts, including academic reform, on the part of the presidents. I was the president of Indiana University during much of that time, and I was involved in a very quiet way with other presidents who were concerned about this.

One of the things we looked at was the large television contract. The latest CBS contract is for $6 billion—that's with a *B*—over 11 years for the postseason basketball tournament. I think that big a revenue stream made it more difficult to get control, but it did begin to happen. Finally, in about the year 2000, we said we're not going to be able to take control of the NCAA until a sitting university president heads up the organization. They had a search and, lo and behold, I emerged. I had no expectation I would become involved that way, but how could I resist? So in 2003 I started the job.

Myles Brand, who has been president of the University of Oregon and Indiana University, was named president of the NCAA in 2002. His selection was part of an effort on the part of university presidents around the country to exercise greater control over college sports.

One reason they wanted a university president to take over was to help align the athletic departments, particularly those with high visibility in basketball and football, with the missions of the institutions. I want to bring college sports back into higher education. We're not a professional league. I have no problem with professional sports—I enjoy them—but

I've always said that you can't get many people to go back to campus on a Saturday afternoon to see their old biology lab, even if it's the best in the country. You need sports to bind people with their alma mater.

they're different from college sports. What we need to understand is that we are the only country in the world where we combine secondary education and college education with sports. It doesn't happen anywhere else. It's a great tradition, and a lot of people learn their values playing high school sports, but over the years, particularly since the media became more involved, we've seen college sports act like professional sports.

One of the things almost no one understands is that a vast majority of universities are not breaking even on sports. About 50 schools in Division I claim they're in the black or breaking even, but even that's not true. When you take into account things like bonded indebtedness, facilities maintenance, and so on, maybe 12 or 15 are in the black. All the others can't balance their

I don't care if you have a multimillion-dollar contract; you'll have a better life if you get an education.

books. Is that bad? Well, no. The classics department loses money, the physics department loses money. If something is part of the university and it's providing genuine educational value to those who participate in it, then the school should be prepared to pay for it. Anyone who thinks college is only about going to class or reading textbooks doesn't understand what a college education is all about. It's embedded in the culture of learning, of networking, of becoming an adult.

And as a bonus, it adds a tremendous amount to college life, to the continuing attachment people feel to their schools. I've always said that you can't get many people to go back to campus on a Saturday afternoon to see their old biology lab, even if it's the best in the country. (laughs) You need sports to bind people with their alma mater.

Of all the sports that are played in college, only two produce any revenue—football and men's basketball. And that revenue is used to support all the other sports. We redistribute the revenue to student-athletes who participate in a range of sports. So are we a business? Well, on the revenue side, we'd better be, and so should every other not-for-profit organization. We're talking about $500 or $600 million per year, so if we didn't do our job on the revenue side, we'd be fiscally irresponsible. But on the expenditure side, we do things differently because we're not paying players.

My goal is to be an advocate for college sports within the context of higher education, not separate from it. And we've already been able to make some changes. For example, we've raised the bar students have to pass academically to play, and we've stopped a number of recruiting problems by putting in much tougher rules. By "we," I mean the college presidents.

What I think we have to realize is that we spend a lot of time talking about a very small handful of players. Take basketball, for instance. There are five hundred thousand young men playing in high school. Of those, five thousand will be good enough to play Division I college basketball. That's 1 percent. Of those five thousand, only fifty will ever get even a tryout with the NBA. So 1 percent of 1 percent of high school players get a tryout, and *that* doesn't mean they're going to make it. It's exciting to talk about those who do, but what about all the others?

I think we're getting traction on this issue. We're getting the sense that people are beginning to understand that everyone should get an education. I don't care if you have a multimillion-dollar contract; you'll have a better life if you get an education. And we realize that not everyone will finish school right away. We're encouraging athletes to consider themselves welcome to come back to finish their educations. We're not there yet. It may take a few more years, but I'm optimistic.

I think March Madness is great. We have young men playing their hearts out, and it couldn't be more exciting. And here's something that I think has improved college basketball lately. A lot of people, myself included, were concerned that when kids started going directly from high school to the NBA it would ruin the game. But instead, something really ironic has happened. The young people they took from high school have changed the NBA, and not necessarily for the better, because they're often less skilled and need more time for development. They tend to be the big men.

This has made college basketball a more guard-oriented game, which makes it more team-oriented. Now, to me, there is nothing more fun than watching a team-oriented game between two closely matched teams with terrific coaches, like Jim Boeheim or Roy Williams or Mike Krzyzewksi. That's what we've been getting in the tournament lately, these great, very close games.

Did you see what the kids were doing in the tournament this year? The called it "popping" the jerseys. Popping the school name in front of the television cameras so that people would identify them with their team. What they were saying was, "Remember us." To me, that's the wonder of college sports. It's not the size of my contract, it's my team.

I see a couple of things on the horizon in the next five to ten years. First, I see the development of stadiums with a different configuration. Rather than a dish, which they use for football, it can be configured in a more up-and-down way that is conducive to basketball. There's one like that in Austin, Texas, now, and Indianapolis is building a new stadium that will look like that. The sight lines will be much better, and they'll have huge HDTV screens so even if you're far away you'll feel like you're part of the action.

I'm very hopeful for the future. I see the Final Four getting bigger and bigger—more entertainment, more college spirit, more alumni participating, more viewership. I think it's going to keep getting better and better.

CHAPTER 51

David Stern: Where the Colleges and the NBA Meet

San Antonio, Texas, June 2005

You couldn't grow up in New York when I did and not be a college basketball fan. There were Satch Sanders and Happy Hairston at NYU, Chet Forte at Columbia, and Bill Bradley at Princeton. And there were St. John's and Rutgers, which were never very good. They were like the Washington Generals playing the Harlem Globetrotters. I was a Knicks fan too, but we were never at a loss when it came to college basketball. I always loved the game, although I went from being a 5'9" forward to a 5'9" guard when I was 12 because I stopped growing. I couldn't play anyway, which is why I became a lawyer. (laughs)

Kids growing up today don't understand the concept of seeing one game a week on television, which was the way it was back then. Our players get more exposure in a week than they used to get in a season, because there were only three networks and they were so tightly controlled. They didn't see the benefit of showing more games.

I know how much you struggled getting the game on the air and selling ads, Eddie, but by the time I went to the NBA as general counsel in the late eighties, college basketball had become the darling of the sports sponsors and was viewed ahead of us. I remember we went to the ad agency representing an automobile sponsor, and they told us they didn't want our game because we had too many black players. We said, "Number one, if you look at the rosters of college teams, they're starting to change, and number two, our audience is not just African American, it's a sports audience." But they said, "No, we're staying with the college game."

So our goal became to make the NBA like the college game. We wanted them to be parallel, part of the same process, and to have sports fans understand that there was a bridge the players crossed from college to the pros. I remember the day I thought we made the breakthrough. I was watching a college game with some friends, and someone said, "This kid is going to be a lottery pick." They had made the connection. Soon people were talking about who was going to get Magic Johnson, who was going to

Since David Stern was named commissioner of the National Basketball Association in 1984, the league has enjoyed tremendous growth and helped spread the gospel of basketball around the world. Photograph courtesy of the National Basketball Association.

get Kareem Abdul-Jabbar, who was going to get Larry Bird. That was great for us.

The NCAA was not exactly welcoming to us in those days, you know. Walter Byers had a rule—I'm not sure it isn't even still in effect—that you couldn't do a commercial for the NBA during college games. You couldn't have pro players in a commercial shown during a college game. They used to kick us off, and all we could say was, "OK, our time will come."

Historically, we understood how much bigger college basketball was than the NBA. The Knicks used to be an afterthought to college games in Madison Square Garden, and, in fact, the NBA was basically created as an afterthought to the NHL. It started back in the late forties with a bunch of hockey owners sitting around saying, "Let's fill the building. Let's get some more dates." There weren't any rock concerts then.

I loved it when people started debating, is college basketball better, or is the NBA better? It gave people something to write and talk about. Someone once asked me, "How do you feel about the competition

Someone once asked me, "How do you feel about the competition from college basketball?" I said, "What competition? They're showcasing the future stars of our All-Star games."

from college basketball?" I said, "What competition? They're showcasing the future stars of our All-Star games." That's true for the women's college game and the WNBA too. We even moved the start of our playoffs back so we wouldn't be going up against the NCAA Tournament.

March Madness is so great, isn't it? Everybody's talking about basketball, which is wonderful. I don't want to sound jealous, although maybe I am a little, but one thing I think people underestimate is the impact the office pool has. Even people who don't know whether the ball is stuffed or inflated get interested in that part of it—making friendly wagers, let's say.

Everything we've done to promote and market the game is something we've learned from somebody else. And we certainly learned a lot from you, Eddie. The way you went out hustling sponsors made us see we should go directly to them too. When there were just three networks, the sponsors used to say, "Here's the money, good-bye, leave us alone." But gradually we came to see there was something bigger out there that would benefit all of us.

I remember once we were talking to a marketing person for a fast-food company, and he said, "I don't understand why you're pitching us. You've already got your money from the network." We said, yes, but we want you to do promotions with us rather than just buy 30-second spots. We want you to see the synergy that's involved here. Today we have a marketing department that works with all our teams and shares information on sponsorships, group sales, telemarketing, customer retention, game presentation, and all the rest of it. What we realized is that if we're not as interested in our game as we should be, then no one else is going to be interested.

I think you understood something very important at the earliest possible time. You saw that basketball was enormously appealing to the people who were at the games and who watched it on television locally, and you said, why not do big games on a national basis at a time when the networks weren't paying any attention? You also saw that the best seat in all of sports is a courtside seat at a basketball game, and that TV captures that seat. Not to knock any other sport, but there are no helmets, no hats, no long sleeves, no long pants. It's just a bunch of guys running around in what almost could be their underwear.

When you look at what televising a basketball game is now compared to when you were doing it with

Not to knock any other sport, but there are no helmets, no hats, no long sleeves, no long pants. It's just a bunch of guys running around in what almost could be their underwear.

three cameras, you must laugh. We have cameras attached to the top of the backboard, to the bottom of the scoreboard, to wires that swing back and forth above the court, as well as on the floor capturing the action from below. It's a 10-camera production, and that's just for a local telecast during the regular season.

And the game lends itself to storytelling because it's the ultimate unscripted drama. We were reality programming before there *was* reality programming.

Think about it. Your reality might be Elvin Hayes versus Kareem Abdul-Jabbar, or Digger Phelps versus John Wooden, or the two teams in the NBA Finals. We owe a lot of that to you, Eddie.

Now that you're out of college basketball, I have just one more thing I want to ask you. Can I sell you an NBA team? (laughs)

The caption for the first picture should read, "Eddie Einhorn as a member of the 1956 Philadelphia Warriors." Just kidding. I was on a team of newspaper and radio guys who played before a Warriors game.

My first publicity photo (above) was taken when I was a student at the University of Pennsylvania and broadcasting the 1957 NCAA championship to a small national network of radio stations.

Somehow, I talked basketball Hall of Famer George Mikan into being my analyst for that tournament. I was on a small budget then and was happy to learn that if I called an announcer a "guest analyst" instead of a "color man," I didn't have to pay him.

Even though I was deeply involved in broadcasting basketball, I had always loved baseball. In 1956 I had the thrill of interviewing Jackie Robinson. All photographs courtesy of Eddie Einhorn.

BIG LEAGUE CARDS ⊕

SOX

EDDIE EINHORN
CHICAGO WHITE SOX   1986

What's the point of being the owner of a baseball team if you can't have a baseball card made up with you in uniform? Another one of the perks of being an owner is having the opportunity to meet your boyhood heroes, like Joe DiMaggio.

It doesn't get any better than this—hoisting the American League Championship trophy with Jerry Reinsdorf (right), with whom I bought the White Sox in 1981, and former general manager Roland Hemond, then, after beating the Houston Astros, holding the 2005 World Series trophy with my family: son-in-law Darryl Jacobson, daughter Jennifer, son Jeff, and wife Ann. That's Julian Lopez, the man who kept me alive by donating his kidney, standing behind me.

Here I am with my old friend NBA commissioner David Stern and my kidney doctor, Gerry Appel, at the 2005 NBA playoffs. Even though college basketball was such an important part of my life, I have always loved the pro game, too. White Sox photographs courtesy of Ron Vesely/Chicago White Sox.

In 1974 and 1975 we used my daughter Jennifer as our mascot for TVS' network identifications and for our promotional spots. Here she is shown at ages two and three. In 1975 my son Jeff joined her. Hey, when you own the company, you can get away with a lot. The colleges loved the personal touch, though, and before long, Jennifer and Jeff were getting fan mail from all over the country. We sneaked this last shot on the air when I sold TVS, and we called it "The End." All photographs courtesy of Eddie Einhorn.